JOHN DONNE

Paradoxes and Problems

ANNO DNI. 1591.
ÆTATIS SVÆ·18

ANTES MVDADO
MVERTO QVE

This was for youth, Strength, Mirth, and wit that Time
Most count their golden Age; but t'was not thine.
Thine was thy later yeares, so much refind
From youths Drosse, Mirth, & wit; as thy pure mind
Thought (like the Angels) nothing but the Praise
Of thy Creator, in those last, best Dayes.
Witnes this Booke, (thy Embleme) which begins
With Love; but endes, with Sighes, & Teares for sins.

Will: Marshall sculpsit.   IZ:WA

JOHN DONNE

1591; from an engraving by William Marshall (? after an original by Nicholas
Hilliard) prefixed to Poems, *1635*

JOHN DONNE

Paradoxes

AND

Problems

EDITED WITH
INTRODUCTION AND COMMENTARY
BY
HELEN PETERS

CLARENDON PRESS · OXFORD
1980

Oxford University Press, Walton Street, Oxford OX2 6DP

OXFORD LONDON GLASGOW
NEW YORK TORONTO MELBOURNE WELLINGTON
KUALA LUMPUR SINGAPORE JAKARTA HONG KONG TOKYO
DELHI BOMBAY CALCUTTA MADRAS KARACHI
NAIROBI DAR ES SALAAM CAPE TOWN

Published in the United States by
Oxford University Press, New York

British Library Cataloguing in Publication Data

Donne, John
Paradoxes and problems. – (Oxford English texts)
I. Title II. Peters, Helen III. Series
828'.3'08   PR2247.P3   79-40844

ISBN 0-19-812753-7

Printed in Great Britain by
Latimer Trend & Company Ltd Plymouth

PREFACE

THIS edition of Donne's *Paradoxes and Problems* has developed from a doctoral thesis presented to the University of Oxford in 1977. The canon of these early prose works and the other juvenilia which have come to be associated with them is examined, the most probable dates of composition are proposed, a critical text is established and provided with a Commentary, and both Paradox and Problem forms and Donne's use of them are discussed.

Examination of the canon has led me to exclude as of doubtful authenticity two Paradoxes, 'A Defence of Womens Inconstancy' and 'That Virginity is a Vertue' and the two Characters, the 'Essay of Valour', and 'News from the very Country'.

In the General Introduction I have argued that the Paradoxes were written in the early 1590s and the Problems between 1603 and 1609 or 1610. Consequently, it is not surprising that they present different textual problems; their manuscript distribution is not identical and while the canon of the Paradoxes is consistent, that of the Problems varies, with different manuscripts containing from six to nineteen. The Problems also differ from the Paradoxes in that four of them show revision mainly in the form of excision of material; this I have attributed to Donne. Both Paradoxes and Problems are alike in that their least reliable text is that preserved in the early editions of 1633 and 1652. For this reason, the use of the first edition as copy-text— the usual procedure in editing Donne's poems—has been abandoned; the Westmoreland MS is used as copy-text for the Paradoxes and the O'Flaherty MS as copy-text for the Problems. Both are printed in the order in which they are contained in the copy-texts. In the case of the Problems which show signs of revision, both unrevised and revised

versions are given where these differ sufficiently to require
both.

In the Commentary I have attempted to defend the read-
ings chosen in the text, to paraphrase difficult passages, and
to show analogies with other texts of Donne and of his
contemporaries. The interesting (and for a commentator
difficult) thing about Donne's Paradoxes and Problems is
that while the purpose of these works was to surprise or
even shock the reader, the materials used were contemporary
common knowledge, leaving one frustrated at being unable
to track down what should be obvious. My greatest debts
in preparing the Commentary are to Helen Gardner and
John Carey who patiently suggested various sources that I
might try.

The literary Paradox has a long, well documented, and
readily accessible history. The literary Problem is less well
served and I have had to piece together something of the
history of this neglected form. The works that proved of
greatest use in this task were Brian Lawn's *The Salernitan
Questions: An Introduction to the History of Medieval and
Renaissance Problem Literature*, which Helen Gardner
suggested to me, and T. F. Crane's *Italian Social Customs
of the Sixteenth Century and their Influence on the Literatures of
Europe*.

The editing of the *Paradoxes and Problems* was begun by
Evelyn Simpson in the 1920s, but put aside when she began
to edit Donne's Sermons. As she was unable to return to
editing these early prose works, she passed them on to R. C.
Bald who had intended to prepare a critical text and textual
introduction for the Renaissance English Text Society. He
was unable to undertake this work, and at his death, his
materials including Evelyn Simpson's early work and the
microfilms and photostats which Bald had collected were
given to Helen Gardner, who later handed them on to me to
prepare an edition under her direction. The Renaissance
English Text Society has generously allowed me to use this
material.

I am indebted to the trustees of the Henry W. and Albert A. Berg Collection, The New York Public Library, Astor, Lenox, and Tilden Foundations for permission to use the Westmoreland MS as copy-text for the Paradoxes; to the Houghton Library, Harvard University for permission to use the O'Flaherty MS as copy-text for the Problems and to quote variants from the Dobell and Stephens MSS; to the Huntington Library for permission to discuss variants from the Bridgewater MS; to The James Marshall and Marie-Louise Osborn Collection, Yale University Library for permission to quote variants from the Osborn MSS; to The Board of Trinity College, Dublin for permission to quote variants from the Trinity College, Dublin, MS; to the Master and Fellows of Trinity College, Cambridge, for permission to quote variants from the Trinity College, Cambridge, MS; to the British Library for permission to quote variants from Stowe MS 962 and Additional MS 25707; to the Bedford Estates Office, London for permission to discuss variants in the commonplace-book of the fourth Earl of Bedford; and to the Bodleian Library which provided me with the bulk of the material required.

Many people helped me to prepare this edition, notably the Fellows of Somerville College who answered questions on topics many and various; John Sparrow and A. J. Smith who examined this work in its thesis form and made many valuable comments and corrections; John Carey who supervised my work on the General Introduction and Commentary; and chiefly, Helen Gardner who suggested that I might undertake this edition, and who gave unstintingly of her advice and encouragement during the period of its preparation. Finally I gratefully acknowledge the financial assistance of The Canada Council and of the Mary Somerville Research Fellowship, Somerville College. This work bears no dedication; if it did, it would be to the man who has inspired and encouraged me in many ways —G. M. Story, and Gloucester.

Department of English,   H. P.
University of Ottawa.

CONTENTS

REFERENCES
AND ABBREVIATIONS

QUOTATIONS from Donne's poems are taken from: *The Divine Poems,* edited by Helen Gardner (Oxford, 2nd ed., 1978); *The Elegies and the Songs and Sonnets,* edited by Helen Gardner (Oxford, 1965 [rpt. 1970]); *The Poems of John Donne,* edited by H. J. C. Grierson, 2 vols (Oxford, 1912 [rpt. 1958]); *The Satires, Epigrams and Verse Letters,* edited by W. Milgate (Oxford, 1967); *The Epithalamions, Anniversaries and Epicedes,* edited by W. Milgate (Oxford, 1978). These are referred to as:

> *Divine Poems*
> *Elegies etc.*
> Grierson
> *Satires etc.*
> *Epithalamions etc.*

Quotations from Donne's prose works are taken from the following texts: *Biathanatos,* 1646 (facsimile rpt., New York, 1930); *Pseudo-Martyr* (1610) (facsimile rpt., Delmar, N.Y., 1974); *The Sermons of John Donne,* edited by G. R. Potter and Evelyn M. Simpson, 10 vols (California, 1953–61); *Essays in Divinity,* edited by Evelyn M. Simpson (Oxford, 1952 [rpt. 1967]); *Devotions upon Emergent Occasions,* edited by John Sparrow (Cambridge, 1923). These are referred to as:

> *Biathanatos*
> *Pseudo-Martyr*
> *Sermons*
> Simpson, *Essays*
> Sparrow, *Devotions.*

Quotations from Donne's letters are taken from *Letters to Severall Persons of Honour,* 1651; *Poems, By J. D.,* 1633; *A collection of Letters, made by Sr Tobie Mathews K^t,* 1660. These are referred to as:

> *Letters,* 1651
> *Poems,* 1633
> *Tobie Mathew Collection.*

OTHER REFERENCES:

Aristotle   *Works,* eds. W. D. Ross *et al.,* 1927–52.

Bald	*John Donne: A Life*, R. C. Bald (Oxford, 1970).
Burton	*The Anatomy of Melancholy*, Robert Burton, Everyman edition, 1932 [rpt. 1972].
Crane	*Italian Social Customs of the Sixteenth Century*, T. F. Crane (New Haven, Conn., 1920).
Gosse	*The Life and Letters of John Donne*, Edmund Gosse, 2 vols., 1899.
Hayward	*John Donne Dean of St. Paul's Complete Poetry and Selected Prose*, edited by John Hayward, 1929 [rpt. 1962].
Lawn	*The Salernitan Questions*, Brian Lawn (Oxford, 1963).
Paradossi, 1544	*Paradossi cioè, sententie fuori del comun parere, Novellamente venute in luce ...*, Ortensio Lando (Venice, 1544).
Problemi	*Problemi naturali, e morali*, Hieronimo Garimberto (Venice, 1549).
Prose Works	*A Study of the Prose Works of John Donne*, Evelyn M. Simpson, 2nd edition (Oxford, 1948 [rpt. 1962]).
Quattro libri, 1556	*Quattro libri de dubbi con le solutioni a ciascun dubbio accomodate*, Ortensio Lando (Venice, 1556).
Shakespeare	*Works*, Arden editions.
Tilley	*A Dictionary of the Proverbs in England in the Sixteenth and Seventeenth Centuries*, M. P. Tilley (Ann Arbor, Mich., 1950).

PERIODICALS:

ELN	*English Language Notes.*
JEGP	*Journal of English and Germanic Philology.*
MLN	*Modern Language Notes.*
MLQ	*Modern Language Quarterly.*
MLR	*Modern Language Review.*
MP	*Modern Philology.*
N&Q	*Notes and Queries.*
OED	*Oxford English Dictionary.*
PBSA	*Papers of the Bibliographical Society of America.*
PQ	*Philological Quarterly.*
PMLA	*Publications of the Modern Language Association of America.*
RES	*Review of English Studies.*

GENERAL INTRODUCTION

To the lovers of his poetry Donne's *Paradoxes and Problems* are the most interesting of all his shorter prose works. This interest arises in part because they are early works of 'Jack Donne' written at different periods of his younger life, and in part because there are similarities in mood, tone, technique, and subject-matter with much of the poetry.

The Paradoxes appear to have been written in the early 1590s when Donne was a student at Thavies and Lincoln's Inns, somewhat proud, aware of his superior abilities, and confident, one feels, of a promising future. This is the period of the Satires and Elegies, and there are parallels with these works, as in Paradox VII, ll. 44–9 and Satire III.[1] The relationship between the literary Paradoxes and the paradoxical Elegies such as 'Loves Progress' where the lover is urged to begin his suit at his lady's foot rather than her face, 'The Anagram' where an ugly wife is to be preferred, and 'The Autumnal' where old age in a woman is praised, is difficult to miss, but Donne's love of paradox never left him. It is evident in many of the Holy Sonnets, and in his later life as a preacher, Donne's joy in the paradoxical nature of the Christian religion is apparent in his Sermons.

The Problems were written later than the Paradoxes. By their allusion to contemporary events and by their mention in letters, several Problems can be assigned to the period between 1603 and 1609 or 1610. It is probable that they were all written during that time. This period was a gloomy

---

1   thrise
  Colder then Salamanders, like divine
  Children in th'oven, fires of Spaine, 'and the line,
  Whose countries limbecks to our bodies bee,
  Canst thou for gaine beare? and must every hee
  Which cryes not, 'Goddesse,' to thy Mistresse, draw,
  Or eate thy poysonous words? courage of straw!
                                          ll. 22–8

time in Donne's life for he lived in Mitcham with a sickly wife and an increasing family, without any proper means of support. The Problems convey none of the self-confidence of the Paradoxes and appear to be the somewhat bitter works of a disappointed man. In them, with a mixture of cynicism and humour, Donne explores social, moral, and scientific questions of the early seventeenth century. In answer to each question posed in the title of the Problems, he presents either an argument or a series of independent sentences each of which offers a possible, if outrageous, answer.

To assess Donne's *Paradoxes and Problems*, it is necessary to review briefly the history of each form, to look at Donne's use of each, and to ask why he wrote them. Also, the inclusion in the canon of some of the works which have been commonly associated with the *Paradoxes and Problems* must be questioned.

I. PARADOXES

Two forms of literary Paradox can be identified, both of which can be traced from the Classical period. The earliest recorded form is seen in the mock encomiums of Helen of Troy written by the Greek writers Gorgias (*c.*483–376 BC) and Isocrates (436–338 BC).[1] These mock encomiums were the predecessors of many other works of false praise, some of which were listed by Erasmus in a sixteenth-century defence of the humour and triviality of the theme. In a letter concerning his *Moriae encomium*, written to Sir Thomas More he wrote:

Now as for those who find the triviality and humour of the theme offensive, I should like them to reflect that this is no vein of my own invention, but reflects the habitual practice of great writers of the past; inasmuch as Homer, all those centuries ago, wrote in jesting vein his

[1] Rosalie Colie, *Paradoxia Epidemica: The Renaissance Tradition of Paradox* (Princeton, N.J., 1966), 8, noted that paradoxically these mock encomiums led to Helen's becoming a proper subject of praise—'paradox became orthodox'.

Battle of the Frogs and Mice, Virgil of the Gnats and the *Moretum*, Ovid of the Walnut; in addition encomiums on Busiris were written by Polycrates and his critic Isocrates, on injustice by Glaucon, on Thersites and the quartan ague by Favorinus, on Baldness by Synesius, on the Fly and the Art of Being a Parasite by Lucian; and finally Seneca wrote a playful apotheosis of Claudius the emperor, Plutarch a jesting dialogue of Gryllus with Ulysses, Lucian and Apuleius an 'Ass' apiece, and someone or other the 'Testament of Grunnius Corocotta the piglet', mentioned also by St Jerome.[1]

Mock encomiums were also written in the Middle Ages, for example Hucbald of St. Amand's wrote *Ecloga de laudibus calvitii*, c.880, dedicated to Charles the Bald, in which every word begins with the letter 'c'. Wine, fleas, lice, and bedbugs were praised by Michael Psellus in the eleventh century, and fleas, lice, and bedbugs by Joannes Tzetzes in Μυίας ἐγκώμιον in the twelfth century.[2] Another form of literary Paradox argued against received opinion. This was used by Cicero (106–43 BC) in *Paradoxa Stoicorum*, a serious work on important ethical doctrines of Stoic philosophy. In six essays Cicero argued 'contra opinionem omnium' that, for example, virtue is sufficient for happiness, transgressions are equal, and right actions are equal in magnitude, and only the wise man is rich.

Both forms of Classical Paradox were popular during the Renaissance. The earliest and most influential of the mock encomiums was Erasmus' *Moriae encomium*, written in 1509, first published in 1511, and translated as *The Praise of Folie* by Sir Thomas Chaloner in 1549. Erasmus' work is more complex than its Classical predecessors. It is a parody of rhetoric, a satiric indictment of European society, an oration seeking to lift men to the contemplation of the heavenly Jerusalem, and a dramatic monologue whose satiric device is to use a woman speaker. It is Folly praising

---

[1] Erasmus, 'Correspondence 1501–1514', *Collected Works*, ii, trans. R. A. B. Mynors and D. F. S. Thomson (Toronto, 1975), 163.

[2] Cited by A. S. Pease, 'Things without Honor', *Classical Philology*, xxi (1926), 40–1, and H. K. Miller, 'The Paradoxical Encomium with Special Reference to its Vogue in England', *MP* liii (1956), 149–50.

Folly or *Moria*, or More, because Folly like More is wise, hence it is both parody and eulogy, no praise, and praise.[1] Despite its complexity, the work was the chief instigator of the numerous mock encomiums which were later written in England. Other continental mock encomiums were translated into English in the sixteenth century. These include Henry Cornelius Agrippa's work translated by James Sandford as 'A Digression in prayse of the Asse', cap. 202 in *Of the Vanitie and uncertaintie of Artes and Sciences*, 1569; Abraham Fleming's translation of Synesius' *Calvitii encomium* as *A Paradoxe, Proving by reason and example, that Baldnesse is much better than bushie haire*, 1579; and an anonymous translation of Adriano Banchieri's *La nobilità dell'asino* as *The Noblenesse of the Asse*, 1595.[2]

The other form of Paradox was reintroduced into Italy by Ortensio Lando in the sixteenth century. His first published work, *Cicero relegatus et Cicero revocatus*, 1534, consisted of two dialogues, the one condemning and the other condoning Cicero's style. In 1543 he published his *Paradossi cioè, sentensie fuori del comun parere, novellamente venute in luce*, consisting of thirty Paradoxes in two books. Topics covered include that it is better to be poor than rich (Paradox I), ugly than beautiful (II), ignorant than wise (III), drunk than sober (VII), that it is not odious to have a dishonest wife (XI), that it is better to die than to live a long life (XIV), that it is bad not to be beaten (XVII), that it is not reprehensible to be a bastard (XVIII), that it is better to be at war than at peace (XX), that woman is more excellent than man (XXV), and that it is better to be timid than bold (XXVI). Lando's Paradoxes are in the tradition of Cicero, as they promote views contrary to those generally accepted

---

[1] See Sister M. Geraldine, 'Erasmus and the Tradition of Paradox', *SP* lxi (1964), 41–2.

[2] Donne knew these three works. In the manuscript commonplace book of his *Catalogus librorum aulicorum* (Cambridge, TCC. MS B. 14.22) is written '*Baldus in laudem Calvitii; Agrippa de vanitate Scientiarum; et Encomium Asini per eundem*', an addition which is thought to be Donne's. See R. E. Bennett, 'The Addition to Donne's *Catalogus Librorum*', *MLN* xlviii (1933), 167–8.

by contemporary society, are basically moral,[1] and are some-
times argued with great erudition[2] and wit. They are not
mere witty and ingenious trifles. Although, or perhaps
because, they are the only known continental Renaissance
form of Paradox that argues against received opinion, they
were popular[3] and appeared in several Italian editions.
Twenty-five of them were translated into French in 1553 by
Charles Estienne as *Paradoxes, ce sont propos contre la
commune opinion*,[4] and in 1593 the first twelve Paradoxes in
Estienne's edition were translated by A[nthony] M[unday]
as *The Defence of Contraries: Paradoxes against common
opinion*.[5] Further English translation of Lando's *Paradossi*
appeared in the seventeenth and eighteenth centuries.[6]

Besides being influenced by translations of written con-
tinental Paradoxes, English writers, who began to write
literary Paradoxes in the late sixteenth century, also drew
upon an oral or subliterary tradition of paradoxical en-

[1] Sister Geraldine (p. 47) noted that once Lando has 'protested his non-sincerity, [he]
seems to take on a rather convincing tone of earnestness, and in most cases it is the abuse of
good, not the good itself, which he condemns'.

[2] W. G. Rice, 'The *Paradossi* of Ortensio Lando', *Essays and Studies in English, University
of Michigan Publications*, viii (1932), 64, noted that to assist in his arguments Lando is
'usually able to summon a cloud of witnesses to his aid, to cite instances from ancient or
contemporary history which will bolster up his case'.

[3] The *Paradossi* proved so popular that Lando published a confutation of them titled
Confutazione del libro de paradossi nuovamente composta [no place, date, or printer]. Cited by
P. F. Grendler, *Critics of the Italian World 1530–1560: Anton Francesco Doni, Nicolò Franco
and Ortensio Lando* (Madison, Wisc., 1969), 223.

[4] Estienne omitted Paradoxes 11 and 27–30 and added a Paradox of his own invention on
lawyers. He also altered Italian names and incidents to French examples.

[5] Munday printed those Paradoxes that argue that poverty is better than riches, that it is
better to be ugly than beautiful, ignorant than wise, blind than enlightened, mad than wise,
that it is not evil for a prince to lose his state, that it is better to be drunk than sober, to have
a barren than a fertile wife, to live in exile rather than in one's native land, that it is better
to be weak than healthy, that weeping is better than laughing, and scarcity is better than
abundance. In a table that followed the text of these Paradoxes, Munday promised that the
text of the remaining fourteen Paradoxes found in the French edition would follow in a
second volume. In 1602 Munday's text was reissued with a new title-page, but as the only
known copy (in the Bodleian Library) is defective, consisting of the opening thirty-four pages,
it is not known whether Lando included the text of the fourteen Paradoxes.

[6] Translations of seven Paradoxes were published in Thomas Milles, *The Treasurie of
Auncient and Moderne Times*, 1613. A single Paradox was printed in *Hygiasticon*, Cambridge,
1634, reprinted in *The Temperate Man*, 1678, and again as *The Frugal Life*, intro. W. E. A.
Axon, 1899. Another Paradox was printed by John Hall in *Paradoxes by J. De la Salle*, 1653.
Finally six of Lando's Paradoxes were printed by John Dunton in *Athenian Sport: Or, Two
Thousand Paradoxes Merrily Argued, To Amuse and Divert the Age*, 1707. This latter work
also included the eleven Paradoxes that occur in Donne's *Paradoxes and Problems*, 1633; see
Textual Introduction, p. lxxxiv.

comiums in ballad form which go back at least as far as the
fifteenth century. These ballads praise subjects such as
money, copper noses, and bottled ale.[1] More important,
however, for the writers concerned were the verbal Paradoxes
which served as entertainment of the university and Inns
of Court wits. Paradoxes were a fashionable feature of the
Inns of Court Revels in the late sixteenth and early seven-
teenth centuries, and as late as 1618 a character named
Paradox was the leading figure in the revels at Gray's Inn.[2]
    While Paradoxes appear to have been acceptable at the
Inns of Court, their position in the university was apparently
rather dubious. Gabriel Harvey, in a letter written in 1573
to Dr John Young of Pembroke College, Cambridge,
defended himself from the accusations of Thomas Nevil,
a Fellow of Pembroke, who used 'a forth reason also against
me; and that forsooth was this: that I was a great and
continual patron of paradoxis and a main defender of
straung opinions, and that communly against Aristotle
too'.[3] His defence rests upon his claim never to have
invented Paradoxes, but merely to have made use of those
which had been propounded earlier by various sixteenth-
century philosophers.
    In 1593 Harvey published an encomium of an ass in the
third section of *Pierce's Supererogation, Or A New Prayse of
The Old Asse*. Other paradoxical or mock encomiums followed
Harvey's. Sir John Harington wrote a praise of the water-
closet in *A New Discourse Of A Stale Subject; Called the
Metamorphosis of Ajax*, 1596. Richard Barnfield, who cited
Erasmus as his model, wrote a poem titled *The Encomion of
Lady Pecunia, Or The Praise of Money*, 1598, and Thomas
Nashe wrote a 'Praise of Red Herring' in *Lenten Stuffe*,
1599.[4] These four literary Paradoxes derive from *Moriae
encomium*. The writers stress the triviality of their themes as

---

[1] See Miller, 155–6.
[2] Cited by P. J. Finkelpearl, *John Marston of the Middle Temple* (Cambridge, Mass., 1969),
228.
[3] *Letter-Book*, ed. E. J. L. Scott (Camden Society, NS, 33, 1884), 10.
[4] Cited by Miller, 156.

Erasmus had done, Harvey by an ironical attack on Paradoxes and their writers,[1] Harington in the 'Answer' to his Paradox by listing the topics of recent continental Paradoxes,[2] and Nashe by devoting two pages of his Paradox to the naming of both Classical and contemporary writers in the field.[3]

Although he wrote his Paradoxes later than Donne, Sir William Cornwallis deserves mention here, because he wrote both mock encomiums which were published in three editions in 1616 and 1617 of subjects such as sadness, the French pox, and King Richard III,[4] and also Paradoxes that argued against received opinion, namely, 'That a great redd nose is an ornament to the face', 'That it is a happines to be in debt', 'That miserie is true Fœlicity' and 'That Inconstancy is more commendable then Constancie'.[5] These latter, which were written in 1600 when Cornwall was twenty-two years of age,[6] are the more interesting, partially because they show very clearly the influence of Ortensio Lando's *Paradossi*, being moral and over-documented,[7] and partially because, although he wished to emphasize the trivial and harmless nature of Paradoxes,[8] he also claimed that he wrote them for a serious purpose, 'seinge Opinion

---

[1] *Works*, ed. A. B. Grosart (1884), ii. 244–5.

[2] Sig. A6.

[3] *Works*, ed. R. B. McKerrow (1957 [rpt. 1966]), iii. 176–8.

[4] *Essays Or rather, Encomions*, 1616; *Essays of Certaine Paradoxes*, 1616; and *Essays Of Certaine Paradoxes. The Second Impression*, 1617.

[5] These Paradoxes are preserved in the commonplace-book of Sir Stephen Powle (Tanner MS 169, ff. 132–7, Bodleian Library). They were first published in R. E. Bennett, 'Four Paradoxes by William Cornwallis, the Younger', *Harvard Studies and Notes*, xiii (1931), 223–40.

[6] Tanner MS 169, f. 132; Bennett, 219.

[7] Cornwallis also, as Bennett noted (pp. 231–5), incorporated the actual arguments used by Lando in five of the *Paradossi* into the Paradox 'That miserie is true Fœlicity'.

[8] In a letter to John Hobart, a relation, probably written in February 1600 or 1601 Cornwallis wrote:

for my Paradoxes, beleve me had I thowght they shoulde have bine knowen for myne, I woulde thoug[h] not in them, yet in keepinge them secreatt have sh[ew]ed some littill discretion: I knowe their weaknes to unmeet objeackts for your Syght . . . the inteant whearfore I seant them was one[ly] to Paralell christmas games, or some such sport*es* wherunto that tyme is Commonly much addickted, yet [it] pleaseth you to lyke them, but I thinke rathir me, thoug[h] neythir the love that is cast away eythir uppon them or me, is love but charity; rathir an almes, then the wort[h] retornead . . . I have seant you this week two, if your letters will betray you soe much to desier any more, 2 weekly I will poyson you wi*th*all. (Tanner MS 283, f. 204; Bennett, 220.)

of a litle nothinge is become soe mightie that like a
Monarchesse she tyrannizeth over Judgement I have been
undertaken to anatomize and confute some few of her
traditions'.[1] Against this background we must now look at
Donne's Paradoxes; what were his sources, how did his
Paradoxes work, what was his attitude to them, why and
when did he write them?

The influence of three authors is apparent in Donne's
Paradoxes. The first is Martial whom he quotes six times in
the Paradoxes and once in the Problems,[2] and whose
epigrammatic and sometimes bawdy quality is reproduced
in the brevity and wit of the Paradoxes. The second is
Erasmus whose scattering of proverbs throughout *Moriae
encomium* Donne copied in his Paradoxes and to whom he
made reference in Paradox VII.[3] Most important, however,
is Ortensio Lando, whose *Paradossi* Donne appears to have
used as his starting-point. Donne's Paradoxes with their
outrageous wit outstrip Lando's earlier efforts; for example,
Paradox II which defends women's painting may have arisen
from Lando's *Paradosso* II, 'Che meglio sia l'esser brutto,
che bello', where Lando had written 'havendogli Iddio fatto
sì bella gratia d'esser brutte, esse proccacciano con peregrine
foggie, con biacca, con lisci, con olii . . . d'apparer belle'.[4]
In Paradox VI on the body and the mind, Donne toys with
the neo-Platonic concept of a fair mind in a fair body,
possibly playing with Lando's serious assertion in his
Paradosso II, that many persons with noble minds (Aesop,
Zeno, Aristotle, and Socrates) had deformed bodies. In the
same Paradox Donne may be mocking the occurrence of a

---

[1] 'Preface' to 'That Inconstancy is more commendable then Constancie', Tanner MS 169,
f. 135ᵛ; Bennett, 237.
[2] Paradoxes V, VII (twice), IX (twice), X and Problem X. See Evelyn M. Simpson,
'Donne's Reading of Martial', *A Garland for John Donne*, ed. T. Spencer (Gloucester, Mass.,
1931 [rpt. 1958]), 44–9.
[3] 'by much laughing thou mayst know ther is a foole, not that the laughers are fooles, but
that amongst them ther is some foole at whome wise men laugh. Which mov'd *Erasmus* to
put this as the first argument in the mouthe of his Folly, that she made beholders laughe'
(ll. 8–12).
[4] 'God gave them the grace of being ugly; they procure with strange fashions, white
make-up, cosmetics, oils . . . to appear beautiful', *Paradossi cioè, sententie fuori del comun
parere, Novellamente venute in luce* (Venice, 1544), f. 13.

noble mind in a sickly body because of Lando's praise of this combination in *Paradosso* X, 'Meglio è d'esser debole e mal sano, che robusto e gagliardo', where Lando had written 'in un fragil corpo dimuora spesso una mente nobile: un'animo prudente e un spirito magnifico e generoso atto con la debiltà, non solo a tentare, ma a condure anche a fine ogni bella e honorata impresa'.[1]

Clearly Donne wrote the form of Paradox that argued against received opinion, rather than the mock encomium, although false praise is part of his method. In general, Donne's Paradoxes open with a vigorous statement that bears either directly or indirectly on the point at issue. The arguments move quickly, one leading on to the next; some are developed while others are not, so that there is variety in pace. Donne's arguments are not always easy.[2] The Paradoxes close, generally, with an exceedingly witty twist that evolves from the preceding arguments but that surprises the reader with its audacity. The language of the Paradoxes is direct and colloquial, yet Donne's rhetorical abilities are obvious in his moderate use of balance, alliteration, repetition, etc. which serve to create a striking phrase. Various features of paradoxical writing occur throughout the Paradoxes. For example, mock praise occurs in Paradox VI on the gifts of the body as opposed to those of the mind, and in Paradox VII on laughter among wise men. There is a change of standards in Paradox II on women's painting, and word-play on the word 'paint' occurs in the same Paradox. There is contradiction in Paradox I that all things kill themselves, and false logic in Paradox VI on the merits of the gifts of the body over those of the mind.

Two conflicting views have been given on why Donne wrote his Paradoxes. Evelyn Simpson argued that these

---

[1] 'A noble mind often dwells in a frail body; a prudent mind and a magnificent and generous spirit fit for the weak, not only to attempt, but also to bring to conclusion, every beautiful and honourable enterprise', *Paradossi*, f. 40ᵛ.

[2] Donne's 'reasoning does not follow the beaten way of the paradox, and is more difficult to grasp', E. N. S. Thompson, 'Paradoxes and Problems', *The Seventeenth Century English Essay, University of Iowa Humanistic Studies*, iii, no. 3 (1926), 102.

works, though witty, were written with a serious intent.[1]
Noting that Paradox V, 'That only Cowards dare dye' is
opposed by Paradox I, 'That all things kill themselves', she
argued 'this refutation of his own contention mirrors for us
the strife within Donne's own mind.'[2] P. N. Siegal, on the
other hand, argued that Donne's Paradoxes are

propositions, destructive of the Platonic–Stoic–Aristotelian–Christian
frame of reference of the Elizabethans, in which the universe was a
divine harmony created by God, in which nature furnished the laws
of man's being, and in which it was one of man's duties to learn to die
bravely, secure in his faith.[3]

He claimed further that Evelyn Simpson's view was too
serious, that Donne

is not concerned with having his paradoxes and problems be consistent
with each other. His subtle mind is playing with different concepts of
the relationship between the sexes, the nature of good and evil, the
cosmological order, death, and using them with a devastating skepticism
to display his mental dexterity in puncturing traditional ideals. While
this jugglery with ideas reveals an early fascination with philosophical
problems which later tormented him so much, it should not be
mistaken for something other than intellectual jugglery.[4]

The true answer lies somewhere between these two opinions;
the Paradoxes are neither entirely serious nor merely
intellectual jugglery. The inquiring attitude manifested is
related to the scepticism and searching after truth shown in
Lando's *Paradossi* and in English scientific writers of the
sixteenth century such as Bacon. However, like nearly all
Donne's poetry, they were written to answer Donne's own
questions, to give himself delight and satisfaction, and to
give delight to his friends.

The *Paradoxes and Problems* were published under the

---

[1] 'Donne's *Paradoxes and Problems*', *A Garland for John Donne*, ed. T. Spencer (Gloucester, Mass., 1931 [rpt. 1958]), 23–43.
[2] Ibid. 39.
[3] 'Donne's *Paradoxes and Problems*', *PQ* xxviii (1949), 510.
[4] Ibid. 511.

title *Juvenilia* with the date 1633 on the title-page. This title
is defensive: to excuse these impertinent pieces as written in
the youth of the newly dead Dean of St. Paul's. Even
twenty years later, when these works were published by
Donne's son, they were accompanied by Epigrams said to
have been written by Donne, *Ignatius His Conclave*, but more
importantly by the *Essays in Divinity*. The volume was
described by the younger Donne as consisting of '*Things of
the* least *and* greatest *weight*', the *Paradoxes and Problems*
being the '*Primroses and* violets *of the Spring* [which]
entertain Us with more Delight, then the Fruits *of the Autumn*'.[1]
Donne himself would have been horrified at the publication
of works that he had written for the amusement of himself
and his friends, and had kept close.

Donne's concern for his Paradoxes and his desire to
restrict their circulation is seen in a letter possibly written in
1600 which had accompanied the text of ten Paradoxes:[2]

> except I receve by your next letter an assurance upon the religion of
> your frendship that no coppy shalbee taken for any respect of these or
> any other my compositions sent to you, I shall sinn against my
> conscience if I send you any more . . . I am desirous to hyde them
> with out any over reconing of them or there maker.

He appeared to feel that his interest in Paradoxes was
reprehensible:

> Only in obedience I send you some of my paradoxes; I love you and
> myself and them to well to send them willingly for they carry with

---

[1] 'Dedicatory Epistle', *Paradoxes, Problemes, Essays, Characters*, 1652, sigs. A2–A2ᵛ.

[2] This letter was dated by Evelyn Simpson who printed its text in *A Study of the Prose
Works of John Donne* (Oxford, 1948), 316–17. It occupied f. 308ᵛ of Sir Henry Wotton's
commonplace-book, known as the Burley MS, which was destroyed by fire in 1908. The
recipient of the letter was identified by Evelyn Simpson as being Wotton himself because he
was a friend of Donne's and because the letter and accompanying Paradoxes were copied in his
commonplace-book. I. A. Shapiro has informed me that he does not think that the letter was
written to Wotton, although he cannot identify the person to whom it may have been sent,
and also that he considers 1600 to be the earliest possible date that the letter could have been
written. Certainly, the second half of the letter chides the recipient for his interest in Aretino's
sonnets, and it is difficult to believe either that Wotton would not have known these works
before 1600 (at the earliest), or that Donne would have addressed him in the admonishing tone
used. One must also wonder whether Wotton would have had a copy made against Donne's
expressed wish to the contrary.

them a confession of there lightnes. and *your* trouble and my shame . . .
and to my satyrs there belongs some feare and to some elegies and
these p*er*haps shame. against both w*h*ich affections although I be tough
enough yet I have a ridling disposition to bee ashamed of feare and
afrayd of shame.

However, like Cornwallis in the preface to his Paradox on
Inconstancy,[1] he stressed that the writing of Paradoxes was
serious because of the disposition of the age:

indeed they were made rather to deceave tyme then her daughth*er*
truth: although they have beene written in an age when any thing is
strong enough to overthrow her.

Finally, he showed in the same letter what Paradoxes are and
how they function:[2]

if they make yo*u* to find better reasons against them they do there
office: for they are but swaggerers: quiet enough if yo*u* resist them. if
p*er*chance they be pretyly guilt, th*a*t is there best for they are not
hatcht: they are rather alaru*m*s to truth to arme her then enemies: and
they have only this advantadg to scape fro*m* being caled ill things th*a*t
they are nothings: therfore take heed of allowing any of them least
yo*u* make another.

Although this letter appears not to have been written before
1600, there is no evidence to suggest that the accompanying
Paradoxes were contemporary with it. Indeed, the recipient
of the letter had recently developed an interest in Aretino's
sonnets,[3] works which had been known by the educated
circle of wits in England since the early 1590s, and there is
no reason to suppose that he was not equally behind the times
in his interest in Donne's Paradoxes. The similarity which
the Paradoxes bear to the Elegies and Satires, both usually
dated in the early 1590s, argues for their having been
written at the same time. Donne associates the three in his

---

[1] See above, pp. xxi–xxii.
[2] Donne's analysis of the function of Paradox has been noted by A. E. Malloch, 'The
Techniques and Function of the Renaissance Paradox', *SP* liii (1956), 192.
[3] See above, p. xxv, n. 2.

letter quoted extensively above, 'to my satyrs there belongs some feare and to some elegies and these perhaps shame'. I would suggest, therefore, that the Paradoxes were written early in the 1590s. Although Donne tried to restrict the circulation of his Paradoxes, apparently successfully till the end of the sixteenth century, by the early seventeenth century knowledge of them was increasing. John Manningham, who was not a member of Donne's circle, copied into his Diary in 1603 extracts of Paradoxes II and VII.[1]

II. PROBLEMS

The Paradoxes were written by Donne the young man-about-town. The Problems were written by an older and a sadder man, amusing himself during his 'exile' in Surrey. The Problem, like the Paradox, has a long history, but unlike that of the Paradox the history of the literary Problem has never been traced by critics of English literature, and cannot therefore be treated here quite as briefly.

The Problem was first used by Aristotle in the fourth century BC as a method of education. His book of Problems, lost long ago, was referred to by himself in *Meteorologica*[2] and by his successors such as Cicero, Plutarch, and Aulus Gellius.[3] The Problem tradition of question and answer which Aristotle began continued, despite the loss of his actual book of Problems, throughout the remaining centuries BC and into the Christian era. During this period Problems were used, and their number increased, by teachers particularly in the sciences. The discovery of the first manuscript of the pseudo-Aristotelian *Problemata* in the ninth century[4] and of the fuller collection consisting of

---

[1] See R. E. Bennett, 'John Manningham and Donne's Paradoxes', *MLN* xlvi (1931), 309–13.
[2] ii, 6; iii. 3.
[3] Cicero, *Tusculan Disputations*, i. 33; Plutarch, *Quaestiones conviviales*, iii. 3; Gellius, *Noctes Atticae*, i. 11; xix. 2 and 4; xx. 4.
[4] This collection is now referred to as the *Vetustissima translatio*.

thirty-eight books in the thirteenth,[1] merely added impetus to a tradition already well established.

The use of the Problem in education has been traced by Brian Lawn,[2] using as his focal point the medical school at Salerno,[3] and tracing the increasing bulk of Problems—questions and answers which were designed to teach—and their spread throughout Europe. These Problems, which dealt with a variety of scientific topics, meteorology, astronomy, physics, anthropology, medicine, zoology, physiology, botany, and to some extent with moral and philosophical issues, were written by a succession of writers including Alexander of Aphrodisias, Seneca, St. Basil, Adelard of Bath, William of Conches, and Albertus Magnus.[4] Throughout the Middle Ages, Problems were the preserve of the small part of the European population that attended the universities. In 1483 a book called Aristotle's *Problemata* was published. The *Problemata* bear no resemblance to Aristotle's works; among the various authorities cited are Hippocrates, Galen, the eleventh-century Arabian translator Constantinus Africanus, and the thirteenth-century teacher Albertus Magnus. The publication of this book, however, spread the information contained in Problems beyond the confines of the universities. The Latin text was rapidly translated into German, French, and English,[5] and so became available to a larger audience.

In the twelfth century the educational Problem also

---

[1] This collection is what we now know as Aristotle's *Problemata*, (*Works*, vii, eds. W. D. Ross *et al.*). According to E. S. Forster, 'The Pseudo-Aristotelian Problems, their nature and composition', *Classical Quarterly*, xxii (1928), 163–5, the *Problemata* were compiled gradually, not earlier than the first century BC and possibly as late as the fifth or sixth century AD, and consist of genuine Aristotelian Problems, fragments of Aristotle's works in problem form, borrowings from the writings of 'Hippocrates' and Theophrastus, and the writings of Aristotle's followers.

[2] *The Salernitan Questions: An Introduction to the History of Medieval and Renaissance Problem Literature*, Oxford, 1963.

[3] The school was founded before the end of the tenth century, came into prominence in the twelfth century, and its authority lasted throughout the Renaissance.

[4] Alexander of Aphrodisias, *Problems*; Seneca, *Naturales quaestiones*; St. Basil, Homilies on the *Hexaemeron*; Adelard of Bath, *Quaestiones naturales*; William of Conches, *De philosophia*; Albertus Magnus, Commentary on *De animalibus*.

[5] Lawn, 100–1, records six German incunables of the Problems, the earliest French edition in 1554, and the first English edition in 1595.

developed into another form, that of the disputed question. This was adopted by all university faculties as a means by which the student could sharpen his skill in dialectic. The various disciplines of the different faculties were sometimes intermingled in disputations, so that, for example, students of the theology faculty in Paris debated in the *Quodlibeta* such questions as:

whether birth in the eighth month is as good as that in the ninth or seventh, whether a wise father generally begets a foolish son, why the tall are dull, the short quick-witted, why one laughs about trifles but not about serious matters, why wounds bleed in the presence of the murderer, why men go bald, and have beards, but women are without these characteristics, whether whole or finely divided foods are better for eating, and questions about vision, optics (the formation of images in mirrors), the actions of lightning, fascination, and sleep-walking.[1]

The disputed question remained a mainstay of scholastic education up to the early part of the seventeenth century. Disputations were part of education in sixteenth- and seventeenth-century Oxford and Cambridge, and were held both privately by the colleges and publicly by the universities.[2] College disputations were less formal than the university events and were sometimes run with little ceremony. Symonds D'Ewes[3] complained of having prepared himself with great diligence and also prayer to act as a respondent to a 'prime student', Mr Gervase Neville, only to have the moderator stop the dispute before D'Ewes had been able to complete his argument or indeed to say 'one-half' of what he had prepared. On the other hand, the conduct or misconduct of the spectators could be noted and reported, as Gabriel Harvey[4] found when Thomas Nevil complained of his 'putting on of [his] hat at problem', thus forcing

---

[1] Lawn, 87–8.
[2] The most complete accounts of the disputation during the period at Oxford and Cambridge are given by W. T. Costello, *The Scholastic Curriculum at Early Seventeenth-Century Cambridge* (Cambridge, Mass. 1958), 14–31, and M. H. Curtis, *Oxford and Cambridge in Transition 1558–1642* (Oxford, 1959 [rpt. 1965]), 89–99.
[3] *College Life in the Time of James the First* (1851), 67–8.
[4] *Letter-Book*, 12.

Harvey to explain that he had covered his head because he had been suffering from a cold. Students were permitted to choose their own questions for disputing if they wished, but there was a certain decorum to be observed both in choosing particular topics and in expressing opinions on them. Harvey complained:

Unles we wil onli admit of that to be done whitch we our selvs onli have dun, in philosophical disputations to give popular and plausible theams, de nobilitate, de amore, de gloria, de liberalitate, and a few the like, more fit for schollars declamations to discurs uppon then semli for masters problems to dispute uppon: and more gudli and famus for the show then ether convenient for the time, or meet for the place, or profitable for the persons. Sutch matters have bene thurrouly canvissid long ago . . . me thinks it were more fruteful for us and commodius for our auditors to handle sum sad and witti controversi. But I never found ani fault with them for duelling in there own stale quaestions. I wuld it miht have pleasd them as litle to envi me for mi nu fresh paradoxis.[1]

Besides the prescribed college and university exercises, there were also elaborate and ceremonial displays of argumentative skill and wit put on both for the visits of royalty and other important dignitaries to the universities and for the special disputations held annually on the eve of Commencement Day, *in vesperiis*, and on Commencement Day itself, *in comitiis*. At these events, a prevaricator was introduced into the university disputations at Cambridge.[2] This official humourist spoke before the disputation, his function being to amuse the audience by playing verbally upon the question to be disputed. The prevaricators were normally students whose efforts sometimes strayed beyond the realms of good taste, mimicking and jeering at professors and graduates, and making fun of university statutes. At Oxford, too, humour was introduced into disputations. The incepting Masters of Arts disputed *in vesperiis* and in *comitiis* with both serious and comic intent.

[1] *Letter-Book*, 11.
[2] Costello, 27.

While the disputes held *in vesperiis* were serious, 'the
tedium of the Comitia was relieved by discussions intended
to produce laughter and give opportunity for buffoonery'.[1]
Donne, as a student at Oxford in the middle 1580s and
possibly later at Cambridge, would have been familiar with
the disputation. Undoubtedly, through this particular form
of the Problem he developed the 'skill in dialectic, most
obvious in his *Paradoxes and Problems*, [which] is employed
in season and out of season through all his writings'.[2]

In addition to its educational forms the Problem also
developed as a means of social diversion, designed both to
entertain and to sharpen one's wits, among friends, during
leisure hours. This tradition can be traced back as far as the
nine books of *Quaestiones conviviales* in Plutarch's *Moralia*,
which consider Problems suitable for conversation at the
dinner table. Conversation at these social gatherings must
not be too complicated in its arguments because it must
include all the guests. Among the hundreds of questions
proposed by Plutarch are: why is it held that love teaches
a poet (i. 5), why old men are very fond of strong wine
(i. 7), whether the hen or the egg comes first (ii. 3), whether
women are colder in temperament than men or hotter
(iii. 4), whether the sea is richer in delicacies than the land
(iv. 4). In each case the question is posed by a member of the
company, and various possible theories are put forth by
other guests, who argue for and against the different answers
suggested.

Some three-quarters of a century after Plutarch, Aulus
Gellius included Problems in his *Noctes Atticae*. Several of
Gellius' Problems are presented as educational questions
on medical, meteorological, physical, grammatical, and other
topics, each question being provided with one or more
possible answers. Others are presented as a feature of social

---

[1] Andrew Clark, *Register of the University of Oxford*, ii, pt. 1 (1571–1622) (Oxford, 1887), 84.

[2] R. C. Bald, *John Donne: A Life* (Oxford, 1970), 48. Cf. Donne himself, 'nay goe backe to our owne times, when you went to Schoole, or to the University; and remember but your owne, or your fellowes Themes, or Problemes, or Commonplaces', *Sermons*, viii, 238.

gatherings similar to Plutarch's 'table talk'. In bk. xviii, ch. 2, Gellius described how, as a student in Athens, he and his fellow Roman students spent the holiday period of the Saturnalia in the Greek capital, and frequently met to dine for their amusement and further advancement at the home of their teacher, the philosopher Calvenus Taurus. To these dinners each guest was expected to bring as his contribution to the evening a question which could be discussed by the gathering. The questions were to be 'neither weighty nor serious, but certain neat but trifling ἐνθυμημάτια, or problems, which would pique a mind enlivened with wine'.[1] Questions discussed concerned:

an obscure saying of some early poet, amusing rather than perplexing; some point in ancient history; the correction of some tenet of philosophy which was commonly misinterpreted, the solution of some sophistical catch, the investigation of a rare and unusual word, or of an obscure use of the tense of a verb of plain meaning.[2]

Actual questions mentioned as having been asked by Gellius include what Plato meant when he said in *The Republic* that women should be common property, sophistical catches such as 'What you have not lost, that you have. You have not lost horns; therefore you have horns', and 'What I am, that you are not. I am a man; therefore you are not a man', and 'When I lie and admit that I lie, do I lie or speak the truth?', what kind of plant the asphodel in Hesiod's *Works and Days* was, and what Hesiod meant in saying that the half was worth more than the whole.[3] During the evening, laurel wreaths and crowns were awarded to those members of the company who solved any of the Problems. Early in the fifth century, Macrobius wrote the *Saturnalia* for the purpose of educating his son. The main theme of the work is Virgil's greatness, but bk. ii, chs. 13 to 20 of bk. iii, and bk. vii consist of Problems, mainly of a scientific nature, which are

---

[1] vii. 13. 4.
[2] xviii. 2. 6.
[3] xviii. 2. 8–14.

discussed during and after dinner, seriously but with good humour, by a group of twelve men. The questions, dealing with topics such as the causes of baldness and of grey hair, the effects of fear on the blood, why oil freezes when wine and vinegar do not, and so on, are posed by a member of the group who requests solutions from the others present. This work provides a bridge between the educational Problem and the amusing one, Macrobius drew on both Plutarch's *Quaestiones* and Gellius' *Noctes Atticae*.

The next recorded use of the Problem as a social device is in the sixteenth century in Italy.[1] However, the classical tradition of the amusing or entertaining Problems may have been preserved during the medieval period as the *tenzon*, a type of love poetry first recorded in twelfth-century Provence.[2] *Tenzons* consisted of questions and answers in musical form, performed by musicians in the halls of feudal courts and great houses during and after dinner.[3] It was one of two types of question-and-answer poetry, and in it one poet defended himself against the attack of another. The other form of the genre was the *partimen* or *joc-partit* in which two poets debated upon a topic proposed by one of them. *Jocs-partitz* spread to northern France, Portugal, Spain, and Italy in the twelfth and thirteenth centuries. In Spain and Italy the form was of question and answer rather than debate. The Spanish poems, *preguntas* or *recuestas* and *respuestas*, concerned theological points as well as love, while in Italy the main concern of the *proposte* and *risposte*, written in sonnet form, concerned love. In general, while love was the most popular subject of *tenzon* poetry, other topics were disputed. These include, for example, which is worthier, a baron who enriches his own people but does nothing for strangers, or one who gives all he has away and ignores his

---

[1] The occurrence is discussed by T. F. Crane, *Italian Social Customs of the Sixteenth Century and their Influence on the Literatures of Europe* (New Haven, Conn., 1920). I am indebted to this account.

[2] Crane argues that the *tenzon* was the origin of the vogue for questions and answers as a means of social diversion in Italy. I see it as a bridge between the Classical and Renaissance traditions of Problems.

[3] *Tenzons* are discussed by Crane, pp. 8–52.

own people? Which is preferable, military prowess, learning, or liberality? Whether wealth or learning is to be preferred?[1] Towards the first half of the fourteenth century Boccaccio in *Il Filocolo* presented a series of thirteen questions and answers on love, posed by a group of ladies and gentlemen who were entertaining themselves in a country house. This setting was very popular possibly because the scene sketched by Boccaccio was 'a picture of one of the favorite diversions of Neapolitan society'.[2] Boccaccio also referred to the custom of questions in the introduction of *Il Filostrato*, and his works were the first of a large number of books published in Venice which show questions used as parlour games.[3] The form spread to England in the sixteenth century and is seen in works of Robert Greene, Thomas Lodge, and John Heywood.[4]

Questions were also used as a means of social diversion in the Italian Academies founded in the fifteenth century. These institutions began as learned bodies to study the history and philosophy of ancient Greece and Rome, but in the sixteenth century they became primarily social organizations with a greater interest in Italian literature, more especially poetry, than in the writings of Classical times. Their influence on Italian literature was great. The academies took their titles from the membership's facetious view of itself; hence, for example, the *Gelati* (Frozen Ones) of Bologna, the *Intronati* (Stunned Ones) of Siena, and the *Ricovrati* (Refugees) of Venice and Padua.[5]

The activities of the academies included lectures, orations, essays, poems, and questions, the latter being used both as academic exercises and as social diversion. Academic

[1] Crane, 23.

[2] Crane, 89.

[3] For example, Giovanni di Gherardo di Prato's *Paradiso degli alberti*, 1389; Giuseppe Betussi's *Il raverta*, 1562; Ludovico Domenichi's *Dialogo di amore*, 1562; Girolamo Parabosco's *I diporti*, 1564; Sabadino degli Arienti's *Le porretane*, 1531; and various novels of Matteo Bandello.

[4] Greene, *Euphues his Censure to Philautus*, 1587; Morando: *The Tritameron on Love*, 1597; Lodge, *A Margarite of America*, 1592; Heywood, *The Play of Love*, 1533; and *A Dialogue Concerning Witty and Witless*, date unknown.

[5] Crane, 142–3.

question writers included Benedetto Varchi, who gave lectures containing nearly thirty questions on love in the middle of the sixteenth century, and Tasso, who composed fifty questions on love to celebrate the wedding of the Duke of Ferrara's sister in 1570.[1] Tasso's questions were published and were also debated on, in the presence of the court, at the Academy of Ferrara. At the *Congrega dei Rozzi* (Congregation of Rustics) at Siena questions also formed part of the social diversion of the members. These questions, which were called 'cases' or 'doubts', were debated and recorded by a member of the society who had been designated to write them out. The questions were usually extracted from a story that had been told by one of the members. They covered a variety of topics and could be coarse.[2]

The foundation of Academies spread from Italy to France where, in Paris, the Academy of Poetry and Music, founded early in the sixteenth century, was revived in 1576 as the Academy of the Palace. The opening discourse of this revival was by Ronsard on the superiority of moral over intellectual virtue.[3]

In the sixteenth century the interest in Problems which had been shown by Italian society in their parlour games and Academies, and by the general public by their interest in Aristotle's *Problemata*,[4] led to the writing of books of Problems in the vernacular. The two most important books of Problems were written in Italy[5] and both enjoyed a wide circulation. The first was *Problemi naturali, e morali* (Venice, 1549), by Hieronimo Garimberto, and the second was by Ortensio Lando, also the writer of Paradoxes, whose *Quattro*

---

[1] Crane, 144–7.
[2] Ibid. 157–8.
[3] Ibid. 486.
[4] See above, p. xxviii.
[5] Lawn records (pp. 135–8) several Problem books written in Spain, in the manner of the old *preguntas* and *respuestas*. The questions were nearly always in verse and the answers were either in verse or prose. Works cited include: Lopez de Corella, *Secretos de filosophia y medicina* (Tarragona, 1539); Lopez de Yanguas, *Cincuenta bivas preguntas* (Medina, *c.*1540); Lopez de Villalobos, *Libro de los problemas* (Zamora, 1543); Luys de Escobar, *Las quatrocientas respuestas a otras tantas preguntas* (Valladolid, 1545); Agustin de Ruescas, *Dialogo en verso intitulado Centiloquio de Problemas* (Alcala, 1546); Alonso de Fuentes, *Summa de philosophia natural* (Seville, 1547).

xxxvi GENERAL INTRODUCTION

libri de dubbi con le solutioni a ciascun dubbio accomodate was
first published in Venice in 1552.[1]

Garimberto wrote 131 Problems which he answered at
considerable length, explaining that he did so because he was
writing for the unlearned, and could not omit those
principles which one could assume that the learned would
know, and also because he had to include certain charming
and easy things to clarify obscure meanings and to delight
the reader and so invite him to read.[2] Among the topics he
deals with are questions on the generation of man, man's
senses, animals in general and in particular, man in general
and in particular, meteorology, musical instruments, moral
issues, love and friendship, cowardliness, and rashness.
Garimberto's method in Problem III, for example, on why
all corruptible things, which are alike in growing weak, vary
in the measure of their endurance,[3] is to give all the reasons
which can possibly be considered for this variation. There
are, he claims, 'due cause; delle quali l'una è estrinseca, e
l'altra intrinseca'. The extrinsic reason involves the varied
aspect of the stars and the conjunction of the planets (*il
vario aspetto delle stelle, e la congiontione de pianeti*), while of
several possible intrinsic reasons four are given; first,
endurance ... because being enduring they are better at
resisting division (*la durezza ... perchè essendo dure resistono
più alla divisione*); the second is the good mixture of
moisture with heat and earthy dryness (*la seconda è la
buona commistione dell'humido col caldo, e secco terrestre*);
the third is to have similar parts, like precious stones, metal,
and the like, which are very enduring (*la terza è haver parti
similari, come le pietre, metalli, e simili; i quali durano assai*);

---

[1] Although the work was called *Quattro libri*... this edition contains only three books, on nature, on miscellaneous topics mostly moral, and on religion. The book on love was presumably censored. The second edition, Venice, 1556, is complete. A small part of the work was published in Latin as *Miscellaneae quaestiones* (Venice, 1550).

[2] 'Perchiochè con gli indotti non si possono lasciar à dietro alcuni principii i quali si presuppongono per ricevuti ne i litterati; ne si poco pretermettere cert'altre cose dilettevoli e facili, per facilitar i sensi oscuri, e dilettar i lettori; e dilettando invitar lor à leggere', Dedicatory Epistle, sig. *ii.

[3] 'D'onde viene, che tutte le cose corruttibili conformando nel venir meno, variano nella misura del durare', 4.

the fourth reason is the proportion of space which it occupies (*la quarta ragione è la proportione del luogo, che contiene*). Similarly, in Problem VII on why only man laughs,[1] Garimberto gives various scientific reasons which have developed from theories originally put forth by Aristotle and Galen. In all his Problems the treatment is serious, the answers showing a history of theories on a given topic as well as Garimberto's own solutions.

The second of these works is Ortensio Lando's collection of 'doubts'. This work, divided into four books on love, nature, miscellaneous subjects mainly moral, and religion, was translated into French under the title *Questions diverses, et responses d'icelles*, Lyons, 1558. From French, the *Dubbi* were translated as *Delectable demaundes, and pleasant Questions, with their severall Aunswers, in matters of Love, Naturall Causes, with Morall and politique devises*, 1566 and 1596, and as *Margariton: A Rich Treasure Discovered of Problemes and their Resolves*, 1640. Neither the French nor the English editions were attributed to Lando and neither contains the fourth book on religious matters.

Like Garimberto's, Lando's work serves as a history of answers to given questions and also gives many answers of the author's own invention. However, the *Dubbi* are more amusing than the *Problemi*. Lando appears to have designed his book as an aid to memory; the format is simple and each question is given a single answer. The following are illustrative of the wide range of topics covered by Lando: Why bastards are frequently more ingenious than legitimate children?[2] It is because the power from which they are generated is more intense (*la virtù di chi genera vista più intenta*) because furtive embraces have more ardour, not being distracted (*i furtivi abbracciamenti con maggior ardore: non essendo adunque distratti*). Who is more constant in love, man or woman?[3] Man being of body and mind firmer in all

---

[1] 'Si cerca per che cosa tra gli animali solamente l'huomo habbia il riso', 9.
[2] 'Perchè sono spesso siate [sic] i bastardi più ingeniosi che i legittimi non sono?'. Quattro libri de dubbi (Venice, 1556), 16. See above, p. xxxvi, n. i.
[3] 'Chi è più costante nell'amore; l'huomo, o la Donna?', 22.

his affairs, is also naturally of greater constancy and more perseverance in love (*Essendo l'huomo: e di corpo, e di animo più robusto in qualunque sua operatione dirò che anche naturalmente egli sia di maggiore costanza e più perseverante in amore*). Why did the poets picture the lecherous god Pan limping on the feet of a goat?[1] To signify that he was lecherous (*Per significarsi, che lussurioso fosse*). Why are there so many bawds?[2] The reason is that many have more desire to belong to others than to themselves (*N'e cagione il ritruovarne tante che hanno voglia d'esser più d'altrui, che di lor stesse*).

Donne appears to have been the earliest to write literary Problems in English and his works derive from the Problem tradition. The first and most obvious debt is to the scholastic disputation of his university years, which developed and sharpened his skill in dialectic, but Donne also owes much to the written tradition of Problem literature.

Donne made use of the subject-matter of his predecessors. His Problems deal with the scientific topics of the educational Problem, such as, for example, astronomy in Problems X and XI on 'Venus Star', and medicine in Problem XIII, 'Why doth the Poxe so much affect to undermine the nose'. From the pseudo-science of the vernacular Problem, Donne drew his Problems IV, 'Why doth not Gold soyle the fingers', and XII on the 'Variety of Green'. Problem V, 'Why dye none for love now', is on love, and Problems XIX on the 'Devil and Jesuits', VI on 'Laymen's Study of Divinity', and XV on the 'Length of Puritans' Sermons' deal with theological matters. More specifically, Donne used several points in his Problems which had been used in earlier writings in the genre. For example, his reference to Aulus Gellius in Problem XII on the 'Variety of Green' refers to Gellius' Problem 'For what reason our forefathers inserted the aspirate *h* in certain

---

[1] 'Perchè finsero i Poeti, che il lussurioso Dio Pan vada con i piedi di capra zoppicando?', 18.

[2] 'Per qual cagione si truovano tante ruffiane?', 42.

verbs and nouns'.[1] Possibly his reference to Horace and his use of mirrors in Problem X on 'Venus Star' derives from Seneca's censure of Hostius Quadra and his infamous use of mirrors.[2] The reference to the longer sounding of bells made of pure metal in Problem VIII, 'Why are the fayrest falsest', may stem from a Problem by Scipion Dupleix.[3] Several points may have been taken from Ortensio Lando's Problems. Donne's Problem IX on the 'Fortune of Bastards' appears to have derived both from Lando's Problem on the same subject[4] and from his *Paradosso* 'Non è cosa biasmevole l'esser bastardo'.[5] Finally, Donne's Problem VII on 'Women's Souls' which mentions speech as an attribute of man alone, although the idea was commonplace, could have been suggested by Hieronimo Garimberto's Problem IX.[6]

In their structure literary Problems show two forms, both of which stretch from the Classical period to the Renaissance. One is a long form which attempts to answer the question posed by argument, using quotations and drawing on the conclusions of earlier writers. This form was used by writers such as Seneca and Aulus Gellius in the Classical period and by Garimberto in the sixteenth century. The other form is short and suggests possible answers to the question asked by one or more independent sentences which may themselves be posed as questions. This latter is the form of Aristotle's *Problemata* and of Lando's *Quattro libri*. Both forms were used by Donne. In the long form of his Problems, Donne in, for example, Problems VII on 'Women's Souls', and X and XI on 'Venus Star', like Seneca, used other writers as authorities sometimes naming them but at other times not

---

[1] *Noctes Atticae*, ii, 3.

[2] *Naturales quaestiones*, i. 16. 1–9.

[3] *La Curiosité Naturelle; rédigée en questions selon l'ordre alphabétique* (Paris, 1606), translated as *The Resolver; or Curiosities of Nature*, 1635, 94.

[4] *Quattro libri*, 16; see above, p. xxxvii.

[5] *Paradossi*, no. xviii; see Commentary, pp. 103-4.

[6] *Problemi*, 12; 'Qual è la cagione che la natura habbia dato all'huomo la voce, e'l parlare, e al resto de gli animali solamente la voce' (what is the reason that nature has given voice and speech to man, and to the rest of the animals, only voice).

identifying them.[1] Like Seneca and Gellius too, in his
Problems X and XI on 'Venus Star' Donne quoted snatches
of poetry to draw an analogy or make a point,[2] and in
Problems VI on 'Laymen's Study of Divinity' and VII on
'Women's Souls' he referred to historical events in order to
illustrate points.[3] These Problems may be regarded as
parodies of the educational Problem.

In writing his short Problems, Donne wrote burlesques of
the Peripatetic method. Problems such as II the 'Sir Walter
Ralegh' Problem, IV 'Why doth not Gold soyle the
fingers' and V 'Why dye none for love now' are brief works
consisting of a question presented in the title and answered
by a few sentences in the manner of Aristotle and Lando.
There is no developed argument, no attempt at expansion
and no citing of either relevant theories or previous
examples.

Donne used both parody of the long educational Problem
and burlesque of the short Peripatetic form in four
Problems, numbers X and XI on 'Venus Star', XII on the
'Variety of Green', and XVIII on 'Women and Feathers'.
The long version of Problem XII on the 'Variety of Green',
for example, has a 'scientific' introduction dealing with the
Aristotelian colour-system followed by a list of various
metaphoric meanings of the colour 'green'. Problem XVIII
on 'Women and Feathers' begins the contrast of *Similis
Simili*, which is not, and *verisimile*, which is, the level of
truth to which Donne says he aspires in his Problems. This
opening is followed by a list of those men who show
women's undesirable features. The long forms of both
Problems cite as authorities, Ronsard, Gellius, and Petrarch
in Problem XII, and Petrarch (whose works are quoted),
Varro, Aristotle, Plato, and Speusippus in Problem XVIII.
In the short forms of Problems XII and XVIII, these
passages have been stripped away, leaving the former about

---

[1] Cf. Seneca, *Naturales quaestiones*, iva 2. 26–8.
[2] Cf. Seneca, *Naturales quaestiones*, i. 5. 6 and i. 8. 8; Gellius, *Noctes Atticae*, i. 12. 12–16.
[3] Cf. Seneca, *Naturales quaestiones*, i. 15. 5–6; Gellius, *Noctes Atticae*, i. 12. 9–13.

one-third and the latter less than a quarter of their original lengths. The short forms consist of a few possible answers to the questions asked, each answer being suggested in individual sentences.

The long versions of the four Problems, X, XI, XII, and XVIII, as well as appearing in some of the accepted Donne manuscripts,[1] are also found in Lodewijk Rouzee's Latin translation of Donne's Problems, which Rouzee had made from a manuscript to which he had gained access among Donne's circle of friends in 1609 or 1610.[2] Extracts of these versions also appear in the fourth Earl of Bedford's commonplace book.[3] Evelyn Simpson, who did not have the advantage of these two sources, argued for the authenticity of the long versions of these Problems. She suggested that Donne wrote his Problems loosely at first, then pruned and tightened in revision, and that he eliminated material in these four Problems as he 'did not wish to over-weight these "light squibs" as he called the *Problems* with a heavy apparatus of quotations from Ronsard, Petrarch, Aulus Gellius, Lactantius and the like'.[4] She suggested further that Donne eliminated the hostility shown towards women in Problem XVIII on 'Women and Feathers' and the bitterness shown towards the court in Problem XII on the 'Variety of Green', so causing the Problems to lose most of their sting, through fear of offending a possible patroness or other persons who were in a position to help him rehabilitate his career.[5]

Donne's letters show evidence, in support of Evelyn Simpson's views, of his concern over various works both that their circulation should be restricted,[6] and that some

---

[1] See Textual Introduction, pp. lxxviii–lxxix.
[2] See Appendix.
[3] This manuscript was discovered by Conrad Russell whose information was passed on to me by A. J. Smith.
[4] Evelyn M. Simpson, 'More Manuscripts of Donne's *Paradoxes and Problems*', *RES* x (1934), 295.
[5] Ibid. 291, and 'Two Manuscripts of Donne's *Paradoxes and Problems*', *RES* iii (1927), 140.
[6] As seen in the letter which had accompanied the Paradoxes, see above, p. xxv.

should be returned to him in order that he might revise them.[1] In a letter to Sir Henry Goodyer he wrote:

Though their unworthinesse, and your own ease be advocates for me with you, yet I must adde my entreaty, that you let goe no copy of my Problems, till I review them. If it be too late, at least be able to tell me who hath them.[2]

The evidence suggests that Donne did revise these Problems, most probably from fear of the backlash of offence. However, the long versions of these Problems do not appear to be 'loose writing', but rather attempts at parody of the educational Problem on topics which he later thought, probably because of his concern about them, might be more appropriately treated as burlesques of the Peripatetic form.

Besides these four Problems which were revised, two more, Problems XVII on 'John of Salisbury' and XIX on the 'Devil and Jesuits', are not found in all the manuscripts.[3] Evelyn Simpson noted that the style of 'John of Salisbury' is 'clearly that of Donne's early prose' because of its 'inordinately long first sentence, with its parentheses and subordinate and co-ordinate clauses'.[4] She also noted the bitter attitude towards the court in this and other of Donne's Problems and remarked on 'the likeness which this problem bears to the whole of Donne's prose work written between 1600 and 1608'.[5] She suggested that 'John of Salisbury' failed to achieve wide circulation possibly because its

---

[1] 'Interim seponas oro chartulas meas, quas cum sponsione citae redhibitionis (ut barbarè, sed cum ingeniosissimo Appollinari loquar) accepisti. Inter quas, si epigrammata mea Latina, et Catalogus librorum satyricus non sunt, non sunt; extremum iuditium, hoc est, manum ultimam iamiam subiturae sunt. Earum nonnulae Purgatorium suum passurae, ut correctiores emanent' (Meanwhile reserve I beg my little papers which you accepted with a solemn promise of rapid returning (in order that, I should speak rudely but in the most ingenious manner of Appollinarius). Among which, if my Latin epigrams and satirical catalogue of books are not, they are no longer; this is the final judgement, that now they will undergo final writing. Some of them will suffer their Purgatory in order to emerge more correct), *Poems*, 1633, 352.

[2] *Letters*, 1651, 108.

[3] See Textual Introduction, pp. lxxviii–lxxix.

[4] 'Two MSS. etc.', 137.

[5] Ibid.

bitterness was expressed more forcibly in other Problems, or, more likely, because of the obscurity of its subject.[1] The 'Devil and Jesuits' Problem is clearly Donne's on the basis of tone and style, and also because of the relation the topic bears to *Ignatius His Conclave*. Donne may have attempted to discard the Problem because he had dealt with much of its substance in *Ignatius*, published anonymously in 1611.

A final Problem exists in both long and short forms, number II on 'Sir Walter Ralegh'. The long version contains two extra sentences which read in part 'Or because, like a Bird in a Cage, hee takes his tunes from every passenger that last whistled', which refers to a comment by Prince Henry who was Ralegh's friend.[2] The Prince's comment was widely reported. I have argued in the Textual Introduction[3] that the text in the manuscripts that contain the extra sentences could not be the original version of the Problem, and rather, that these sentences were added to the Problem. Because the saying was widespread they were not necessarily added by Donne.

The overwhelming impression of Donne's Problems is of their moral tone. Donne wrote Problems on moral issues, numbers VII and VIII on 'Women's Souls' and 'Why are the fayrest falsest', and in many other Problems he criticized certain aspects of the life he saw around him. His moral tone varies from the amused tolerance of Problem XV 'Why Puritans make long Sermons' and XIX on the 'Devil and Jesuits' to a tone of bitter hostility towards the court in Problem I on 'Atheism among Courtiers', III on 'Great Men Preferring Bawds', IX on 'Bastards', the early version of Problem XII on the 'Variety of Green', and so on. Also obvious in Donne's Problems is his wit and verbal skill. For example, he uses a turn of phrase in Problem VIII 'Why are the fayrest falsest', a verbal twist in XVII on 'John of

---

[1] 'Two MSS. etc.', 138.
[2] Henry 'did so far applaud the advice of *Rawly*, as to say *No King but his Father would keep such a Bird in a Cage*', Francis Osborne, *Historical Memoires on the Reigns of Queen Elizabeth, and King James* (1658), 141–2.
[3] See below, pp. lxxviii–lxxix.

Salisbury', word-play in the early version of Problem XVIII on 'Women and Feathers', and a relentlessly logical construction in Problem III on 'Great Men Preferring Bawds', all of which serve to surprise and entertain the reader. The language of Donne's Problems, like that of his Paradoxes is direct and colloquial. His sentences can be brief and simple or long and involved and some of his arguments are not easy to follow.

Why did Donne write these Problems with their cynical and bitter tone and sense of sadness which is not found in the earlier and gayer Paradoxes? Clearly his intent was not that of Garimberto and Lando whose works were published in order to teach and amuse a large audience. Like most of his writings, the Problems appear to have been written to satisfy, and with their dark humour to entertain, Donne and the friends to whom he sent copies.

The date of composition of the Problems is easier to document than is the date of the Paradoxes. References in some Problems mark the date of their writing as being the period between 1603 and 1609 or 1610. For example, Problem II on 'Sir Walter Ralegh' must have been written after 1603 because of its reference to Ralegh's trial and possibly as late as 1609 when Ralegh was writing his *History of the World*. Problem XII on the 'Variety of Green' was most likely written early in King James's reign, for 'newe men Ennobled from Grasiers' probably refers to the conferring by James of many knighthoods in order to raise revenue for the Crown. Problem X 'Why Venus starre onely doth cast a Shadowe' has been dated 1606 or possibly 1607 on the basis of its reference to Kepler's *De stella tertii honoris in cygno* which was appended to *De stella nova in pede Serpentarii*, Prague, 1606.[1] Problem XIX on the 'Devil and Jesuits' was almost certainly written before the publication of *Ignatius His Conclave* in 1611.

Problems can also be dated by Donne's references to them in letters. In 1607 he wrote two letters to Sir Henry

---

[1] See Evelyn Simpson, *Prose Works*, 120, 147.

Goodyer which read in part: 'I end with a probleme, whose errand is, to aske for his fellowes' (*Poems*, 1633, 358; *Letters*, 1651, 99) and 'I pray reade these two problemes: for such light flashes as these have beene my hawkings in my Surry journies' (*Poems*, 1633, 361; *Letters*, 1651, 88).[1] Another letter refers to Problems: 'else let this probleme supply, which was occasioned by you, of women wearing stones; which, it seems, you were afraid women should read' (*Letters*, 1651, 108). The accompanying Problem may have been the 'Women and Feathers' Problem, or possibly, 'Why are the fayrest falsest'. In *Letters*, 1651, this letter was headed 'To Sr G. M.' which Edmund Gosse expanded to 'George More'.[2] As the letter was friendly, he dated it 1603 or 1604 by which time Donne and his father-in-law were on reasonable terms. This expansion of Gosse's was clearly incorrect and John Hayward in the Nonesuch Donne identified the recipient as Sir Henry Goodyer,[3] but did not alter Gosse's proposed date of its composition.[4] I. A. Shapiro has informed me that precise dating for this letter has so far proved to be impossible, but he thinks it most likely to be *c.*1608–9.

A final piece of evidence provides a *terminus ante quem* for the bulk of the Problems. This evidence is Lodewijk Rouzee's claim in the Preface of his book of Problems which contains a Latin translation of thirteen of Donne's Problems, that he had obtained his copy of those Problems six or seven years before the publication of his book in 1616—that is 1609 or 1610.[5]

III. DUBIA

Certain works have been associated with Donne's *Paradoxes*

---

[1] *Letters*, 1651, reads 'sorry' for 'Surry'.
[2] *The Life and Letters of John Donne* (1899), i, 122–3.
[3] *Complete Poetry and Selected Prose* (2nd impression, 1929), 448. Hayward's note, p. 787, refers to the letter as having been sent to More.
[4] See *John Donne: Selected Prose*, selected by Evelyn Simpson, eds. Helen Gardner and Timothy Healy (Oxford, 1967), 121.
[5] See Appendix.

and Problems whose right to inclusion in the canon of the 'Juvenilia' must be questioned. These works include two Paradoxes ('A Defence of Womens Inconstancy' and 'That Virginity is a Vertue'), two Characters (of 'A Scot' and of 'A Dunce'), 'An Essay of Valour', and 'Newes from the very Country'.

There is no textual evidence to argue for the acceptance of the two Paradoxes as Donne's work. 'A Defence of Womens Inconstancy' is found in the Stephens MS as Paradox XI and in the three seventeenth-century editions as Paradox I.[1] The Stephens MS includes as Donne's work several spurious pieces, and it seems likely that the 'Inconstancy' Paradox belongs to this category.[2] Extracts of the Paradox are found in Edward Pudsey's commonplace-book[3] as being 'out of the defenc of womens inconstancye' from a revel held at the Middle Temple *c.*1610;[4] Donne is unlikely to have written for Inns of Court revels at that date. There is also a reference to a defence of women's inconstancy in 1598,[5] Cornwallis wrote a Paradox 'That Inconstancy is more commendable then Constancie' and John Marston included a set piece on inconstancy in *The Fawne*. This multiplicity of works on inconstancy would suggest that the topic was a standard part of revels at the legal Inns, and that 'A Defence of Womens Inconstancy' could have been written by any wit at the Middle Temple, probably close to the time of the revel in which it appeared.

'That Virginity is a Vertue' is not found in any of the Donne manuscripts. It appears only in the third edition of the *Paradoxes and Problems* at the end of the section of juvenilia, after the 'Essay of Valour' and preceded by a

---

[1] I argue in the textual introduction that the first edition was printed from a manuscript very similar to Stephens, and that each subsequent edition was printed, except for new material added, from the preceding.

[2] One Satire, six Elegies, and thirteen other poems which are not accepted as Donne's appear in Stephens undifferentiated from the genuine Donne material.

[3] MS Eng. poet. d. 3, f. 87.

[4] See P. F. Finkelpearl, 'The Use of the Middle Temple's Christmas Revels in Marston's *The Fawne*', *SP* lxiv (1967), 206.

[5] 'This night [Tuesday, 3 Jan 1598] one had like to have commended women for their inconstancy, but he was disappointed', *Le Prince D'Amour* (1660), 85.

blank page. A marginal note reads 'Place this after Paradox
XI. fol. 37', which clearly was not done. The Paradox
appears from its position to have been found when all the
Paradoxes and Problems had been printed, and to have been
hastily added to the collection. This Paradox, like the
piece on 'Inconstancy', appears to have been written later
than the ten accepted Paradoxes, because of the following
passage, 'An Ape is a ridiculous and an unprofitable Beast,
whose flesh is not good for meat, nor its back for burden, nor
is it commodius to keep an house'. This passage seems
almost certain to have been copied from an addition of
Edward Topsell to his translation of Conrad Gesner's
Historiae animalium, lib. I, de quadrupedibus vivparis which
was published in 1607.[1]

It is immediately noticeable that 'A Defence of Womens
Inconstancy' and 'That Virginity is a Vertue' are two to
three times longer than the ten accepted Paradoxes. They
also differ in style. Instead of the vigorous opening and witty
ending, 'A Defence of Womens Inconstancy' opens with
an error in expression; the author confesses women to be
inconstant but maintains 'that *Inconstancie* is a bad Qualitye
... against any man', when he means to maintain that it is
not a bad quality. Some of the arguments are at least
paradoxical moving by 'fabricated argument which consists
of discrete statements equivocally united',[2] and spurious
comparisons and puns,[3] but these are not the normal
characteristics of Donne's paradoxical method, which is far
more complex and interesting. The Paradox ends weakly
with the plea that the name 'Inconstancy' be changed to
'Variety'. 'That Virginity is a Vertue' opens with a dull
sentence distinguishing that virginity which the author
considers to be a vertue from that which he regards as a vice.
Throughout the Paradox the sentiments are too qualified to

---

[1] *The Historie of Foure-Footed Beastes*, 2, Apes 'are held for a subtill, ironical, ridiculous and unprofitable Beast, whose flesh is not good for meate as a sheepe, neither his backe for burthen as an Asses, nor yet commodious to keepe a house like a Dog'.
[2] Malloch, 195.
[3] Michale McCanles, 'Paradox in Donne', *SR* xiii (1966), 278–9.

have the fresh vigour found in Donne's Paradoxes. The ending, which claims that the virgin upon marriage shall change her name to the more honourable one of 'A Wife' is similarly lacking in freshness and wit.

Of the remaining four works, the two Characters, of 'A Scot' and of 'A Dunce', appear in the largest number of Donne manuscripts: the Group II manuscript Stowe 962, and the Group III manuscripts Bridgewater, Dobell, and O'Flaherty (none of which are, however, absolutely sound in canon), as well as in the Stephens MS and in the third edition of Donne's *Paradoxes and Problems*, 1652. As one of the Characters, of 'A Dunce', was printed anonymously in all editions of Sir Thomas Overbury's *Characters* from 1622 on, it appears that these works, if not written specifically for the Overbury book, were composed under its influence. In comparison with the *Paradoxes and Problems*, the Characters are simple and easy to comment upon. They contain none of the obscurity and little of the wit that characterize the *Paradoxes and Problems*, and it is difficult to know whether Donne wrote them.

Textual evidence for the inclusion of the 'Essay of Valour' among Donne's juvenilia is weak. The text occurs in the Stephens MS, the third edition of the *Paradoxes and Problems*, 1652, anonymously in all editions of Overbury's Characters from 1622 on, and as ' "Valour Anatomized in a Fancie", by Sir Philip Sidney, 1581' in *Cottoni posthuma*, 1651. The work is clearly not Sidney's.[1] The Essay is more complicated than the Characters, but several of the obscurities in the text appear to be caused more by textual corruption than by the witty or ingenious reasoning of the author. The tone of this work is cynical, not unlike that of Donne's Problems, but it is difficult to accept it unequivocally as his.

' "Newes from the very Country" by J. D.' was first published in a section titled 'Newes From Any Whence' in the 1614 editions of Overbury's *Characters* and appears in all

---

[1] See *Sir Philip Sidney: Miscellaneous Prose*, eds. Katherine Duncan-Jones and Jan van Dorsten (Oxford, 1973), 159.

subsequent editions. It was printed as Donne's in *Poems, By J. D.*, 1650. The bulk of its text, although not in the same order, was copied along with other extracts of 'Newes From Any Whence' in a series of anecdotes in Sir Henry Wotton's commonplace-book, the Burley MS. None of the authors are named. The entire section from the commonplace-book was printed by L. P. Smith in his *Life and Letters of Sir Henry Wotton*, 1907, under the heading 'Table Talk', Appendix IV, Section C. 'Newes from the very Country' consists of a collection of anecdotes, many very cynical, which contrast the life of the country with that of London. It is a difficult work with several obscure passages, but with few of the flashes of wit that are associated with Donne. It is difficult to believe that Donne was its author.[1]

The *Paradoxes and Problems* are very different from these six works, and, in comparison, differ only slightly from each other. This difference between the *Paradoxes and Problems* is primarily one of tone—the Paradoxes showing a gay and superior attitude while the Problems show a moral and cynical tone. Both *Paradoxes and Problems*, however, are characterized by verbal skill and wit, by difficulty and obscurity, and throughout both Donne's lively inquiring mind and highly developed, if sometimes dark, sense of humour are manifested.

---

[1] However, cf. John Sparrow, 'Donne's Table-Talk', *London Mercury*, xviii (1928), 39–46, and below, p. lxxxviii, n.2.

TEXTUAL INTRODUCTION

An editor of Donne's *Paradoxes and Problems* is faced with a different problem from that which faces an editor of his Poems. Although the first edition of the Poems in 1633 needs correction from manuscript copies, its manuscript sources belonged to sound traditions and its text is superior to that of any extant manuscript, with the possible exception of the Westmoreland MS which contains very few of the poems. The first edition of the *Paradoxes and Problems* in 1633 (*1633a*), omits half the Problems and presents a text with many obviously corrupt and obscure passages. The second edition (*1633b*) and the third (*1652*) were based, except for the new material added in each, on the previously printed text. As Evelyn Simpson discovered in her work on the seventeen manuscripts she had found, the first edition was printed from a manuscript which must have been very close indeed to the Stephens MS, which was justly stigmatized by Grierson as the worst manuscript of the poems he had seen, 'the fullest of obvious and absurd blunders'. Whereas an editor of the poems has to improve the text of the first edition by analysis of its manuscript sources and removal of errors and sophistications, an editor of the *Paradoxes and Problems* has to construct a text.

Evelyn Simpson began work on the *Paradoxes and Problems* in the 1920s. She intended to produce an edition in line with, though on a smaller scale than, Grierson's edition of the Poems. In this attempt she was assisted by Grierson who lent her his collations of the Paradoxes in the Burley MS, which he had made some years before the manuscript itself was destroyed by fire, as well as collations of the Trinity College, Cambridge, and Trinity College, Dublin, MSS. There does not appear to have been any collaboration between herself and Grierson on an edition of the *Paradoxes and Problems*, and she wrote in the Textual Introduction to her projected edition that she alone was responsible for the use made of, and conclusions drawn from, Grierson's collations. In the early 1940s, having collated the manuscripts, she discovered that they frequently disagreed with both *1633a* and each other. She attempted to construct a critical text and had produced a draft text and apparatus for the Paradoxes, using *1633a* as her copy-text, and had made a beginning at collecting notes for a commentary on the Paradoxes and the Problems when she laid the work aside in order to edit Donne's Sermons. Unable to take it up again, she passed her materials on to R. C. Bald, who put them aside until he should have finished his biography of Donne. At his death in 1965, the materials were given to Helen Gardner who later handed them on to me to prepare an edition under her direction. I am, then, a successor of earlier and able scholars. I have been given unrestricted access to my predecessors' material, enjoying the benefit of their collection of microfilms and photostats of several manuscripts, and having the advantage of consulting the typescript of Evelyn Simpson's proposed edition. In order to construct my text, however, I have relied on her collations only in the case of the Burley MS which is no longer extant, otherwise I have recollated all available manuscripts, including some witnesses which she had not used,[1] and the early printed texts in order to arrive at a critical text, conforming to modern editorial principles.

Although, hitherto, there has been no critical text, the *Paradoxes and Problems* have been published, in whole or in part, eight times since Grierson's edition of Donne's

---

[1] The witnesses which were not used by Evelyn Simpson are as follows: the Norton MS, the Osborn MSS *O 2* and *O 1* (Osborn 1 was formerly known as the King MS), Rouzee, a Latin translation by Lodewijk Rouzee of thirteen of Donne's Problems published in Leiden in 1616, the fourth Earl of Bedford's commonplace-book, Historical Manuscripts Commission, 26, and Edward Pudsey's commonplace-book. Two further unimportant manuscripts of the *Paradoxes and Problems* are owned by the Bodleian Library. One contains extracts copied from the second edition (MS Eng. poet. e. 112); it was formerly in the Library of the Long Island Historical Society, Brooklyn, New York. The other contains only a text of Paradox II which appears to be a copy of the text in the Westmoreland MS (MS Don. c. 54). I have not included the readings of these two manuscripts in the apparatus.

poetry in 1912. Geoffrey Keynes's Nonesuch edition of the *Paradoxes and Problems* (1923) was based on *1633b*, adding the extra material found in *1652* and the 'Sir Walter Ralegh' Problem first printed in Edmund Gosse's *The Life and Letters of John Donne* (1899), ii. 52–3. The 'Women's Inconstancy' Paradox and 'That women ought to paint themselves' were printed as 'Jack Donne *A Defence of Women for their Inconstancy and their Paintings* (1925). John Hayward printed eight Paradoxes, numbers, 1, 2, 4, 6, 8, 10, 11, 12, which appear in this edition as numbers 11, 2, 8, 10, 4, 7, 6 and 12, 11 and 12 printed as 'Dubia'; five Problems, 2, 6, 9, 11, and 16, renumbered in this edition 15, 7, 11, 13, 1; two Characters, the 'Essay of Valour' and 'Newes from the very Country' in his Nonesuch *Complete Poetry and Selected Prose of John Donne* (1929), 335–53, 413–20. He based his text on the third edition (*1652*) incoporating certain substantive and accidental features from the first edition. No apparatus is given, but in his notes Hayward discusses some alterations which he had made. These appear to come not only from the first edition, but also from manuscript readings which Evelyn Simpson had proposed in her article 'Two Manuscripts of Donne's *Paradoxes and Problems*', *RES* iii (1927), 129–45 and her *A Study of the Prose Works of John Donne* (1924), ch. vi. In the article (p. 136), she printed the text of the 'John of Salisbury' Problem for the first time. In 1936 a facsimile of the first edition, *Juvenilia*, with a bibliographical note by R. E. Bennett was published in New York. Charles D. O'Malley privately printed one Problem 'Why doth the pox soe much affect to undermine the nose?' (San Francisco, Calif., 1943). The text of the first edition is anthologized in *English Prose 1600–1660*, edited by Victor Harris and Itrat Husain (New York, 1965), 241–58. The closest approach to a critical text is that of eleven Paradoxes and the seven Problems numbered in this edition 15, 12, 7, 18, 4, 1, 2 in Donne's *Selected Prose*, selected by Evelyn Simpson and edited by Helen Gardner and Timothy Healy

(Oxford, 1967), 5–22. The editors reprinted from the Nonesuch edition of 1923, admitting into the text those readings from the manuscripts which Evelyn Simpson had reported not only in the sources available to Hayward, but also from her later article 'More Manuscripts of Donne's *Paradoxes and Problems*', *RES*x (1934), 288–300, 412–16.

I. MANUSCRIPTS

The *Paradoxes and Problems* were first published after Donne's death and were printed from a poor manuscript. Thus the manuscripts containing the texts of these works are essential in the production of a reliable text.[1] Most of the manuscripts which contain the *Paradoxes and Problems* are, or aim to be, collections of the poet's writings, the most important exceptions being the Burley MS *(Bur)*,[2] Sir Henry Wotton's commonplace-book amongst whose varied contents were poems, letters, ten Paradoxes by Donne, and extracts of 'Newes from the very Country'; the Ashmole MS *(Ash 826)* which contains a text of the nineteen Problems amongst its miscellaneous collections; and the Latin text, Rouzee *(R)*, which prints thirteen Problems as numbers 1,

---

[1] Although I have worked mainly with microfilms and photostats, I have seen all the manuscripts with the exception of Bridgewater *(B)*. For a full list of sigla, present locations of manuscripts, and shelf marks, see below, pp. ic–c.

[2] *Bur* perished in the fire that destroyed part of Burley-on-the-Hill in 1908. Its historical documents had previously been listed by Alfred J. Horwood *(Historical Manuscripts Commission*, Seventh Report, 1878, 516). Logan Pearsall Smith reproduced the material connected directly with Wotton in his *Life and Letters of Sir Henry Wotton*, Oxford, 1907. He gives an amusing account in his *Unforgotten Years* (1938), 218–23, of finding the manuscript in Burley-on-the-Hill and of later examining the manuscript at the Clarendon Press with Grierson. He reports that he suggested to Grierson's horror that they could insert among the table-talk a chance remark about Bacon as a playwright which might set the Baconians agog. The story is reprinted in *The Oxford Book of Literary Anecdotes*, ed. James Sutherland (Oxford, 1975), 18–21. Smith had arranged for the Oxford University Press to purchase the copyright of the manuscript, and among Donne's letters and some of his poetry which were transcribed by order of the Press was a letter which had accompanied a text of the ten Paradoxes. The Paradoxes were not copied. The transcription made, which I have not seen, as well as photostats of the transcript, which I have examined, have been mislaid at the Press. Evelyn Simpson printed Donne's letters and discussed the manuscript in her *A Study of the Prose Works of John Donne* (2nd edn., 1948), 291–336. She also described *Bur* in 'More Manuscripts etc.', 297–300. Grierson collated the text of the Paradoxes, in *Bur* against the *Juvenilia*, but all these collations except for his annotations on an off-print of Simpson, 'Two Manuscripts etc.', have disappeared. Evelyn Simpson had, however, made a copy of Grierson's collations which she used in her apparatus, and it is on these sources that I have to rely for readings of *Bur*.

4, 12, 20, 22, 28, 29, 35, 36, 38, 45, 47, and 50 of Rouzee's works. The Donne collections belong to Grierson's Groups II and III; no manuscripts of Group I contain the *Paradoxes and Problems*.

Both Paradoxes and Problems are found in the Group II manuscripts, Stowe MS 962 (*S 962*), Trinity College, Cambridge MS (*TCC*), with its copy Additional MS 18647 (*A 18*), and Trinity College, Dublin MS (*TCD*), with its copies Norton MS (*N*) and Wyburd MS (*Wy*). *S 962* differs from the other Group II manuscripts in that it contains the texts of two Problems and of the two Characters which are not otherwise found in Group II. Both Paradoxes and Problems appear in the following Group III manuscripts: Bridgewater (*B*), Dobell (*Dob*), and O'Flaherty (*O'F*), which also contain the texts of the two Characters, Osborn (*O 2*), Phillipps (*P*), and Stephens (*S*). *S* also contains texts of the two Characters and is the only manuscript to contain a text of the 'Essay of Valour'.

Paradoxes, along with extracts from 'Newes from the very Country' were found in Burley (*Bur*), and Paradoxes only in Westmoreland (*W*). Extracts from a single Paradox occur in the Pudsey commonplace-book (*Pud*).

Problems only are found in Ashmole MS 826 (*Ash 826*), Osborn MS (*O 1*), in the Latin translation Rouzee (*R*), and in Additional MS 25707 (*A 25*) and Tanner MS 299 (*Tan*) which each contain a single Problem. Extracts of Problems occur in the commonplace-book of the fourth Earl of Bedford (*HMC 26*).

Only Groups II and III manuscripts contain both Paradoxes and Problems. But manuscripts outside these groups, which contain only Paradoxes or only Problems are of great importance in establishing the text. It is therefore necessary, at the cost of some repetition, to discuss the transmission of the text of the Paradoxes and of that of the Problems separately, and to add a brief section which discusses the transmission of two Paradoxes, the two Characters, the 'Essay of Valour', and 'Newes from the very

Country' which are printed in this edition as Dubia.

A. *Paradoxes*

The most important manuscripts in establishing the text of the Paradoxes are Westmoreland (*W*) and Burley (*Bur*). *W* is a well-punctuated fair copy in the hand of Donne's friend Rowland Woodward.[1] It cannot have been made much before 1620 at the earliest. It consists of poems which have been arranged and copied under their kinds:[2] the Satires, the Elegies, the Lincoln's Inn Epithalamium, Verse-letters to Donne's men friends, some not extant elsewhere, and the two sets of Holy Sonnets, including three sonnets not found in any other manuscript, one of which is the sonnet on the death of Anne Donne in 1617. After the verse comes prose, the ten Paradoxes written in the order in which they are printed in this edition, followed by a single lyric.

Woodward appears to have been copying out, possibly for presentation to his patron Westmoreland, material which had come into his possession at different times. Most of the works, including the Paradoxes, were written before 1600, but the two sets of Holy Sonnets date from considerably later. It seems certain that the copy behind the pre-1600 material in *W* was itself early, for letters to Sir Henry Wotton, who was knighted in 1603, are headed to 'Mr H. W.' and the Lincoln's Inn Epithalamium is entitled simply 'Epithalamium' as if it were the only one Donne had written and did not need to be distinguished from the Epithalamiums of 1613 as it usually is by the addition of 'made at Lincoln's Inn'.

Whether Woodward was copying from works in Donne's own hand which he had given him, or from copies he had

---

[1] This was suggested by E. H. M. Cox, *The Library of Edmund Gosse* (1924), 98, and established by Alan MacColl; see Gardner, *Elegies etc.* lxxii, n. 2. P. J. Croft and R. E. Alton have confirmed the attribution. *W* is described in Gardner, *Divine Poems*, lxxviii–lxxxi, *Elegies etc.* lxxii, and Simpson, 'More Manuscripts etc.', 297–300.

[2] The Verse-Letters have been brought together and are not in order of composition. Woodward has included among these early Verse-Letters the later letter 'To E. of D. with six holy Sonnets'.

himself made from works which Donne had lent him to copy, *W* must be very close to the holograph.[1] Even if it had not such high extrinsic authority, it would have high intrinsic authority from the excellence of the text it presents.

Bur was written in the various hands of Wotton's secretaries. It was his commonplace-book and appears to have contained copies of the letters and documents generally found in such collections; it included, for example, Sidney's letter to Queen Elizabeth on the Alençon marriage (1580) and Ralegh's apology for the Guiana expedition (1617). The contents were not arranged in chronological order, but appear to have been copied in a random fashion probably as they were come by. The manuscript also contained copies of papers relating to Wotton's embassy in Venice (1604–10)—these include a section of anecdotes among which are extracts of 'Newes from the very Country', Wotton's poems and letters, as well as poems and letters sent to him, some of which are Donne's. *Bur* also contained a letter from Donne, possibly written in 1600, to an unknown recipient which accompanied the text of ten Paradoxes which Donne had made, or caused to have made, because he had been requested to do so.[2] The transcription of this letter made for the Clarendon Press was followed by the copyist's note 'Here follow Donne's Paradoxes "That all things kill themselves" etc.'

---

[1] R. E. Alton and P. J. Croft examined photostats of this manuscript for me. They noted that Woodward, in copying Donne's 'Epigrams', made a sloping dash after each epigram in the manner in which Donne had marked off his verses in the holograph 'Letter to the Lady Carey and Mrs. Essex Riche'. They also noted that throughout the manuscript Woodward had formed his *k*s with loops that dropped below the line and looped forward in a clockwise motion. This *k* was like that used by Donne and was not a normal form of the letter in sixteenth- and seventeenth-century hands. These two features suggest that Woodward may have been copying from Donne's own hand and was influenced by it. I have looked at a few other samples of Woodward's hand: notably those letters preserved in the Public Record Office, dating from the years 1620 to 1630 (for example, S.P., Dom., Jas. I, 14, 115 and 16, 169 and others cited by M. C. Deas in 'A Note on Rowland Woodward, the Friend of Donne', *RES* vii (1931), 454–7) and a letter written by Woodward for Sir Henry Wotton when Woodward was serving as Wotton's secretary and dated 8 July 1605 (Stowe MS 168/62). An extract from this letter was printed by L. P. Smith, *The Life and Letters of Sir Henry Wotton* (Oxford, 1907), i. 329–30. The use of the 'Donne *k*' in Wotton's letter but not in Woodward's own, which I noticed, could indicate that it was a feature of his formal writing practice but not of his private.

[2] See above pp. xxv–xxvi.

Besides Donne's Paradoxes and private letters to Wotton, *Bur* contained his fourth Satire, Elegies, and Epigrams—a smaller collection of works than that found in *W*. Neither of these two early collections include lyrics.

The text in *W* is excellent, and although we have only the Simpson copies of Grierson's collations to judge by, so was the text in *Bur*. These manuscripts were almost certainly very close to Donne's holograph, and they at times agree in a reading not found in witnesses that are further removed from the poet's papers. Thus, for instance in Paradox VIII, this reading which is found only in *W* and *Bur* is obviously correct: 'foule may be riche and vertuous, poore may be vertuous and faire, vicious may be faire and riche'.[1] Donne's point is that the contraries of the three categories of the good can each have the goodness of the other two (the contrary of foul being fair, of poor being rich, and of vicious being vertuous). The other witnesses read 'faire, maybe ritch and vertuous. Poore may be...' obscuring the point of the passage. Again in Paradox I, 31–2, where *W* and *Bur* read '(for no perfection indures) and all things labor to this perfection' the other manuscripts and the editions read '(for noe affection indures, and all things labour to this perfection)'. Common readings of *W* and *Bur* range from these which are obviously correct to those which are not obviously superior such as 'Survayes and examinations' for 'examinations, and surveyes' in Paradox II, 9, and 'controversies only' for 'controversie' in Paradox IX, 26.

W and *Bur* do not always agree. But occasionally one or the other, though in error, partially supports the other. In Paradox VI, 19, where *W* reads 'hath this maime' (i.e. injury, defect), *Bur* has a minim error and reads 'hath this mayne'. The other witnesses complicate the minim error further by reversing *y* and *n* and reading 'hath still many' or 'still hath many' (*TCC*).

Neither *W* nor *Bur* is free from scribal errors, but each

---

[1] ll. 33–4. Woodward corrected himself in error; he first wrote 'poore may be vertuous and riche' but drew two lines through 'riche' and wrote 'faire'.

manuscript has variant readings which are difficult to regard as scribal and which I believe reflect the possibility that W is the earliest extant version of the text, and Bur, which is also early, contains alterations made by Donne when he was preparing a copy of the Paradoxes. I judge W to be earlier, not only because of the quality of its text, but because two blanks[1] left in the texts of Paradoxes V and VIII indicate that Woodward was unable to read what Donne had written,[2] and while conceivably difficulties could have been caused by tears in the paper or blots, it is not unlikely that Woodward's copy was an early draft, still in the process of composition, in which words were illegible because they had been crossed out and rewritten. The copy behind Bur was made either by or for Donne. Differences between a few readings of Bur and the other witnesses would suggest that Donne improved occasional obscure passages in preparing the text. Thus in Paradox VI, 42, 'Sociable' (Bur) for 'flexible to companies' (Σ), 'flexible to [blank]' (S) which was 'corrected' to '*flexible* to *complaints*' ($1633+$) appears to be such a revision. Donne also appears to have changed his text in Paradox II, 39–41. The point made in all the witnesses but Bur 'Thou didst love her: if thou beginst to hate her then it is because she is not painted' is rather obscure. In Bur the sense is clarified: 'Thou didest love her; if thou begin to hate when it [i.e. the paint] falls thou hatest her because shee is not painted'.

As well as readings such as these, Bur contains many other peculiar readings some of which seem to be minor alterations of the readings common to the other manuscripts, and others which appear to be scribal errors. It is difficult to

---

[1] In Paradox V, 14–16, W reads 'a brave, and a fiery [*blank*] which is indeed a cowardly, an earthly, and a groveling Spiritt'. What Woodward could not read and leaves a blank for, Bur provides: 'a brave a fiery sparkling and a clyming resolution which is indeed . . . ' thus supplying the three necessary opposites for 'cowardly', 'earthly', and 'groveling'. The other witnesses reflect the confusion of W, reading 'a very brave, and a very clyminge which is indeed . . .' This is nonsense. In Paradox VIII, 22, W reads 'prostitute her owne [*blank*] to all'. All the other witnesses agree that the missing word is 'amiablenes'.

[2] Whether Woodward was copying W directly from Donne's holograph or from a copy which he had previously made of his friend's works should not affect the argument.

determine in a few of these unique readings which are Donne's changes, which are his (or his copyist's) errors, and which are the blunders of the scribe of *Bur*. There is no way of knowing whether Grierson noted all the variant readings of *Bur* against the edition of *Juvenilia* which he used in collation. It is also impossible to know whether Evelyn Simpson copied all the readings that Grierson had noted. The punctuation of the readings of *Bur* in the copies which she had made of Grierson's collations is very light. Similarly, those letters in *Bur* which are attributed definitely to Donne and printed in *Prose Works*[1] are lightly punctuated, and six poems from the manuscript printed by Grierson lack punctuation altogether.[2] As Donne punctuated carefully,[3] it can be assumed that the faulty punctuation in *Bur* was the work of one of Wotton's secretaries.[4]

The Clarendon Press transcriber of Donne's letters noted after his transcription of the letter which had accompanied the Paradoxes that the Paradox, 'That all things kill themselves', came first. However, Evelyn Simpson's notes in the Osborn Collection, Yale University, indicate that the order of the Paradoxes in *Bur* was the same as that in *W*.

i

To Grierson's Group II manuscripts,[5] Trinity College, Cambridge (*TCC*), and its copy Additional MS 18647 (*A 18*) and Trinity College, Dublin (*TCD*), and its copy Norton (*N*), two more manuscripts can be added. Wyburd (*Wy*) is another copy of *TCD* and Stowe MS 962 (*S 962*)

---

[1] pp. 303–23.
[2] Grierson, i. 437–43. The poems that Grierson titled 'My Love', 'O Eyes', 'Fortune, Love, and Time', 'Life a Play' (which had two interrogation marks), and the two poems called in *Bur* 'Epi: B: Jo:' and 'Epi: Hen: Princ: Hug° Holland' were unpunctuated in the manuscript.
[3] Evelyn M. Simpson, 'A Note on Donne's Punctuation', *RES* iv (1928), 295–300.
[4] See *Prose Works*, 302. L. P. Smith had identified amongst the various hands in *Bur* one hand which he called D1. Most of Donne's poems were written in this hand as were all the letters which can be attributed definitely to Donne. The letter which had accompanied the Paradoxes was in the D1 hand and it is likely that the Paradoxes were copied by the same scribe.
[5] These are described in Gardner, *Divine Poems*, lxvi–lxviii and *Elegies etc.* lxvii–lxxi, and also briefly in Simpson, 'More Manuscripts etc.', 416.

appears to be collateral with *TCC* and *TCD*. These manu-
scripts contain the same ten Paradoxes in the same order as
in *W* and *Bur*.

Wy is a small poetical miscellany containing poems by
Thomas Carew, a few poems by Donne, and his *Paradoxes
and Problems*.[1] It is written in a scribal italic hand, probably
dating from the mid seventeenth century. Leaves are missing
in at least two places and the manuscript has been rebound,
during which process the leaves were shuffled thus altering
the order in which the *Paradoxes and Problems* appear. *Wy*
contains complete texts of Paradoxes I to III and VIII to X,
the beginning of IV and the end of VII. It also has com-
plete texts of the first eight Problems and the beginning of
the ninth. Since *Wy* was rebound, Paradoxes VII to X
followed immediately by the Problems come first (ff. 50–5ᵛ).
After a few poems, some of which are Donne's, come the
first four Paradoxes (ff. 59–61ᵛ). Foliation is in a modern
hand and followed rebinding. *Wy*, like *N*, as it is dependent
on *TCD*, is not an important witness. *TCD* is written in two
scribal hands, neither of which is the hand of *TCC*. The
bulk of the manuscript was written by one scribe but
twelve of the pages containing the Paradoxes were copied by
the second (ff. 148–53ᵛ). The change from one hand to the
other occurs in mid sentence and it seems highly probable
that the two scribes were working together. The second
scribe was careless and omitted a passage in Paradox III
and another in Paradox VII. In both places a hand which
appears to be that of the first scribe has written the omitted
passages in the margin and marked with carets those places
in the text where the passages belonged. *N* appears to have
been copied before the correction of *TCD* for it omits both
passages. *Wy*, on the other hand, seems to have been copied
after *TCD* was corrected, for the marginalia of *TCD* are
included in its text.

All of the Group II manuscripts were written in different

---

[1] Evelyn Simpson described *Wy* and discussed some of its readings in 'Two Manuscripts
etc.', 131–45.

hands, but all except *S 962* show a curious physical resemblance at the beginning of the Paradoxes where they all read 'Paradoxes' followed by the first title.[1] It looks as if each scribe imitated the writing of the copy he followed, and the unity of style so achieved makes it highly likely that one manuscript lay behind the five. Helen Gardner has suggested that such a manuscript which she called Y was probably an expansion of MS Lansdowne 740 in which the latest datable poems are two elegies on Mrs Bulstrode (1609).[2] Alan MacColl has further suggested that Y was compiled by Sir Robert Ker to whom Donne sent a collection of his poems in 1619, and these Ker added to the nuclear group.[3] The collection continued to grow as Ker obtained new material, of which the latest datable pieces are the 'Hymn to God the Father' (1623), and finally the Hamilton Elegy (1625) written at Ker's request. It is clear an authoritative and late source lay behind the collection as the Group II manuscripts contain poems written by Donne after his ordination, and some texts in these manuscripts have readings which have been judged by all recent editors of Donne as late. The text of the Paradoxes is good, and although not without scribal errors, contains readings which reflect some reworking of them after they were copied in *W* and *Bur*.

The text of the Paradoxes in *S 962* does not have the same physical appearance noted in the *TC* manuscripts.[4] On the first page it is dated 'Feb. 1.' and headed 'Paradoxes of John Done'. The manuscript is really two notebooks, both of which were kept at times contemporaneously, over a period of some three or four years by a single scribe whose handwriting was developing. The notebooks are bound in reverse order so that the earliest writing (f. 37) faces some of

---

[1] R. E. Alton has pointed out this feature to me.
[2] *Divine Poems*, lxvii–lxviii. 149–50.
[3] 'The New Edition of Donne's Love Poems', *Essays in Criticism*, xvii (1967), 259, and 'The Circulation of Donne's Poems in Manuscript', *John Donne: Essays in Celebration*, ed. A. J. Smith (1972), 35.
[4] Following Grierson, the agreement of *TCD* and *TCC* is designated *TC*.

the latest (f. 35).[1] The larger manuscript which was begun first is bound second. Its leaves, originally foliated 2 to 208, were refoliated 37 to 243 when the smaller manuscript was bound to it. Its first leaf is missing but the stub is plainly visible. This manuscript is a miscellany containing poems by Donne and others such as Corbet and Strode. Helen Gardner has examined the text and found it so late and of such mixed traditions that it could have been copied from a manuscript corrected from either the first or second edition of the poems, or copied from the editions themselves.[2] On the last page but one is a poem on the death of John Pultenay, dated 1637, and as the manuscript was probably written over three to four years, it does not antedate the *Poems* of 1633, so the scribe could have used its text as well as that of the second edition of 1635 as sources.

The smaller manuscript, which is bound first, contains the *Paradoxes and Problems*, the two Characters (of a Scot and of a Dunce), followed by several other Characters from Earle's *Microcosmographie* (1628). These are indexed. The scribe took great pains with his manuscript, and although he made several copying errors he corrected most of them. On the pages that follow the index of the manuscript he added various poems at a later date. It is not possible to tell from the hand how much time had elapsed between the copying of the *Paradoxes and Problems* and of the poems; it could have been weeks or years. As in the larger section of the manuscript, one of the poems is on the death of John Pultenay, 1637. Although this notebook, like its companion, was probably written after the publication of the *Paradoxes and Problems* in 1633, its text is unlike that of the editions. The text preserved in *S 962* is the same as that preserved in *TC*,[3] and where *TCC* and *TCD* differ, *S 962* is closer to *TCC*. Neither manuscript could have been copied from the other.

---

[1] P. J. Croft has examined this manuscript in the British Library for me.

[2] Gardner, *Divine Poems*, lxxvi and *Elegies etc.* lxxxi.

[3] The inclusion of *S 962* in Group II is argued by its agreement with *TC* in many readings of which the following are examples: in Paradox II, 28–9, these manuscripts agree in reading 'Is not the Earths face in the most pleasing season painted?' when this sentence is omitted

ii

Seven remaining manuscripts contain texts of the Paradoxes. Three of these were unknown to Grierson; the other four belong in his Group III manuscript collections of Donne's poems. The four are Bridgewater (*B*), O'Flaherty (*O'F*), Phillipps (*P*), and Stephens (*S*). The three unknown to Grierson are Dobell (*Dob*) whose text is similar to *O'F* and *B*, Osborn (*O 2*) whose text is like that of *P*, and Pudsey (*Pud*) which contains extracts of a single Paradox. In the text of the Paradoxes, as Helen Gardner found in her study of Donne's poems, Group III manuscripts are not a group in the sense that they descend from a common ancestor, but they are a group in the sense that they agree in preserving a tradition of the text which is distinct from that preserved in other groups.[1] The text of the *Paradoxes and Problems* in *B*, *Dob*, *O'F*, however, appears to descend from a common exemplar which also contained the text of the two Characters, and I wish to restrict the title of Group III to these three manuscripts.

The three are ambitious collections: *B* contains all the material which its collector could gather up to 1620 when the manuscript was probably copied. It is, although beautifully bound,[2] a mechanical, laboured, scribal copy, full

in all other manuscripts with the exception of *Bur* which reads '... season new painted'; they agree twice in minim errors in quotations from Martial, reading '*Camus*' for '*Canius*' in Paradox VII, 24, and '*mane*' for '*inane*' in Paradox IX, 1 (this reading is not included in the apparatus); they read 'means, Art and industrie' for 'mans art and industry' in Paradox IV, 48, and 'Ministry' for 'misery' in Paradox IX, 27.

[1] Gardner, *Divine Poems*, lxix–lxxiv and *Elegies etc*. lxxi–lxxv. *O'F* is described in Simpson, 'Two Manuscripts etc.', 134–45, and *B*, *Dob*, *O'F* in Simpson, 'More Manuscripts etc.', 289–93, 412.

[2] D. F. Foxon has carefully examined this manuscript for me. He reports that the binding is contemporary vellum-covered boards with double gilt fillets on the covers and spine and gilt patterned edges to the boards. The initials 'F B' appear on both front and back covers flanking the remains of a coloured cartouche. He suggests that 'F B' stands for Frances Bridgewater (d. 11 Mar. 1636) whose husband John Egerton succeeded to the title of Viscount Brackley 15 Mar. 1617 and was created Earl of Bridgewater, 27 May 1617. The text is on fine writing-paper which has gilt edges and gilt ruling throughout. There is an elaborate gilt pattern on folio 3, which is the first leaf of the first text gathering, leaving a blank in which 'Dr: Donne' is written by the same hand which wrote 'J. Bridgewater' on the flyleaf. The manuscript originally had striped pink and blue ribbon ties. Foxon suggests that the elegance of the manuscript points to its being a presentation copy. He adds, however, that it could have been given to the Countess as a blank but ruled book. There are many such elegant blank books at least later in the century although they are not normally as thick as this one.

of silly errors, omissions, and inaccuracies. *Dob*, which belonged to and was annotated by William Balam who also owned and annotated *C* 57,[1] contains examples of virtually every form which Donne is known to have written, including sermons. Most of the manuscript, including the *Paradoxes and Problems* is written in a beautiful mixed secretary hand, and although not without errors, it is a good witness to the Group III tradition. *B* and *Dob* share a common arrangement in the order of the Paradoxes which is neither that of *W*, *Bur*, and Group II, nor that of *O'F*. Also comprehensive, the best-arranged, and, except for *W*, the best-punctuated manuscript is *O'F*, which was finished on 12 October 1632. It is an 'edited' manuscript which looks as if it were prepared to serve as copy for an edition, but it shows no physical signs of such use. It is an expansion of the Luttrell MS, drawing material not in Luttrell from various sources, one of which was a Group II manuscript. The *Paradoxes and Problems* were not copied from either source, Luttrell does not contain them, and the text in *O'F* is very unlike the text in Group II. The Paradoxes in O'F must have been copied from a manuscript very like that behind *B* and *Dob*. The exemplar of *B* and *Dob* was thought by Evelyn Simpson to be a single manuscript.[2]

O'F shows signs of correction which appear to have been made by the scribe as he was copying. Sometimes a word is crossed out and the correct word follows it immediately on the line, sometimes the correct word is written above that which is struck out. Not all the corrections arise from the scribe's checking his copy; some are sophistications which he has inserted in place of a reading in his copy which he has rejected. There is no sign of later correction from the first edition such as Helen Gardner had noted in the poems.

Despite the agreement of *B*, *Dob*, *O'F* in a large number

---

[1] *C* 57, Cambridge University Library, Add. MS 5778. For a recent discussion of *Dob*, see Mabel Potter, 'A Seventeenth-Century Literary Critic of John Donne: The Dobell Manuscript Re-examined', *Harvard Library Bulletin*, xxiii (1975), 63–89.
[2] Unpublished material.

of readings,[1] the three manuscripts do not always agree. Disagreement is caused in part by the numerous scribal blunders in *B*, but also by the sophistications which the scribe of *O'F* introduced into his text. Of the three manuscripts of Group III, *Dob* appears to be the best representative, as it is, though not without errors, the most free of blunders and sophistications.[2] The text preserved in Group III is not as good as that in *W*, *Bur*, and Group II, yet the distinct tradition of the text in this group must be considered against the readings of the better witnesses.

iii

Osborn (*O 2*) and Phillipps (*P*) most probably are, as Grierson suggested of *P*, examples of those collections of poems which seventeenth-century gentlemen had caused to be prepared. They are both pocket-sized manuscripts whose chief contents are various works of Donne. Collation shows that both manuscripts were copied from a single source[3] which contained many errors that both *O 2* and *P* perpetrate. *O 2*, which is more neatly written than *P* and which shows fewer independent errors, omits two of the ten Paradoxes.[4] The order in which the Paradoxes appear in these two manuscripts is peculiar to each and unlike the order of any other extant manuscript. *P*, which bears the date, 1623, on its first page, and *O 2* are far removed from Donne's papers. Through the veil of errors it can be seen that the text is in

---

[1] An ultimate common original behind the three manuscripts is indicated by readings such as the omission of 'sodain' in 'sodain deflowrers' in Paradox II, 17, 'out of nothinge it is' for 'out of it nothing is' in Paradox I, 36, 'weake' for 'unable' in 'how unable a guide', Paradox IV, 15, 'accounted lovers' for 'called lovers' and 'knowne some' for 'noted some' in Paradox VII, 28, 32.

[2] In the text of the Paradoxes there are 198 instances of disagreement among the manuscripts of Group III. On four of these occasions all three manuscripts read differently; *Dob*, *B* agree together against *O'F* 80 times; *Dob*, *O'F* agree against *B* in 85 instances; and in only 29 readings does *Dob* read against *O'F*, *B* in agreement.

[3] *Elegies etc.* lxxv–lxxvii. Helen Gardner discussed the relationship of the text of the poems in *O 2* and *P* with the Carnaby MS (*Cy*) and the Haslewood–Kingsborough MS (*HK*). *O 2*, *P*, *Cy* represent a corruption of the text in *HK*. However, neither *HK* nor *Cy* contains the *Paradoxes and Problems*. *P* is described in Simpson, 'More Manuscripts etc.', 413–14.

[4] *O 2* omits 'That women ought to paint themselves' and 'That it is possible to find some vertue in some women'.

general close to that of Group III but independent of it, for *O 2* and *P* occasionally agree with the better manuscripts against this group. In one instance, in Paradox IX, 3, *O 2* and *P* alone agree with *W*, *Bur* in correctly quoting a passage from Martial; they read '*Factum, dum negat haec, videt beatum*' (*W* reads '*vidit*') when all the other manuscripts and the editions read '*factum vidit dum negat haec beatum*'. *P* and *O 2*, though full of dittography, homoeoteleuton, and other features of scribal inaccuracy, are free of scribal sophistication, and the independence of their text makes them a useful check on the other traditions.

iv

Grierson described *S* as 'the worst [manuscript], the fullest of obvious and absurd blunders' showing 'more evidences of stupid editing than [are] in *P*'.[1] It is a manuscript whose readings bear only a very general witness to the Group III tradition, and those readings would not normally be included in a textual apparatus. In editing the Paradoxes, *S* cannot be ignored, for a manuscript very like it was copy for the first edition. *S*, which lacks a leaf so that the end of Paradox VIII along with the beginning of Paradox IX are missing, contains the usual ten Paradoxes in an order unlike that of any other witness. It is the only manuscript to contain the Paradox called 'A Defence of Womens Inconstancy' which is number eleven in its text following the usual ten, and is also the only manuscript which contains the text of the 'Essay of Valour' which is copied between the text of the two Characters.

Although the text in *S* is very like the text in *1633a*, *S* was not used as copy for the edition; it shows no signs of compositor's marks, and since each witness has errors of its own, there is no possibility that either was copied from the other.[2] *S* is dated at the end '19 July 1620'. Similarities

---

[1] Grierson, ii, cv.
[2] In Paradox X, 16, *S* reads '*Dispersers*' against 'other *dispensers*' the reading of *1633a*

between *S* and *1633a* are both typographical and sub-
stantive. *S*, which uses extensive italicization like that of
1633a, is the only manuscript to use italics for words other
than Latin quotations, proper names, and titles. The other
manuscripts employ italics only for these purposes, and then
not consistently. *S* and *1633a* agree against the other
manuscripts in the use of parenthesis in 'Ruyne; and
Deformitie (the tyrannous *Ravishers*, the sudden deflowrers
of all *Women*)...' in Paradox II, 16–17. Substantive
variant readings include the nonsensical 'forecastinge that
Ball upon Ida' for 'for casting that ball upon *Ide*' in Paradox
IX, 36–7, and 'sensible change in men' for 'for sensible
change in me', Paradox III, 3. In some readings *S* represents
an intermediate stage between the other manuscripts and
the editions. In Paradox V, 17–18, for example, in a
passage about slaves who are chained to a galley and who
'thirst their deathes', *S* uses an archaic form 'thrist' for
'thirst', and the compositor set 'thrust'.[2] In Paradox II, 6–7,
W, *Bur*, and Group II manuscripts read 'wary and con-
ceald, offending without witnes'. Group III manuscripts
and *P* read '... concealinge offendinge ...' having changed
the 'ed' of 'concealed' to 'inge' because of the following
present participle. *S* reads '... Concealinge offendinges ...'
which the compositor saw was an error and 'corrected' to
'... concealing offendors ...'.

The value of *S* is as an intermediary between the other
manuscripts and the editions, showing how some of the
errors in the editions arose.

---

and the other manuscripts. In the same Paradox, l. 22, *S* omits 'and beeing them selves
overthrowne'. On the other hand, in Paradox V, l. 4, *S* agrees with the other manuscripts in
reading 'necessited' where *1633a* reads 'of necessity'. Again, in the same Paradox, l. 11, *S*
and the other manuscripts read 'Valyantes' against '*Gallants*' in *1633a*. In Paradox X, *1633a*
omits two separate passages which are present in all the manuscripts including *S*: 'yea in the
worst and most prostitute sorte of them' and 'but they are both good scourges for bad men',
ll. 19–20, 28–9.

  [2] This, and other readings of *S*, are discussed in Simpson, 'More Manuscripts etc.', 414–16.

v

The theory of the transmission of the Paradoxes in manuscript can be summarized by the following stemma.

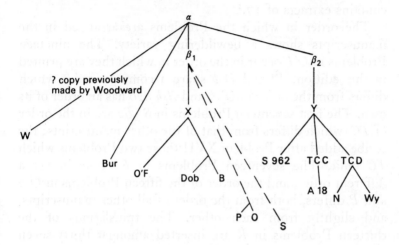

B. Problems

Unlike the manuscripts containing the Paradoxes which are, except for *S*, consistent in their canon, the manuscripts of the Problems contain varying numbers and slightly different collections of Problems. There are no clearly superior manuscripts such as *W* and *Bur*. There is, furthermore, a Latin collection of Problems, published in 1616, which contains Latin translations of thirteen of Donne's Problems, with alterations and additions made by the translator in the course of his translating. Finally, in the texts of four Problems, there is evidence of large-scale revision, mainly but not entirely in the form of excision of material. This feature does not occur in Donne's poetry or in the Paradoxes, where only occasional reworking of a word or passage is seen.

The largest collection, of 19 Problems, is found in *Ash 826*, *B*, *Dob*, *O'F*, and *S 962*; *TCC* and its copy *A 18*, and

TCD with its copy *N*, along with *S* have 17.[1] *O 2* and *P* contain 15,[2] *O 1* has 6, and *A 25* and Tan contain 1 each.[3] *R*, the Latin translation, contains 13 Problems.[4] Finally, the fourth Earl of Bedford's commonplace book, *HMC 26*, contains extracts of 17.[5]

The order in which the Problems are arranged in the manuscripts shows a bewildering variety. The nineteen Problems in *O'F* occur in the order in which they are printed in this edition. *B*[6] and *Dob* share a common order which differs from the order in *O'F*, and *Ash 826* has an order of its own. The first seventeen Problems in *S 962* are in the order of *TC*, which differs from that of the other manuscripts; the scribe added after Problem XVII those two Problems which *TC* omit. The seventeen Problems in *S* occur in yet a different order, and the order of the fifteen Problems in *O 2* and *P* differs, both from the order of all other manuscripts, and slightly from each other. The translations of the thirteen Problems in *R* are inserted amongst thirty-seven other Problems and are in an order peculiar to themselves, and the seventeen extracts in *HNC 26* are also in a unique order.

---

[1] These manuscripts omit the 'John of Salisbury' and the 'Devil and Jesuits' Problems. *Wy*, the other copy of *TCD*, has leaves missing and thus contains only the first eight Problems with the beginning of the ninth, but there is no reason to suppose that it did not originally contain the same seventeen as its fellows.

[2] *O 2* and *P* omit, in addition to the 'John of Salisbury' and the 'Devil and Jesuits' Problems, those Problems on 'Women Delighting in Feathers' and 'Statesmen being Incredible'.

[3] *O 1* contains 'Why doe women delight soe much in feathers', 'Why dye none for love now', 'Why have Bastards best Fortune', 'Why doth not Gold soyle the fingers', 'Why are Courtiers sooner Atheists then men of other Condition', 'Why are Statesmen most Incredible'. *A 25* contains the 'Puritans' Problem and *Tan* the 'Sir Walter Ralegh'.

[4] *R* contains 'Why is there more variety of Greene, then of other Collours', 'Why doth the Poxe so much affect to undermine the nose', 'Why doth not Gold soyle the fingers', 'Why are Courtiers sooner Atheists then men of other Condition', 'Why is Venus Starre multinominous called both Hesperus and Vesper', 'Why Venus starre onely doth cast a Shadowe', 'Why are the fayrest falsest', 'Why did the Devill reserve Jesuits for these latter times', 'Why hath the common opinion affoorded woemen Soules', 'Why doe women delight soe much in feathers', 'Why have Bastards best Fortune', 'Why doe Great Men choose of all dependants to preferre theyr Bawds', 'Why dye none for love now'.

[5] *HMC 26* omits the 'John of Salisbury' and the 'Variety of Green' Problems.

[6] The arrangement in *B* is peculiar; Problems 1 to 15 come first, followed by the Paradoxes and the two Characters, and then Problems 16 to 19. The scribe failed to number Problem 6 and consequently numbered Problems 7 to 15 as 6 to 14. Problems 16 to 19 are unnumbered.

In this variety in the order in which the Problems occur in the various manuscripts, two common arrangements can be seen. In all these manuscripts, with the exception of *Ash 826*, the first six Problems are the same, and occur in the same order. This would suggest that these six circulated as a set. Three additional Problems may also be related, in that their occurrence is restricted, the 'John of Salisbury' the 'Devil and Jesuits' and the 'Women and Feathers' Problems. The 'John of Salisbury' and the 'Devil and Jesuits' occur only in *Ash 826, B, Dob, O'F* and are added at the end of the collection in *S 962*. They appear in *Ash 826, B, Dob, O'F* as numbers seventeen and nineteen with the Problem on 'Women and Feathers' intervening.[1] The 'Women and Feathers' Problem occurs in a much shortened form in *TC* and *S* (and not at all in *O 2* and *P*) while the 'John of Salisbury' and 'Devil and Jesuits' Problems do not appear in *TC, S, O,* and *P*.

The remaining ten Problems differ in their arrangement in the manuscripts, which would suggest that the scribes of these manuscripts were working from collections of papers which they sorted differently.[2]

i

The first witnesses to be discussed in an examination of the manuscripts containing the Problems are *Ash 826, R,* and *HMC 26*. *Ash 826*, which contains nineteen Problems, was discovered by Percy Simpson and was described by Evelyn Simpson who called it *Y*.[3] *R*, which contains thirteen

---

[1] *R* contains the 'Women and Feathers' and the 'Devil and Jesuits' Problems but not the 'John of Salisbury'.

[2] Donne sent his Problems to his friends as he composed them as the following extracts from letters to Sir Henry Goodyer indicate: 'I end with a probleme, whose errand is, to aske for his fellowes' (*Poems*, 1633, 358, *Letters*, 1651, 99) and 'I pray reade these two problemes: for such light flashes as these have beene my hawkings in my Surry journies' (*Poems*, 1633, 361. *Letters*, 1651, 88. The latter reads 'sorry' for 'Surry'). The variety shown therefore amongst the various manuscripts in the order of the Problems should not be surprising.

[3] 'More Manuscripts etc.', 293–97.

Problems, was discovered by R. C. Bald,[1] and *HMC 26* was found by Conrad Russell.[2] The texts of the Problems in *Ash 826* are on three leaves (ff. 249–51, f. 251v being blank). At the end of Problem XIX the word 'Finis' is written, and there is no stub to indicate that the Paradoxes may have accompanied the Problems. The scribe was careless and uneducated, and in some places he has garbled his text so badly that it is virtually unintelligible, a feature which is accentuated by his erratic punctuation.[3] Among many blunders he wrote 'W. K.' for 'W. R.' in Problem II and 'Konsard' for 'Ronsard', Problem XII, 8.[4]

The manuscript from which *R* was translated was a much superior version of the text in *Ash 826*. *R* contains thirteen Problems which were printed along with thirty-seven others to make up a volume of fifty.[5] Rouzee, the translator, wrote some of the other Problems himself, and found the remainder in other sources. In the Preface to his book Rouzee did not name Donne as the author of the thirteen Problems which he said that he had found in England in 1609 or 1610, but he admitted that he had made alterations in, and additions to, these Problems in the course of translating them. Collation of *R* with the other witnesses shows that he made additions to three Problems and alterations as well as

---

[1] R. C. Bald, 'A Latin Version of Donne's Problems', *MP* lxi (1964), 198–203.

[2] Russell passed his discovery on to A. J. Smith who informed me of the existence of the manuscript in March 1978.

[3] In Problem X, for example, *Ash 826* reads 'Is it because her workes are workes of darkenesse Childish and unrefined, times might thinke so' when there should be a question mark after 'darkenesse' and no comma after 'unrefined'.

[4] R. E. Alton has pointed out that Donne's *R* was easily mistakable for *K*. This confusion by the scribe of *Ash 826* could suggest that he was copying directly from Donne's holograph. His following Donne's use of 'yow' for 'you' supports this suggestion. However, the multitude of errors in his text suggests that he was copying from a manuscript made by an equally careless and unlettered scribe who also had difficulty with Donne's *R*.

[5] *Problematum miscellaneorum, Antaristotelicorum, centuria dimidiata, ad dominos studiosos in Academia Leydensi. A Ludovico Rouzaeo directa. Lugduni Batavorum, Ex Officina Godefridi Basson. Anno Domini, 1616.* In the order of this edition, Donne's Problem I is found on p. 38, III on p. 86, IV on p. 26, V on p. 90, VII on p. 64. VIII on p. 62, IX on p. 83, X on p. 51 XI on p. 40, XII on p. 1, XIII on p. 11, XVIII on p. 68 and XIX on p. 54 For a biographical note on Rouzee and his connection with Donne's circle, see Appendix.

additions to three others.[1] That his translation contains only
thirteen Problems should not be surprising, nor taken as
proof that his source did not contain the full nineteen. As
Bald suggested,[2] the 'John of Salisbury' and 'Sir Walter
Ralegh' Problems would have lost some of their point out-
side England, and an attack on Puritan preachers would
have perhaps been impolitic in Holland.

Because of the liberties taken by Rouzee readings
peculiar to R cannot be ascribed to Donne. But where R
supports other manuscripts, it is a useful and valuable
witness.

Ash 826 and R contain long versions of four Problems, the
two on 'Venus Star', and the 'Women and Feathers', and
the 'Variety of Green'. In these four Problems they agree in
several sentences which are not found in other manuscripts.[3]

The many scribal errors in the text of Ash 826 can be
recognized and corrected by comparison with the text in R
in order to give those readings which present an independent
text of the Problems.

The fourth Earl of Bedford must have copied his extracts
of the seventeen Problems that HMC 26 contains from a
manuscript very similar to that which lay behind Ash 826
and R. The manuscript is in his own rather difficult hand. In
the 'Women and Feathers' and 'Venus Star Multinominous'
Problems, he copied extracts of the long versions found

---

[1] Rouzee added an introductory sentence to the Problem which is printed in this edition as
Problem VII, two introductory sentences to Problem XIX, and a concluding paragraph of
two sentences to Problem V. To Problem X he added an introduction of four sentences and
omitted from the middle of the Problem a sentence which occurs in all other witnesses to the
text. He added a sentence in the middle of Problem XI and exchanged the two concluding
sentences containing a quotation from Virgil for a sentence of his own and a verse from
Annibal Cruceius. In Problem XII he altered the order of three sections which otherwise
appear only in Ash 826 and omitted a reference to Petrarch which is found in that manuscript.
The concluding sentence which is found in Ash 826, B, Dob, O'F but which is changed in TC,
S 962, O 2, P, S was omitted by Rouzee and replaced by an ending of seven sentences which
he had invented. I have included in the Appendix two of Rouzee's translations. The first is
Donne's Problem XI (Rouzee's Problem XXII) to which Rouzee made additions and altera-
tions, and the second is Donne's Problem XVIII (Rouzee's XXXVIII) which he rendered
faithfully.

[2] 'A Latin Version etc.', 199.

[3] B, Dob, O'F contain the same text of 'Women and Feathers'; they omit the additional
lines in 'Variety of Green' but share the variant ending of Ash 826 and R. B, Dob, O'F will be
discussed below.

otherwise only in *Ash 826* and *R*. His method in copying
was not consistent as he transcribed different parts of
various Problems: two, 'Sir Walter Ralegh' and 'Puritans'
Sermons' he copied in full, while the other fifteen ('Variety
of Green' and 'John of Salisbury' are omitted) are re-
presented by sometimes the first and last sentences, some-
times the first (or the last) half of a Problem, and sometimes
by individual sentences copied from various parts of a
Problem. The value of the text in *HMC 26* is that it provides,
albeit far from complete, a third witness to the long version
of two Problems. Its readings have not been included in the
apparatus.

ii

TCD, *N* and *TCC*, *A 18* contain seventeen Problems,[1] and
the two Problems which these manuscripts omit, 'John of
Salisbury' and the 'Devil and Jesuits', have been added after
Problem XVII in *S 962*. As in the text of the Paradoxes,
several common readings indicate that the text of the first
seventeen Problems in *S 962* is collateral with the text in
TC.[2] In the four Problems that occur in long versions in
Ash 826 and *R*, the Group II manuscripts have short texts,
consisting, in the 'Women and Feathers' Problem, of but a
few of the sentences that are found in *Ash 826* and *R*.
However, in material common to *Ash 826*, *R* and *TC*, *S 962*,
these witnesses frequently agree in readings against the other
witnesses.

iii

B, *Dob*, *O'F* in the text of the Problems, even more than
in the text of the Paradoxes, preserve a distinct text. In
three Problems the text in *B*, *Dob*, *O'F* differs so substanti-

---

[1] *Wy*, another copy of *TCD*, being defective contains only the first eight Problems and the
beginning of the ninth.
[2] A common source behind *TC* and *S 962* is argued by their agreement in reading 'endevour'
for 'endure', Problem XI, 23, 'Maces' for '*Fasces*', Problem XII, 9, 'more' for 'mercy'
Problem XIII, 3, and 'Graculously' for 'oraculously', Problem XVI, 10.

ally from the texts of the majority of the manuscripts, that their reliance upon a common exemplar is clearly seen.[1] In the 'Women and Feathers' Problem these Group III manuscripts agree with *Ash 826* and *R* in the long version of the text. But in 'Variety of Green' *B*, *Dob*, *O'F* occupy an intermediate position between *Ash 826* and *R* on the one hand, and the other witnesses on the other. They differ from *Ash 826* and *R* in omitting a long introductory passage, but in the final sentence they agree with them against a quite different sentence in the other witnesses. In one other Problem, the 'Sir Walter Ralegh', *B*, *Dob*, *O'F* agree in two final sentences which are otherwise only found in *S* and *Tan*.

Despite their agreement, *B*, *Dob*, *O'F* show minor disagreements with each other, caused mainly by errors in *B* and sophistications in *O'F*. The majority of readings peculiar to *O'F* must be regarded as scribal sophistications. For example, in Problem XVI, 4, the scribe of *O'F* deliberately altered the reading of his copy, changing 'theyr' which he had first written to 'his' in a sentence in which all other witnesses read 'theyr'. This alteration makes it likely that he also 'improved' the final sentence in Problems XV, 15–16, and VII, 25–6, by inserting a phrase that does not occur in any other witness. It must be noted, however, that these readings serve to clarify the sense of the passages. The scribe of *O'F* appears to have undertaken the duty of a copy editor in attempting to free his text from ambiguities. These alterations are easily recognizable by comparison with the readings in *Dob* and *B*. The accidental features of *O'F* are good; its spelling is consistent for the period, and its punctuation is the most rational of all the manuscripts which contain the Problems.

---

[1] *B*, *Dob*, *O'F* also agree in readings in other Problems: 'Lawe robbs' for 'Lawes robb', Problem IX, 18, 'very snuff', for 'snuff', Problem XV, 8, and omission of 'they have' in 'the memory they have of the monny', Problem XIV, 3.

iv

The texts of the fifteen Problems which occur in *O 2* and *P*
appear to be intermediate between Groups II and III. In
those Problems which occur in long and short forms, *O 2*
and *P* contain the short forms of the texts which are found in
TC, *S 962*, but they frequently agree with Group III read-
ings against Group II. *O 2* and *P* have many errors peculiar
to themselves, *P* being more carelessly copied than *O 2*.

   S contains seventeen Problems and is generally a poor
witness to the same version of the text which is somewhat
better preserved in *O 2* and *P*. However, in contrast with *O 2*
and *P*, *S* contains the long version of the 'Sir Walter Ralegh'
Problem as found in *B*, *Dob*, *O'F*. This version of the 'Sir
Walter Ralegh' Problem also appears in *Tan* which contains
no further Problems.[1] The copy behind *S* and *Tan* does not
appear to have been the copy which was behind *B*, *Dob*,
O'F, for, besides agreeing in minor variant readings, *S* and
Tan share a title which is not found in any other manuscript:
'Why was Sir Walter Raleigh thought the fittest Man to
write the History of these Tymes'.

   Collation shows the text in *S* to be similar to the text in
1633a in the nine Problems which they have in common.[2]
As in editing the Paradoxes, therefore, *S* is of value in
editing these nine as an intermediary between the other
manuscripts and the editions. For example, in Problem VI,
8, 'River Ougus' (*Dob*, *B*, *O 2*, *P*) which appears as 'river
Ongus' (*Ash 826*, *TC*, *S 962*) and 'river Ogus' (*O'F*) is
'River oriyns' in *S*. The compositor saw that this was an
error and 'emended' the reading to 'river *Origus*'.

   In those seven Problems which were first printed in *1652*,

---

[1] The Problem was copied in *Tan* in the eighteenth century by the then Bishop Sancroft
who noted above the text "'Tis one of Dr Donne's problemes (but so bitter, that his son—
Jack Donne LL.D. thought not fitt to print it with the Rest;)'. The text is so like that in *S*
that his copy must have either been *S* or a manuscript so like *S* as to be indistinguishable from
it.

[2] *S* omits the 'Devil and Jesuits' Problem which *1633a* contains and contains the 'Sir
Walter Ralegh' Problem which *1633a* omits. Similarities in readings of *S* and *1633a* include
'successyon in Civill Benifits' for 'Succession and civill benefits', Problem IX, 18, and
'watchinge Candles' for 'watch candles', Problem XV, 5–6.

there is no resemblance between the text in the edition and
that in *S*. For those Problems, therefore, *S* presents an
independent witness.

Two further manuscripts of the Problems exist. One,
A 25, contains the text of only one Problem, the 'Puritans'
Problem, which is similar to the text in *Ash 826* but inde-
pendent of it. The other, *O 1*, was formerly known as the
King MS. The date of its composition is not known. Its
variant readings jumble together errors both from the manu-
scripts and from the printed text of the third edition, *1652*,
so that it is difficult to tell what tradition it represents. Of
the six Problems in *O 1*, five were not printed in *1633a*, and
the sixth Problem contains only those lines which were
omitted in *1633a*.[1] Perhaps the scribe owned a copy of the
first edition of the *Paradoxes and Problems*, and by comparing
his book with a copy of the third edition, noticed that his
edition was incomplete. The Problems copied in *O 1* may
therefore represent his attempt to complete the text of the
Problems in *1633a*. Readings of *O 1* have not been included
in the apparatus.

v

The following stemma summarizes the manuscript
transmission of the Problems.

---

[1] The first twenty-three lines of 'Why have Bastards best Fortune' are omitted in *1633a*.

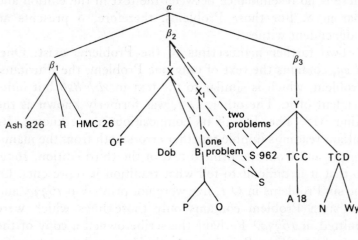

vi

Of the nineteen Problems, twelve occur in virtually the same form in all their witnesses, five occur in variant forms, and the remaining two are of restricted occurrence.[1] Two main variant versions of the five Problems exist—a long and a short form. *Ash 826* and *R* contain long versions of the two Problems on 'Venus Star'; *Ash 826*, *R* and *B, Dob, O'F* agree in a long version of the 'Women and Feathers' Problem;[2] in 'Variety of Green' *Ash 826* and *R* agree together in a long introductory passage which is not found in any other witness, but they agree with *B, Dob, O'F* in an ending which is unlike the ending found in the remaining witnesses. *B, Dob, O'F* agree with *S* and *Tan* in a concluding section of the 'Sir Walter Ralegh' Problem which is omitted in the other witnesses. Finally, there are two Problems of restricted occurrence, 'John of Salisbury' and the 'Devil and Jesuits' which are found in *Ash 826, B, Dob, O'F*, and *S 962*.[3]

My argument concerning the probable order of composi-

---

[1] See above, pp. xlii–xliii.

[2] *HMC 26* supports the long versions of 'Venus Star Multinominous' and 'Women and Feathers' but consists, only of extracts.

[3] The scribe of *S 962* added the two Problems at the end of the collection which it shares with *TC*. The 'Devil and Jesuits' Problem also occurs in *R*.

tion is that Donne first wrote the version that appears in *Ash 826, R, HMC 26,* excised the 'learned' material from this version in order to produce the form that occurs in *B, Dob, O'F,* and later pruned from this version material which could possibly be regarded as offensive to provide the latest version that is found in *TC* and *S 962.* I would further suggest that included among the material eliminated in revision are the full texts of the 'John of Salisbury' and the 'Devil and Jesuits' Problems which occur in *Ash 826, B, Dob, O'F* but not in *TC.*

The text of the 'Sir Walter Ralegh' Problem presents difficulties. In *B, Dob, O'F, S, Tan,* the text of the Problem contains two concluding sentences which are not found in any other witness. If my suggested chronology of the versions is correct, first *Ash 826,* then *B, Dob, O'F,* finally *TC,* then the extra sentences in the intermediate manuscripts could not represent Donne's original version, and I would suggest that somebody, possibly Donne but equally possibly not, added these extra sentences to the exemplar behind *B, Dob, O'F, S, Tan.* That the passage should appear in *S* which otherwise contains only late texts of the Problems should not be surprising. As Donne appears to have sent out his Problems singly and in pairs, and as he requested their return in order that he might review them,[1] it is not unlikely that the manuscripts should contain mixtures of both early and late texts; indeed it is surprising that more manuscripts do not.

It is not possible to date any of the exemplars which lay behind the extant witnesses to the text of the Problems with the exception of the copy that preceded *R.* Rouzee claimed that he had copied the manuscript from which he made his translation in 1609 or 1610.[2]

The revised and omitted Problems can be summarized by the following *stemma.*

---

[1] See above, pp. xli–xlii.
[2] See above, p. xli and Appendix.

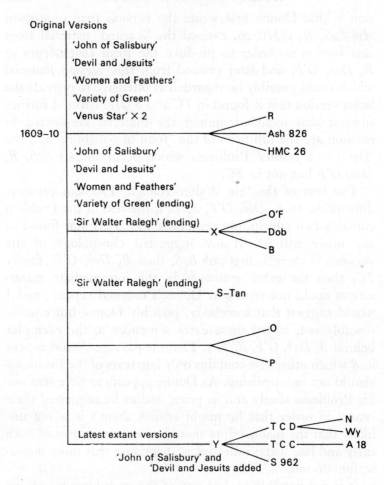

Original Versions

'John of Salisbury'
'Devil and Jesuits'
'Women and Feathers'
'Variety of Green'
'Venus Star' × 2

1609-10

R
Ash 826
HMC 26

'John of Salisbury'
'Devil and Jesuits'
'Women and Feathers'
'Variety of Green' (ending)
'Sir Walter Ralegh' (ending)

X
O'F
Dob
B

'Sir Walter Ralegh' (ending)
S-Tan

O
P

Latest extant versions

TCD
N
Wy

Y
TCC
A 18
S 962

'John of Salisbury' and
'Devil and Jesuits added'

II. EDITIONS

On 13 September 1632 Sir Henry Herbert and two
Wardens granted a licence to John Marriot entitling him to
publish John Donne's *'booke of verses and Poems'* excepting
the five Satires and five Elegies. On 31 October Herbert and
Warden Apsley issued another licence permitting Marriot
to print the five Satires which they had excepted in

September. The book was published in 1633, printed by M[iles] F[letcher]. W. W. Greg has pointed out that licensing and licensers were various both in the function served and in the authority with which the licensers were invested.[1] Licensing could mean, on the one hand, nothing more than that a proposed book was the work of the author involved or that an author gave consent for the publishing of his work, or, on the other hand, it could be a guarantee that the book contained nothing contrary to public policy. Licensers were not equal in their authority—the monarch was absolute; and those like the Archbishop of Canterbury, the Bishop of London, the Privy Council, the Master of the Revels (which Herbert was), had more authority than others such as Wardens, 'correctors', and various clergy who were also appointed. There are cases, too, of a licenser merely assuming the role, as did Francis Bacon who licensed his own *Essays* in 1597. Although the question of authority in licensing is obscure, it seems fair to assume that Herbert had authority as a licenser, who appears, from his dealings with Donne's poems, to have acted as a censor. He does not appear to have consented readily to their publication. The first entry in the *Register*, on 13 September 1632, permits the printing of '*a booke of verses and Poems* . . . and these before excepted', while excepting the five Satires and five Elegies. A second entry permits the printing of the Satires. It appears that Donne's poetry was examined at least three times—the first, not recorded, excepts some works; the second, recorded 13 September 1632, admits these works plus '*verses and poems*' but excepts the five Satires and five Elegies; and the third, on 31 October 1632, permits the Satires. The five Elegies remained under ban.

Before the licence was granted for the Satires, a licence was granted to 'Master Seile' (Henry Seyle), on 24 October 1632, by Herbert and Master Apsley, Warden, for the

[1] Information on licensing comes from Greg's three studies of the subject: 'Samuel Harsnett and Hayward's *Henry IV*', *The Library*, xi (1956), 1–10; *Some Aspects of London Publishing 1550–1650*, 1956, ch. iii, 41–62; and *Licensers for the Press, &c. to 1640*, 1962.

printing of a book called *certaine Paradoxes and Problems in prose* written by J. Donn[e]. This book, a quarto, entitled *Juvenilia: or Certaine Paradoxes and Problemes*, containing eleven Paradoxes and ten Problems with Herbert's *imprimatur* after each section, was published by Seyle in 1633 (*1633a*).[1] It was printed by E[lizabeth] P[urslowe].

The book contained only ten Problems while the extant manuscripts contain more, some fifteen, some seventeen, some nineteen. *S*, a manuscript like that which Seyle must have had, contains seventeen Problems. In the edition, too, the first Problem printed lacks the first twenty-three lines. While it is not impossible that Seyle's manuscript was defective and contained the Problems in such an order that the loss of a few leaves had resulted in the omission of the material which is not printed in the first edition, it is also possible that Herbert refused to license the missing material, although no mention of such an exception is made in the *Register*.

Whether Herbert was responsible for the material that did not appear in *Juvenilia*, he was held to answer for that which it did contain. On 14 November 1632 he was called to appear before the Star Chamber by the Bishop of London at the King's command, to explain 'why hee warranted the booke of D. Duns paradoxes to bee printed'.[2] There is no record of what punishment, if any, was meted out to either Herbert or Henry Seyle, and indeed, Seyle released a second edition in 1633 (*1633b*).[3] It was again in quarto format,

---

[1] D. F. Foxon has pointed out that while the New Year began with Lady Day, 25 March, the publishers' year was usually begun on the beginning of November, with the consequence that books printed between November and March were often given the date of the following year, *Juvenilia*, then, could have been published in November 1632.

[2] It seems likely that the book *was* published before mid November 1632. The demand that Herbert appear before the Star Chamber appears in the *Calendar of Domestic State Papers*, Charles I, ccxxv. 20.

[3] While appearances before the Star Chamber for publishing and licensing offences do not appear to have been common, they were not unheard of. In 1599 Samuel Harsnett, who had approved John Hayward's essay on Henry IV, was questioned by the Chamber and the author imprisoned. A second edition of the work was published before Whitsun 1600, but before its release it was seized and burned by the Bishop of London. In 1634 William Prynne's *Histriomastix: the Players Scourge* cost the author his ears and Thomas Buckner, who licensed the book, was fined fifty pounds under rulings of the Star Chamber. Donne's *Paradoxes and Problems* do not appear to have been such serious offences; the editions were not seized.

printed by E. P., and entitled *Juvenilia or Certaine Paradoxes and Problemes*. It was marked '*The second Edition, corrected*'. The second edition differed from the first in only two important respects: it no longer bore Herbert's *imprimaturs* and the missing twenty-three lines had been restored to the first Problem. Seyle either already had, or was able to procure, that part of the text.

In 1637 Donne's son, in a petition to the Archbishop of Canterbury, attacked the publication of Seyle, Marriot, and Marriot's joint venture with William Sheares, *Ignatius His Conclave*, saying that they were not his father's works. Archbishop Laud responded on 16 December 1637 and granted an injunction against further publication.[1] But in 1652 the younger Donne admitted the authenticity of the *Paradoxes and Problems* by publishing them with one extra Paradox, seven extra Problems, two Characters, and the 'Essay of Valour', in conjunction with the *Essays in Divinity* and *Ignatius*. The combination was, according to Donne's introduction to his father's works, to balance the light-hearted works of youth against the graver efforts of age. The book is a duodecimo, published by Humphrey Moseley and printed by T[homas] N[ewcombe]. It is entitled *Paradoxes, Problemes, Essayes, Characters*, and except for the new material added, which must have come from a manuscript in the younger Donne's possession, it is a reprint of the second edition.

Other early appearances in print of Donne's juvenilia and of works long accepted as having been written by Donne are interesting for the diversity of places in which they occur. '"Newes from the very Country" by J. D.' was printed in the 1614 edition of Sir Thomas Overbury's *Characters* (sigs. G2–G2ᵛ), and in *Poems, By J. D.*, 1650, 369–70. 'An Essay of Valour' and 'The True Character of a Dunce' were printed anonymously in Overbury's *Characters*, 1622, sigs. Q6–R1, G3–G5. Henry Seyle joined the Overbury publisher, Lisle, in 1622, and he probably then possessed

---

[1] See *Calendar of Domestic State Papers*, Charles I, ccclxxxiv. 4.

the manuscript from which he later published the *Paradoxes and Problems*.¹ The bulk of the 'Essay of Valour' appeared as ' "Valour Anatomized in a Fancie", by Sir Philip Sidney, 1581' in Sir Robert Cotton's *Cottoni posthuma*, 1656, 323–7. Cotton's book was printed by Francis Leach for Henry Seyle. John Dunton writing *Athenian Sport: Or, Two Thousand Paradoxes Merrily Argued To Amuse and Divert the Age*, 1707, included among the Paradoxes collected from the writings of 'Illustrious Wits', the eleven Paradoxes that occur in the first edition.² Finally, John Manningham of the Middle Temple copied extracts of four Paradoxes into his *Diary* or commonplace book.³ Of the four only two are known to be Donne's, Paradoxes II and VII.⁴

i

The first edition, *1633a*, contains eleven Paradoxes and ten Problems in an order unlike that in any of the extant manuscripts. In addition to the ten Paradoxes which occur in all the manuscripts, *1633a*, prints as Paradox I 'A Defence of Womens Inconstancy' which does not occur in any known manuscript but *S* where it appears as number XI and *Pud* where extracts have been copied. The ten Problems which are printed in *1633a* are as follows: '*Why have Bastards best Fortune*', '*Why Puritanes make long Sermons*', '*Why did the Divell reserve Jesuites till these latter dayes*', '*Why is there more variety of Greene, than of other colours*', '*Why doe young Laymen so much studie Divinity*', '*Why hath the Common Opinion afforded Women soules*' '*Why are the Fairest, Falsest*', '*Why Venus-starre onely doth cast a shadow*', '*Why is Venus-Starre*

---

¹ See Evelyn M. Simpson, 'John Donne and Sir Thomas Overbury's *Characters*', *MLR* xviii (1923), 410–15.

² G. R. Potter, 'Donne's Paradoxes in 1707', *MLN* lv (1940), 53. But compare Sir Geoffrey Keynes, *A Bibliography of Dr. John Donne*, 4th edn. (1973), 106, who says eight of Donne's Paradoxes are included. Dr. Keynes is in error. The Paradoxes, in the order of this edition, appear as follows: I, 398–9; II, 170; III, 401; IV, 402–3; V, 307–8; VI, 314–15; VII, 308–9; VIII, 395–6; IX, 389–91; X, 399; XI Dubious, 94–7.

³ See John Manningham, *Diary*, ed. John Bruce, Camden Society, os, 99 (1868), 134.

⁴ R. E. Bennett, 'John Manningham and Donne's Paradoxes', *MLN* xlvi (1931), 309–13.

multinominous, called both Hesperus *and* Vesper', '*Why
are New Officers least oppressing*'. Those three Problems
which occur in long and short versions in the manuscripts,
'Variety of Green' and the two on 'Venus Star', appear in the
short form of the text in *1633a*. In the first Problem in
1633a the opening twenty-three lines are omitted.[1] The
manuscript from which *1633a* was printed was very like *S*,
and could have been copy both for the edition and *S*.
Whether this is so, or whether the manuscript behind the
edition is collateral with *S*, it is far from Donne's papers and
an unhappy choice of copy for an edition. Both similarities
and differences in readings between *1633a* and *S* have been
pointed out in the discussions of *S*.[2] *1633a* was printed with
much and frequently disconcerting use of italicization, use of
long *s*, and old usage of *u, v, i, j*.

ii

The second edition, *1633b*, was printed from *1633a*. It
differs chiefly from the first edition in that Herbert's
*imprimatur*s are not present, and the missing lines have been
restored to 'Why have Bastards best Fortune'. It also differs
from *1633a* in trifling spelling alterations and minor
typographical variation, such as less frequent use of italiciza-
tion and modern usage of *u, v, i, j*. Except for a few minor
corrections such as 'weare' for 'wee are', Paradox III, 14,
and 'for casting' for 'forecasting', Paradox IX, 36–7, the
second edition does not otherwise differ from the first.

iii

The third edition, *1652*, reprints the eleven Paradoxes and
ten Problems from *1633b*. It contains an additional
Paradox, 'That Virginity is a Vertue', and also contains the

---

[1] In the second edition where the missing passage is restored, it occupies twenty-three lines;
in this edition it occupies nineteen.

[2] See above, pp. lxvii–lxviii and lxxvi.

texts of seven additional Problems, two Characters, and the 'Essay of Valour'. The Problems which appear as numbers XI to XVII are as follows: '*Why doth the Poxe soe much affect to undermine the Nose*', '*Why die none for Love now*', '*Why do Women delight much in Feathers*',[1] '*Why doth not Gold soyl the fingers*', '*Why do great men of all dependants, chuse to preserve their little Pimps*',[2] '*Why are Courtiers sooner Atheists then men of other conditions*', '*Why are Statesmen most incredulous*'. While the texts of the ten Problems first printed in *1633a* were copied from a manuscript very like *S*, the manuscript behind the seven Problems first printed in *1652* is not readily identifiable. It does not appear to have been *S* nor any other manuscript which I have examined. Whatever its tradition was, its text is not good. The printing of *1652* uses modern *u, v, i, j*. It alters the spelling of its copy *1633b* slightly and uses less italicization.

III. DUBIA

The texts of two Paradoxes are not found in the bulk of the manuscripts that contain the *Paradoxes and Problems*. 'A Defence of Womens Inconstancy' occurs only in *S*, where it is number XI, and extracts of the Paradox appear in Edward Pudsey's commonplace-book (*Pud*), as having been taken from 'the defenc of womens inconstancye' in a Middle Temple Revel *c*.1610. The extracts, from the beginning and end of the work, are not always in the same order as they are in the texts preserved in *S* and *1633*+.[3] On the whole, the extracts in *Pud* serve as a check on the text in the other witnesses. The 'Defence' was printed in the three seventeenth-century editions (*1633*+) as Paradox I. Collation shows that the text in *1633*+ is derivative of a text similar to that in *S*.

---

[1] The Problem occurs in the short version of the text.

[2] While there is some variation amongst the manuscripts in the exact wording of the titles, all the manuscripts agree in reading 'Bawds' for 'little Pimps'.

[3] *Pud* contains ll. 5–7, 3–4, 8–12, 14–17, 72–6, 77–83, 89–91, 87–8.

'That Virginity is a Vertue' appears only in *1652* as the twelfth Paradox. It was printed after the 'Essay of Valour', preceded by a blank page. A marginal note reads 'Place this after Paradox XI. fol 37'. This was not done.

Texts of the two Characters, the 'Essay of Valour' and 'Newes from the very Country' do not occur in many of the manuscripts that contain the Paradoxes and Problems. The two Characters were the most widely circulated, appearing in the Group II manuscript *S 962*, in the Group III manuscripts *B*, *Dob*, *O'F*, and in *S*. The Character of 'A Dunce' was printed anonymously in all editions of Overbury's *Characters* from the eleventh edition of 1622 (*1622*), sigs. G3–G5, and along with the Character of 'A Scot' in the 1652 edition of Donne's Juvenilia, *Paradoxes, Problemes, Essayes, Characters* (*1652*), 65–71. Collation shows the text in *S 962* to be independent of that in *B*, *Dob*, *O'F*, and that both the Group II and the Group III manuscripts have texts that differ from the text in *S* and the editions *1622*, *1652*. The text of the editions, particularly in the Character of 'A Dunce' shows a marked similarity to the text in *S*.

The 'Essay of Valour' has a more limited manuscript circulation appearing only in *S* where its text occurs between the Character of 'A Dunce' and that of 'A Scot'. It was printed anonymously with the Character of 'A Dunce' in the eleventh (*1622*), sigs. Q6–R1, and subsequent editions of Overbury's *Characters*, in *1652*, 72–9, and the bulk of its text appears as ' "Valour Anatomized in a Fancie", by Sir Philip Sidney, 1581' in Sir Robert Cotton's *Cottoni posthuma* 1651 (*1651*), 323–7. The text in *1651* differs from that in *S*, *1622*, *1652* in omitting the opening twenty-five lines and the concluding two. It also appears to be a 'tidied' text, substituting, for example, 'Certainely' for 'Whilome', l. 45 and 'very scum' for '*Catalines*', l. 114. On a few other occasions the reading in *1651* is less difficult than that in *S*, *1622*, *1652*, as, for example, 'and in a free way too, without any danger' for 'and we free from the daunger of yt', ll. 28–9, and 'such an one a lasse dares take, and will desire him' for 'such a one a glass dares take, and shee will desyre him', ll. 64–5. In these instances it appears as if the editor of *1651* has emended difficult passages rather than the text in *1651* being the original version from which the text in *S*, *1622*, *1652* has deviated. The text in *1652* appears to have been copied from that in *1622*, and both represent a corruption of a text similar to that in *S*.

Most of the text of 'Newes from the very Country' was included in a series of anecdotes in *Bur*, 255 and 82–6. These anecdotes were printed by L. P. Smith in his *Life and Letters of Sir Henry Wotton* (Oxford, 1907), under the heading 'Table Talk', Appendix IV, Section C.[1] The first thirty-four jottings from *Bur*, 255, are found in 'Newes From Any Whence' in Overbury's *Characters*; numbers 3–8, 10–12, and 23–9, in Smith's numbering, occurring in 'Newes from the very Country'. The authors were not identified in the manuscript. The other collection of anecdotes, numbers 35–145 (*Bur*, 82–6), contain several references to the assassination of Henry IV of France, so were probably copied in 1610. A fuller version of the text by 'J. D.' was printed in the 'Newes' section in all editions of Overbury's *Characters* from the 1614 edition (*1614*), sigs. G2–G2ᵛ on, and also in the 1650 edition of *Poems, By J. D.* (*1650*), 369–70, published by Donne's son. There is little difference between the texts in *1614* and *1650*, and comparing them with the text of *Bur*, now preserved in Smith's Appendix, shows that the text in *Bur* was nearly complete, but that the sayings were slightly abbreviated, in a different order, and interspersed amongst the other anecdotes. In this format they have lost much of the impact they possessed in Overbury's 'Newes', coming as they did after 'Newes from Court', by T. O. (Overbury), 'Answer to the Court Newes', by A. S., 'Country Newes', by Sr T. R. (Sir Thomas Roe).[2]

---

[1] Noted by Evelyn M. Simpson, 'John Donne and Sir Thomas Overbury's "Characters" ', *MLR* xviii (1923), 410–15.

[2] John Sparrow, 'Donne's Table-Talk', *London Mercury*, xviii (1928), 45, has suggested that Donne wrote the entire thirty-four anecdotes found in *Bur*, 255, and that they were copied there from a manuscript which was different from that which lay behind the Overbury edition of 1614.

IV. CONCLUSIONS

The text of the first edition, *1633a*, is, with that of *S*, the worst witness to the text of the Paradoxes.[1] In addition, its use of italicization is so excessive as to be misleading and its punctuation is faulty. Consequently, although use of the first edition as copy-text is the usual practice in editing Donne,[2] *1633a* has not been used as such for the text of the Paradoxes. I have chosen as copy-text for the Paradoxes the Westmoreland MS, because it preserves the best text of all the witnesses, it is the closest to Donne's holograph, and it is, with the O'Flaherty MS, the best punctuated.[3] Woodward, besides being a close friend of Donne's, was in a sense a professional scribe, having served Sir Henry Wotton as secretary during Wotton's embassy in Venice; therefore his manuscript cannot be considered merely as an amateur's copy.

The principle in editing the Paradoxes is to accept the reading of *W* and *Bur* whenever they agree, because the extrinsic and intrinsic authority of these manuscripts is so high. The text of the Group II manuscripts frequently supports the readings of *W* and *Bur*, and such agreement been taken as proof of the correctness of these readings. When *W* and *Bur* differ, Group II generally supports one or the other. Where this occurs the reading of the manuscript supported by Group II is accepted, unless the reading of *W* seems almost certain to be correct.[4]

---

[1] In two instances the reading of 1633+ has been accepted over that of the manuscripts. In Paradox VII, l. 16, there is general disagreement among the witnesses, and the readings of the manuscripts appear to be in error. In Problem XI, l. 13, the full version of a Latin phrase, found in *1633+* has been preferred over the various abbreviations of the manuscripts.

[2] The text of the 1633 *Poems*, which is good, has been used as copy-text by modern editors of Donne's poetry. Evelyn Simpson chose *1633a* as copy-text for her proposed edition of the *Paradoxes*. The use of manuscripts as copy-text along with problems that arise in recording alterations in manuscripts is discussed in Fredson Bowers, 'Transcription of Manuscripts: The Record of Variants', *SiB* xxix (1976), 212–64.

[3] I have chosen not to modernize the spelling and punctuation in this edition. There is a discussion of the virtues and defects of modernization in J. R. Brown, 'The Rationale of Old-Spelling Editions of the Plays of Shakespeare and his Contemporaries', and Arthur Brown, 'The Rationale of Old-Spelling Editions of the Plays of Shakespeare and his Contemporaries: A Rejoinder', *SiB* xiii (1960), 49–76.

[4] In Paradoxes IV, 52, and VIII, 18, where the reading of copy-text has been accepted over the agreement of *Bur* and Group II, reasons for the choice are given in the notes.

In editing the Problems, the use of *1633a* as copy-text presents an additional difficulty to those it presents in editing the Paradoxes—it contains only half of the Problems. Nor do the Problems occur in the well-authenticated manuscripts *W* and *Bur*. I have chosen *O'F* as copy-text for the Problems, because it contains the full nineteen, and because it is a carefully 'edited' manuscript apparently prepared as copy for an edition, with consistent spelling and a rational system of punctuation.

As *O'F* is a sophisticated manuscript, the principle of editing is to reject all readings peculiar to *O'F* as sophistications and to record them in the apparatus; to adopt the agrement of *Ash 826*, *R* and Group II, which are taken to represent the first and third versions of the text, because of the likelihood that a reading which survives in both versions is correct. On those occasions where the readings of Group III seem clearly correct and have consequently been adopted, reasons for the choice are given in a textual note.

In two of the five Problems which exist in multiple states,[1] *O'F* does not contain what I have taken to be the final version of the text. These two Problems are 'Variety of Green' and the 'Women and Feathers', and for the texts of these two I have used *TCD* as copy-text. I have also used *TCD* as copy-text for the 'Sir Walter Ralegh' Problem as the text in *O'F* contains two extra sentences whose authenticity I am unable to demonstrate.

'A Defence of Womens Inconstancy' I print from *S* as this manuscript preserves the text better than *1633+*. 'That Virginity is a Vertue' is printed from its only known extant source, *1652*.

In editing the two Characters I have used *O'F* as copy-text for the same reasons, and, with the same precautions as I have used it as copy-text for the Problems. The principle of editing the Characters has been to reject all peculiar readings of *O'F* and to record them in the apparatus, and to accept

---

[1] For a detailed discussion on the editing of the Problems in which revision has occurred, see below, pp. xcv–xcvii.

the agreement of *S 962* and Group III wherever this occurs. In editing the 'Essay of Valour' I have chosen *S* as copy-text for in *S* the text is better preserved than it is in *1622* and *1652*. The principle of editing has been to accept the agreement of *S* and *1651*, where they agree, for they frequently agree in readings from which *1622* and *1652* have deviated. With regard to the two passages which are corrupt in *S*, *1622*, *1652* and which appear to have been emended in *1651*, ll. 28–9, 64–5, I have adopted the conjectural emendations given to me by John Sparrow.

In editing 'Newes from the very country' I have used *1614* as copy-text and have recorded the few variant readings of *1650*.

i

The texts of the *Paradoxes and Problems* that follow are based on *W* for the Paradoxes and *O'F* for the Problems. As the punctuation of both *W* and *O'F* is good, emendation of punctuation has been made sparingly, and any alterations made are noted in the apparatus. In spelling and typography, this edition adheres to the practice of the copy-texts and all departures from that practice are recorded in the apparatus except for the following silent alterations: in *W* the spelling 'ey' has been altered to 'eye' and 'dy' to 'dye', while in *O'F* 'ar' has been changed to 'are'; the first word of a sentence has been silently capitalized if this has been neglected by the scribe; in *W*, because Woodward used capital *L* for most words beginning with *l*, the capital has been altered to *l* where there seems to be no point for the use of the capital; ampersand and normal contraction by superscription and abbreviation have been expanded; use of *u*, *v*, *i*, *j* have been modernized and in *O'F* the use of long *s* has been abandoned; in *W* Latin quotations and proper names have been italicized both because this was the normal seventeenth-century printing practice and to conform to the practice of *O'F*.

In order to avoid repetition of the full list of witnesses in the apparatus of each Paradox and Problem, at the beginning of the apparatus of both Paradoxes and Problems lists of the witnesses from which readings are given occur. If a Paradox or a Problem is missing from any of these witnesses, the omission is noted at the beginning of the apparatus of that particular work. Similarly, to avoid repetition at the beginning of the commentary of each Paradox and Problem, a list of the witnesses in which these works occur is given at the beginning of the commentary of both the Paradoxes and the Problems.

The list of witnesses in which the dubious Paradoxes, Characters, Essay, and News occur, being short, is given at the beginning of the critical apparatus of each text and also at the beginning of the commentary on each work.

The witnesses from which readings are given have been selected to represent the Groups and traditions of the text and their readings are recorded by groups rather than alphabetically.

In editing the Paradoxes, *Bur* represents the tradition closest to the copy-text.[1] *TCD* represents Group II and I have followed Grierson in using *TC* to indicate that *TCC* supports *TCD*. When *TCD* and *TCC* differ, both readings are given. *Dob* represents Group III. The readings of *S* are included because of the intermediate position *S* occupies between the other manuscripts and the editions.[2] The readings of the editions are recorded using *1633+* to indicate the agreement of all three. Where they differ their individual readings are given.

---

[1] All variant readings of *Bur* are included in the apparatus because its witness is important and because the manuscript is no longer extant. For readings of *Bur* I have had to rely on Evelyn Simpson's copies of Grierson's collations. The spelling of readings in her notes differs from the spelling in the apparatus in which she used these readings. I follow the spelling of her apparatus. There are instances in which the majority of the manuscripts disagree with the editions and no variant reading is recorded for *Bur*. I have used *? Bur* in the apparatus to denote uncertainty about the reading of *Bur*.

[2] That part of *S* which contains the Paradoxes is tightly bound so that parts of words and even whole words disappear into the binding. When a whole word has disappeared, and it could be of significance, I have indicated my inability to give the reading by placing *? S* in the apparatus. If possibly significant letters are not visible the reading is given thus: 'whe/'.

In editing the Problems, the readings of *Ash 826* are recorded as are those readings of *R* which could reflect what Donne wrote.[1] Readings of *Dob* are given to represent Group III and to serve as a check on the readings of the copy-text. As in editing the Paradoxes, *TCD* represents Group II and *TC* represents the agreement of *TCC* with *TCD*, but in editing the Problems the readings of *S 962* are included. Although the bulk of the text in *S 962* is essentially the same as that of *TC*, *S 962* contains two extra Problems. Where *S 962* shows correction I have printed the corrected form. Readings of *O 2* are recorded to represent the text in *O 2* and *P*, as this text appears to be a much better witness than *S* to a version of the text which is intermediate between that of Groups II and III. As in editing the Paradoxes, the readings of *S* and the editions are recorded. Finally, the readings of two manuscripts which each contain a single Problem, *A 25* and *Tan*, are given.

In editing 'A Defence of Womens Inconstancy' readings of *Pud* and *1633*+ are given. In the Characters readings of *S 962* are recorded, readings of *Dob* are also recorded to represent Group III and to serve as a check on the readings of copy-text. Readings of *S* and *1652*, and in the Character of 'A Dunce' readings of *1622*, are also given. In editing the 'Essay of Valour' where *S* is copy-text, readings are recorded from *1622*, *1652*, and *1651*. Finally, in editing 'Newes from the very Country', *1614* is copy-text and the readings of *1650* are recorded.

The apparatus is selective. Its first purpose is to record all departures from the copy-texts. Its second is to record those variant readings which could possibly be attributed to Donne. The third purpose of the apparatus is to show all rejected readings of the editions and to trace the process of

---

[1] All variant readings of *Ash* 826 and those of *R* which are helpful in establishing the text are recorded because I believe the text in these witnesses to be the earliest extant version of the Problems. In recording the readings of *R* variations in readings caused by translation from English into Latin have been ignored, as have the translator's additions to and alterations in the text. In the apparatus, the readings of *R* are recorded in Latin followed by an English translation enclosed in round brackets, See Appendix for examples of Rouzee's treatment of two of Donne's texts.

deterioriation of a reading from the form which must be correct to the corrupt form in which it occurs in the editions. In the apparatus, when no manuscript is cited in the lemma, the reading retained is that of copy-text and the accidentals of the copy-text are given. Where the reading of the majority of witnesses has been adopted over the reading of copy-text, the accidentals recorded in the lemma have been made to conform to the practice of the copy-text. In recording variants, the accidentals are those of the first manuscript cited, expanding all contractions, abandoning the use of long *s*, but not modernizing *u, v, i, j*. Spelling and punctuation differences in manuscripts other than the first listed are ignored unless such accidental features help to explain variant readings; then they are given in the apparatus, or discussed if extensive in a textual note. *Σ* stands for all the witnesses except those specifically excepted and the accidentals recorded are those of copy-text.[1]

ii

Five of Donne's Problems exist in multiple states and the problem of how to deal with authorial revision is raised. Editors in recent years have become increasingly concerned with the problem of how to present a text that has been revised by the author and consequently exists in two or more versions.[2] Usually they choose as the most authoritative text the version containing the author's final revisions. Yet earlier versions may also have interest and importance and should not be ignored in the preparation of a critical edition. Besides, where an author leaves several versions of an unpublished work, it may not be easy to decide which, if any,

---

[1] In those instances in the Paradoxes where the reading of copy-text supported by *Bur* has been accepted over the reading of the majority, and the majority is indicated by *Σ*, the accidentals given for *Σ* are those of *TCD*.

[2] See, for example, Fredson Bowers, *Textual and Literary Criticism*, Cambridge, 1966; Fredson Bowers, 'Established Texts and Definitive Editions', *PQ* xli (1962), 1–17; Fredson Bowers, 'Textual Criticism', *Aims and Methods of Scholarship*, ed. James Thorpe, New York, 1968; James Thorpe, 'The Aesthetics of Textual Criticism', *PMLA* lxxx (1965), 465–82, reprinted in *Bibliography and Textual Criticism*, ed. by O. M. Brack, Jr., and Warner Barnes (Chicago, Ill., 1969), 102–38.

he could have considered the final text. Faced with a choice of multiple versions, an editor must print that which its author would consider finished. James Thorpe distinguishes complete and incomplete works of art thus:

> Works which are in process can be called potential works of art, while the actual work of art is the one which fulfills the author's intentions. Our only practicable way of distinguishing is to observe whether the author does or does not communicate the work to his usual public. When the author provides us with multiple actual versions of what we commonly think of as a single literary work, he has in fact written separate works, among which there is no simple way to choose the best.[1]

Thorpe's contention is that, for an author who does not publish, 'publication' consists of releasing his work to his regular audience, and his principle can, I believe, be applied to Donne. If only the final revised version were 'published', then however interesting the earlier versions are, they have no authority over the one which the author released. If, on the other hand, an author released his work, made alterations and released it again, and again, all versions of the works can be considered complete, and an editor should be entitled to print either version, or all of them. Donne seems to have lent certain of his works to his friends, then asked that he might have them back in order that he might alter them, and lent them out again. Evidence from his letters shows that he lent his works to friends such as Sir Henry Goodyer, Sir Edward Conway, Sir Henry Wotton, Rowland Woodward, and others, and that he sought the return of his works for review. The versions which he sent to them can, by Thorpe's argument, be considered 'published' and hence complete.[2]

In the five Problems which exist in multiple states I have printed as text the version which I have taken to be the final

---

[1] Brack and Barnes, 137.

[2] The copy of the Problems behind *R* seems likely to have been supplied to Rouzee by Sir Edward Conway. If Donne sent a copy of his Problems to Conway, and it is likely that he did, then the version of the Problems which that manuscript contained, and which is now only preserved in *R* (and independently in *Ash* 826 and partially in *HMC* 26) was 'published'.

version of that text. The readings of the earlier versions are given in a subsidiary position to the final text in a manner which I hope allows the reconstruction of the earlier versions and avoids needless repetition. In Problem II, 'Sir Walter Ralegh', I have used *TCD* as copy-text, giving in the apparatus the two final sentences found in *B*, *Dob*, *O'F*, *S*, and *Tan*.[1] For these extra sentences *O'F* has been used as copy-text. In Problem X, 'Venus Star's Shadow', I have used *O'F* as copy-text. The earlier version in *Ash 826* and *R* contains only two short passages not found in the final text. I have printed these passages from *Ash 826*, corrected where necessary from *R*, in the apparatus of the main text, and have indicated where in that text they belong. In Problem XI, 'Venus Star Multinominous', I have used *O'F* as copy-text. The earlier version in *Ash 826* and *R* is considerably longer than the final form of the text and I have printed the text of *Ash 826* in full, corrected where necessary from *R*,[2] following the short version of the text. In Problem XII, 'Variety of Green', which exists in three variant states, I have abandoned the use of *O'F* as copy-text, and give the text in *TCD*. The intermediate state of this Problem, in *B*, *Dob*, *O'F*, differs from the final version in *TC*, *S 962*, *O 2*, *P*, *S*, and *1633*+ in its closing sentence which is quite different from the concluding sentence in the final version. I have indicated in the apparatus that *B*, *Dob*, *O'F* omit the concluding sentence of the text printed, and I have printed the closing sentence of *B*, *Dob*, *O'F*, in the apparatus using *O'F* as copy-text. The earliest version of the text which occurs in *Ash 826* and *R* has the same ending as *B*, *Dob*, *O'F*, but it is considerably longer. I have printed the text of *Ash 826* in full, following the final text and the variant ending of the intermediate text, correcting the text

---

[1] In this Problem I do not know who added the additional lines.

[2] On three occasions where the text in *Ash* 826 is corrupt, I have admitted readings of *R* into the *Ash* 826 text. The adopted reading of *R* is printed in the text in English, enclosed within square brackets. In the lemma this English reading, enclosed in its brackets, is given, followed by the Latin reading of *R* which is unbracketed.

of *Ash 826* where necessary from *R*.[1] In Problem XVIII, 'Women and Feathers', the final version of the text in *TC*, *S 962*, *S*, *1652* consists of three sentences taken from three different places of the earlier text in *B*, *Dob*, *O'F*, *Ash 826*, and *R*. I have printed the final text from *TCD* but have corrected a corrupt passage in that version from the earlier one. The earlier version of the text is printed in full from *O'F* after the text from *TCD*.

iii

The order of the Paradoxes and Problems differs in the witnesses. The Paradoxes occur in *W*, *Bur*, *TC*, and *S 962* in a common order which differs from that of all other witnesses a common order which differs from that of all other witnesses, of which, besides the editions which copy one another, only *Dob* and *B* agree together.

The same six Problems in identical order occur as numbers one to six in all the manuscripts except *Ash 826*, and the two Problems which are not found in all the manuscripts occur at the end in those manuscripts which contain them. Except for *Dob* and *B* which agree together, and *TC* and *S 962* which also agree, the order of the remaining Problems in the manuscripts varies.

As there seems little or no advantage in either the Paradoxes or the Problems of one arrangement over another, I have followed the order given in the copy-texts.

---

[1] On one occasion a reading of *R*, enclosed in brackets, is admitted to make good a defect in the text of *Ash* 826.

LIST OF SIGLA

Editions of the Paradoxes and Problems:

1633a = First edition of *Juvenilia*, 1633.
1633b = Second edition of *Juvenilia*, 1633.
1652 = Third edition of *Paradoxes, Problemes, Essayes, Characters*, 1652.
1633+ = All editions.

Manuscripts containing both Paradoxes and Problems:

A 18 = Additional MS 18647, British Library.
B = Bridgewater MS, MS EL 6893, Huntington Library.
Dob = Dobell MS, MS Eng. 966/4, Houghton Library, Harvard University.
N = Norton MS, MS Eng. 966/3, Houghton Library, Harvard University.
O 2 = Osborn MS b 148, Osborn Collection, Beinecke Library, Yale University.
O'F = O'Flaherty MS, MS Eng. 966/5, Houghton Library, Harvard University.
P = Phillipps MS, MS Eng. poet. f. 9, Bodleian Library.
Pud = Edward Pudsey's commonplace book, MS Eng. poet. d. 3, Bodleian Library. (Extract of one Paradox.)
S = Stephens MS, MS Eng. 966/6, Houghton Library, Harvard University.
S 962 = Stowe MS 962, British Library.
TCC = Trinity College, Cambridge MS R 3 12.
TCD = Trinity College, Dublin MS 877, formerly MS G 2 21.
TC = Agreement between *TCC* and *TCD*.
Wy = Wyburd MS, MS Eng. poet. e. 112, Bodleian Library.

Manuscripts containing the Paradoxes:

Bur = Burley MS. Formerly in the possession of Mr G. H. Finch at Burley-on-the-Hill where it was destroyed by fire in 1908.
W = Westmoreland MS, Berg Collection, New York Public Library.

Manuscripts containing the Problems:

    A 25 = Additional MS 25707, British Library. (One Problem.)

Ash 826 = Ashmole MS 826, Bodleian Library. Formerly called *Y*.

HMC 26 = Historical Manuscripts Commission 26, Bedford Estates Office.

    O 1 = Osborn MS 1, formerly King MS (*K*), Osborn MS b 114, Osborn Collection, Beinecke Library, Yale University. (Six Problems.)

  Tan = Tanner MS 229, Bodleian Library. (One Problem.)

Latin text of the Problems:

    R = *Problematum miscellaneorum, Antaristotelicorum, centuria dimidiata . . .*, Ludovic Rouzaeus, 1616, 518. a. 44, British Library.

Editions of the Characters, Essay, News:

    1614 = Second edition of Sir Thomas Overbury's *Characters*, 1614. (News.)

    1622 = Eleventh edition of Sir Thomas Overbury's *Characters*, 1622. (One Character, Essay.)

    1650 = Fourth edition, second issue of *Poems, By J. D.*, 1650. (News.)

    1651 = Sir Robert Cotton's *Cottoni posthuma*, 1651. (News.)

    1652 = Third edition of *Paradoxes, Problemes, Essayes, Characters*, 1652. (Two Characters, Essay.)

PARADOXES

PARADOX I

That all things kill themselves

To affect yea to effect their owne deaths, all living
are importun'd. Not by Nature only which perfects them,
but by Art and education which perfects her. Plants quick-
ned and inhabited by the most unworthy Soule, which ther-
fore neyther will, nor worke, affect an end, a perfection,   5
a Death. This they spend their Spirits to attaine; this
attained, they languish and wither. And by how much more
they are by Mans industry warm'd, and cherisht, and pam-
per'd, so much the more early they climbe to this perfect-
ion, this Deathe. And yf between men, not to defend be to   10
kill, what a heinous selfe murder is it, not to defend it
selfe? This defence, because beasts neglect, they kill
themselves: because they exceede us in number, strength,
and lawles liberty. Yea, of horses; and so of other
beasts, they which inherit most courage by beeing bred of   15
galantest parents, and by artificiall nursing are bettered,
will run to their own Deathes, neyther sollicited by
spurrs, which they neede not, nor by honor which they ap-
prehend not. If then the valiant kill himselfe, who can ex-

PARADOXES. *Text from W unless otherwise stated. Readings are given from the following
representative witnesses: W, Bur; TC (TCD with TCC); Dob; S; 1633+ (1633a and b with
1652). When a Paradox is not found in one of these the omission is noted.*

(Paradox V. *1633a*)   1 deaths] death *S, 1633+*   living] ... thinges *Dob, S,
1633+*   5 neyther *ed.*: nether *W*   7–8 more they are by Mans industry
warm'd *Σ*: the more by Mans industry, they are warm'd *W*   8 and cherisht] cherished
S, 1633b, 1652   10 between] amongst *1633+*   11–12 it selfe] the selfe
Bur; see note   13 number, strength, *Σ*: number in strength *W*: strength, number
Bur   14 lawles *Bur, TCD, Dob*: in a ... *W*: a ... *TCC, S, 1633+*   14–15
and so ... inherit] *omit Bur*   14 so of] soe *Dob: omit S, 1633+*   15 which]
that *Dob, S, 1633+*   by *Σ*: for *W*   bred] ? *Bur*: breed *1633a*   16 galantest] gallanter
Dob   are] *omit Bur*   18 spurrs] spur *Bur*   by] *omit TC*   19 himselfe]
themselues *Dob*

cuse the coward? Or how shall man be free from this, since 20
the first man taught us this? Except we cannot kill our
selves because he kill'd us all. Yet least some thing
should repair this common ruine, we kill dayly our bodyes
with Surfets, and our Minds with anguishes. Of our Powers,
remembring kills our Memory. Of affections, Lusting our 25
Lust. Of Vertues, giving kills Liberality. And if
these things kill themselves, they do it in ther best
and supreme perfection: for after perfection immediatly
followes exces: which changes the natures and the names,
and makes them not the same things. If then the best 30
things kill themselves soonest (for no perfection indures)
and all things labor to this perfection, all travaile to
ther owne Death: Yea the frame of the whole World (yf it
weare possible for God to be idle) yet because it begun
must dye: Then in this idlenes imagin in God, what could 35
kill the world, but it selfe, since out of it nothing is.

PARADOX II

That women ought to paint themselves

FOULNES is lothesome; can that be so too which helpes it?
Who forbids his beloved to gird in her wast, to mend by
shooing her uneven lamenes, to burnish her teethe, or to
perfume her breathe? Yet that the face be more precisely
regarded it concernes more. For as open confessing Sinners 5

20 Or] and *Bur*   21 taught *ed.*: tought *W*   23 kill dayly] daily kill *TC*, *Dob*,
S, 1633+   our bodyes] our selues, . . . *TC*   24 anguishes] *Auguishes 1633a*
25 remembring] remembrance *Bur*   26 Lust] Lusts *TC*   27 things] omit
1633b, 1652   28 supreme] extreme *Dob*   after perfection] . . . perfections *TC*
29 changes] changeth *1633*+   the names *Σ*: names *W*   31 perfection] affection
TC, Dob, S, 1633+   32 travaile] ? *Bur*: travell *TCD, Dob, 1633*+   34 yet]
omit *TC*   begun] ? *Bur*: began *TC, 1633*+   35 could] would *TC*   36 out of
it nothing is] out of nothinge it is *Dob*

(Paradox II. *1633a*)   Title: themselves] omit *Dob, S, 1633*+   1 too *Bur*,
TC: omit *W*, *Dob, S, 1633*+   2 gird *TCC, Dob, S, 1633*+: girt *W*, ? *Bur, TCD*
3 shooing] shoaring *Bur*   4 breathe? *ed.*: breathe. *W*

are allwayes punished, but the wary and conceald, offend-
ing without witnes, do it allso without punishment, So the
Secret parts neede les respect; but of the Face discoverd
to all Survayes and examinations ther is not too nice a
jealousy. Nor doth it only draw the busy eye, but allso is   10
most subject to the divinest touche of all, to kissing,
the strange and misticall union of Soules. If She should
prostitute her selfe to a more Worthy Man then thy selfe,
how earnestly and how justly wouldst thou exclaime? Then
for want of this easy and ready way of repayring, to betray   15
her body to ruine and Deformity, the tirannous ravishers
and sodain deflowrers of all Women, what a hainous adultery
is it? What thou lov'st most in her face is color, and this
painting gives that. But thou hat'st it not because it is,
but because thou knowest it: Foole, whome only ignorance   20
makes happy. The Starrs, the Sun, the Skye, whom thou ad-
mirest, alas have no color, but are faire because they seeme
color'd; If this seeming will not satisfy thee in her, thou
hast good assurance of her color, when thou seest her lay
it on. If her face be painted upon a boord or a wall, thou   25
wilt love it, and the boord and the wall. Canst thou lothe
it then, when it smiles, speekes, and kisses, because it is
painted? Is not the earths face in the most pleasing season
new painted? Are we not more delighted with seeing fruits,
and birds, and beasts painted, then with the Naturalls?   30
And do we not with pleasure behold the painted Shapes of

6–7 concealld, offending] concealinge offendinge *Dob*: Concealinge offendinges *S*: concealing
offendors *1633+*   8 neede les] *? Bur*: needs the lesse *S, 1633+*   respect; *ed.*: respect, *W*
9 Survayes and examinations] examinations, and surveyes *TC, Dob, S,1633+*   10 eye]
eyes *Dob, S, 1633+*   10–11 allso is most] alsoe is *TC*: it is also *Dob, S*: it is *1633+*
13 Worthy] vnworthy *Dob, S, 1633+*; *TCC inserts* 'vn'; *see note*   14 how justly]
iustly *1633+*   exclaime] complayne *Bur*   Then] That *S, 1633+*   15 easy] easier
Dob, S, 1633+   and ready way of *Σ*: *omit W*   16 ruine and] *omit Bur*   16–
17 ravishers ... deflowrers] ravisher ... deflowrer *Bur*   17 sodain] *omit Dob*   17–
18 what ... it] what can be a more heynous adultery *Bur*   18 lov'st most *TC, Dob,
S*: most lov'st *W*, *? Bur*: louest *1633+*   this] *omit Dob, S, 1633+*   19 that] it
TC   20 only] *omit 1633+*   21 Starrs ... Sun] Sunne ... starrs *Dob*   Skye *Σ*:
Skies *W*   22 alas] *omit TC*   seeme] ... to be *Dob, S, 1633+*   25 upon] *? Bur*:
on *1633+*   a wall] wall *TC, S, 1633+*   27 then] *omit Dob*   smiles, speekes] speakes,
smiles *Dob, S, 1633+*   28–9 Is ... painted *Bur, TC which omits* new; *sentence
omitted in other MSS and in the editions; see note*   29–30 fruits, and birds] Birds *Bur*:
Birds, and fruits *TC*: byrdes, fruits *Dob, S, 1633+*   30 with the Naturalls] wee are
with naturalls *TC, S, 1633+*: with naturalls *Dob*   31 Shapes] *? Bur*: shape *S, 1633+*

Devills and Monsters, whom trew we durst not regard? We
repayre the ruines of our houses, but first cold tempest
warns us of it, and bites us through it: We mend the
wracke and washe the staines of our apparell, but first   35
our eye, and other body is offended: But by this prov-
idence of women this is prevented. If in kissing or
breathing upon her, the painting fall off, thou art angry:
wilt thou be so, yf it stick on? Thou didst love her: if
thou beginst to hate her then it is because she is not   40
painted. If thou wilt say now, thou didst hate her before,
thou didst hate her and love her together. Be constant in
some thing; and love her who shewes her great love to thee,
by taking this paines to seeme lovely to thee.

PARADOX III

That old Men are more Fantastique then younge

Who reads this Paradox but thinks me more fantastique
then I was yesterday when I did not think thus? And if one
day make this sensible change in me, what will the burden
of many yeares? To be fantastique in yong men, is a
conceitfull distemperature, and a witty madnes: but in old
men whose senses are withered, it becomes naturall,
therfore more full and perfect. For as when we sleepe our
fansy is most strong, so is it in Age, which is a slumber

32 Devills and Monsters] Monsters and Deujlls *Dob, S, 1633+*   33 ruines *Σ*: ruine *W*
33-4 tempest warns ... bites] tempests warns ... bites *TCD, 1633+*: tempests warne ...
bite *TCC, Dob*: Tempests warn/ ... bytes *S*   35 washe the] omit *Dob, S, 1633+*
36 our eye, and other body is *Bur, TC*: our ey and body is *W*: our eyes, and other bodies are
Dob, S, 1633+; *see note*   offended: *ed.*: offended. *W*   37 or *Σ*: and *W*   38
off *ed.*: of *W*   39 so *Σ*: so to, *W*   39-41 if thou ... painted] if thou begin to
hate when it falls thou hatest her because shee is not painted *Bur*   40 it is] 'tis *1633+*
41-2 hate her ... hate her ... love her *TCC, Dob, S, 1633+*: hate ... hate ... love *W*,
? *Bur*: hate her ... hate ... loue her *TCD*   43 her great *Σ*: great *W*: her *Dob*
44 by taking] ? *Bur*: in ... *S, 1633+*: in *TCD*

(Paradox VII. *1633a*)   1 but] omit *Dob*   fantastique] ... now *Bur, S, 1633+*
2 I did not think thus] I thought not this *Bur*   3 make *Σ*: makes *W*   me] men
S, 1633+   4-5 a conceitfull] Conceiptfull *S, 1633+*: conceited *TC, Dob*   7
therfore] and ... *Dob*   8 fansy] fantasie *TC*   is it] ? *Bur*: it is *TC, Dob, 1633+*

of the deepe sleepe of Deathe. They taxe us of inconstancy, which in themselves yong they allow'd; So that reproving that which they did approve, their inconstancy exceeds ours, because they have changd once more then we. Yea, they are more idly busied in conceiting apparell then we, for we when we are melancholy, weare black; when lusty, greene; when forsaken, tawny; pleasing our owne inward affections, leaving them to others indifferent. But they prescribe Laws, and constraine the Noble, the Scholler, the Marchant, and all estates to certaine habits. The old men of our time have chang'd with patience ther own bodyes, much of ther Lawes, much of ther Language, yea ther Religion, yet they accuse us. To be amorous is proper and naturall in a yong man, but in an old man most fantastique. And that ridling humor of Jealousy, which seekes and would not find, which inquires and repents his knowledg, is in them most common yet most fantastique. Yea that which falls never in yong men, is in them most fantastique and naturall; that is Coveteousnes; even at ther journeys end to make great provision. Is any habit in yong men so fantastique as in the hottest Seasons to be double gound and hooded, like our elders? Or seemes it so ridiculous to weare Long haire as to weare none? Truly, as amongst Philosophers, the Sceptique which doubts all is more contentious then eyther the

10

15

20

25

30

11 exceeds] *Bur*: exceedeth *1633*+   12 changd once] once changed *Bur*   12–13 yea, they are] yet . . . *Dob*: yet are they *TC*   13 conceiting] conceited *Dob, S, 1633*+   14 melancholy *Σ*: melancolique *W*   weare] *? Bur*: wee are *1633a*   15 owne *Σ*: . . . only *W*   affections] affection *TC*   16 them] *omit Bur*   they] the Elders *Bur*   17 constraine *ed.*: constraine, *W*   18 certaine habits] a certaine habit *1633*+   20 of ther Language] of language *Bur*: . . . languages *1633*+   21–2 yong man *Σ*: yong, *W*   22 but] *omit TC, Dob*   24 inquiries] *? Bur*: requyres S, *1633*+   25 falls never] never falls *Bur, TCD, Dob*   25–6 in . . . in] *? Bur*: among . . . among *TC*: among . . . amongst *Dob*   26 most *Σ*: both *W*   fantastique and naturall] naturall and fantastique *Bur*   26–7 that is Coveteousnes] *omit Bur*   27 great] *omit Dob*   28 habit in *Bur, TC, Dob*: . . . of *W, S, 1633*+   the] *omit Bur*   29 Seasons] season S   and] or S, *1633*+   like] as *Bur*   30 Or] and *TC, Dob*   31 amongst] . . . the S: among the *Dob, 1633*+   32 doubts] doubt S: doubted *Dob*   is] *? Bur*: was *Dob, S, 1633*+   eyther] *omit Dob*

Dogmatique which affirmes, or Academique which denyes
all, So
are these uncertaine elders, which both call them
fantastique,
which follow others inventions, and them allso which
are led by ther owne humors suggestion, more fantastique
then eyther.

35

PARADOX IV

That Nature is our worst Guide

SHALL she be guide to all creatures which is herselfe
one? Or if she allso have a guide, shall any creature have
a better guide then we? The affections of Lust and Anger,
yea even to erre is naturall: shall we follow these? Can
she be a good guide to us which hath corrupted not us only
but her selfe? Was not the first man by desyre of knowledg
corrupted, even in the white integrity of Nature? And did
not Nature if Nature do any thing, infuse into him this
desyre of knowledg, and so this corruption in him, in her
selfe, in us? If by Nature we shall understand our essence,
our definition, our reasonablenes, then this, beeing alike
common to all men (the ideot and wisard beeing equally
reasonable) why shall not all men having one nature, follow
one course? Or if we shall understand our inclinations,

5

10

33 affirmes] affirmed *Dob*   or] or the *TC, Dob*   denyes] denied *Dob*   34 call] calls
S, 1633+   them] themselues *TC*   35 others] there *Bur*   36 owne]*omit Bur*
humors] humorous *1633+*   37 eyther] other *Dob, 1633+*: *others S*

(Paradox VIII. *1633a*)   2 allso have] haue herselfe *TC, Dob*   5 which]
that *Dob*   hath corrupted not] corrupted not *TC*: corrupteth not *Dob*: hath not Corrupted
S   us only] only vs *Dob*   6 selfe? *ed.*: selfe. *W*   desyre] *? Bur*: the . . . *S, 1633+*
7 white *Bur*: whight *W*: whytest *TC, Dob, S, 1633+*   8 do] did *S, 1633+*   into
Σ: in *W*   9 so] soe *TCC, Dob, S*: sowe *TCD; see note*   9–10 in him . . . in
us] into hym, in vs *S*: in him, into vs *1633+*   10 us? *ed.*: us. *W*   11 our
reasonablenes] our reason, our noblenes *S*: or *reason, noblenesse 1633+*   12 men] *omit*
TC, Dob, S, 1633+   wisard] the . . . *TC, Dob, S, 1633+*   13 shall] showld *TCD, S,*
1633+   having] being *Bur*: . . . equally *TC, Dob, S, 1633+*   one] all one *TCD, Dob, 1633+*
14 course] cawse *TC*

Alas, how unable a guide is that which follows the 15
temperature of our slimy bodyes? For we cannot say that
we derive our inclinations, our minds, our soules, from our
parents by any way. To say it, as All from All, is error
in reason, for then with the first nothing remaynes; or as
part from all is error in experience, for then this part 20
equally imparted to many children, would (like Gavelkind
lands) in few generations become nothing. Or to say it by
communication is error in Divinity; for to communicate
the
ability of communicating whole essence with any but God
is
utter blasphemy. And if thou hast thy fathers nature and 25
inclination, he allso had his fathers, and so climbing up,
all come of one man, all have one nature, all shall embrace
one course. But that cannot be. Therfore our complexions
and whole bodyes we inherit from parents, our inclinations
and minds follow that. For our mind is heavy in our bodyes 30
afflictions, and rejoyceth in the bodyes pleasures: How
then shall this nature governe us, which is governd by the
worst part of us? Nature though we chase it away will
returne. Tis true: but those good motions and inspirations
which be our guides, must be wooed and courted, and 35
wellcomed or els they abandon us. And that old *Tu nihil
invitâ etc.* must not be sayd, thou shalt, but thou wilt do
nothing against nature: so unwilling he notes us to curbe
our naturall appetites. We call our bastards allwayes our

15 unable] weake *Dob*   16 our] *omit TC, Dob*   that] *omit Dob*   17 our soules]
or soules *1633+*   from] to *TC*   18 by] *omit Dob*   it, as] that it is *S, 1633+*
19 as] as a *S*: is a *1633+*   21 like] as *TC, Dob*   22 lands] land *Bur, TCD*
23 the] this *Bur*   25 utter] *? Bur*: vtterlie *S, 1633a*   hast] hadst *Bur*: hit *1633+*
25–6 nature and inclination] inclynations and nature *Bur*   27 come] comes *S, 1633+*
all have] and have *1633b, 1652*   shall] *omit TC Dob*   28 complexions] complexion *Dob*
29 whole *Σ*: *omit W*   parents] our fathers *TC, Dob*   31 the *Bur, TC, Dob*: our
W, S, 1633+   pleasures] pleasure *Bur, S, 1633+*   32 which] that *1633+*   33 we...
away] ofte chaced away it *S, 1633+*   34 returne]... againe *Dob*   35 which be]...
are *TC, Dob*   wooed and *ed.*: woed and *W*: woed, *S, 1633+*   36 old *Tu*] old Axiome
in *Bur*: old *Axiome S, 1633+*; *see note*   37 sayd]... that *TC, Dob*   39 naturall]
owne... *TC, Dob*   39–40 our naturall issue]... issues *Bur*: our naturall children
and yssue *Dob*: vnnaturall children, and issue *TC*   40 designe] *? Bur*: define *S, 1633+*

naturall issue, and we designe a foole by no name so   40
ordinarily as by the name of naturall. And that poore
                                                  knowledg
wherby we but conceive what raine is, what wind, what
thunder, we call Metaphisique, supernaturall. Such small
                                                  things,
such nothings, do we allow to our plaine natures
comprehension. Lastly by following her, we loose the
                                                pleasant and   45
lawfull commodityes of this life, for we shall drinke
water, and eate akornes and rootes, and those not so sweete
and delicate as now by mans art and industry they are
                                                  made.
We shall loose allso the necessityes of Societyes, Lawes,
Arts, and Sciences, which are all the workmanship of man.   50
Yea we shall lack the last best refuge of Misery, Deathe:
because no deathe is naturall; for yf yee will not dare to
call all Deathes violent (though I see not why Sicknesses
be not violences) yet confes that all deathes proceede of
the defect of that, which nature made perfect and would   55
preserve, and therfore are all against Nature.

40-1 no name so ordinarily] nothing so ordinary S, 1633+   41 naturall] a ... Dob
42 but] ? Bur: omit 1633+   42-3 what wind, what thunder] what thunder, what
wynde TC, Dob   43 Metaphisique] Metaphysicall Dob   44 nothings] ? Bur:
nothinge TC, Dob: no things 1633+   plaine] pliant 1633+   45 comprehension]
apprehension Bur, 1633+   46-7 drinke ... rootes] eate acornes, and drinke water,
and feede on rootes Dob: drinke water and eat roots S, 1633+   47 so] omit S, 1633+
48 mans] means, TC   49 allso] omit TC, Dob: all S, 1633+   Lawes] and ... TC,
Dob   51 the Σ: that W   52 yee] wee Bur, TC; see note   53 Deathes]
Death TC, Dob, 1633+   Sicknesses] all ... TC   54 be] are TC, Dob   confes
that] confes Bur: Causes that S: causes of 1633+   deathes] omit Bur   of] from TC,
Dob   55 the Σ: this W   56 are all] all are S: all 1633+

PARADOX V

That only Cowards dare dye

EXTREAMES are equally removed from the meane: So that
headlong desperatnes asmuch offends true valor, as
backward
cowardise. Of which sorte I reckon justly all unenforced
deathes. When will your valiant man dye? necessited? So
cowards suffer what cannot be avoyded. And to run to
death 5
unimportun'd, is to run into the first condemn'd
desperatnes. Will he dye when he is riche and happy?
Then by living
he might do more good. And in afflictions and misery
death
is the chosen refuge of cowards.
Fortiter ille facit qui miser esse potest. 10
But it is taught and practisd amongst our Valiants, that
rather then our reputation suffer any maime, or we any
misery, we shall offer our brests to the canons mouthe, yea
to
our swords points. And this seemes a brave, a fiery
sparkling, and a climbing resolution, which is indeed a
cowardly, 15
an earthly, and a groveling Spiritt. Why do they chaine
these Slaves to the gallyes, but that they thirst their

(Paradox IX. *1633a*)   *Title: only Cowards*] Cowards only *Bur*   3 cowardise]
Cowardliness *Bur*   unenforced] vnforced *TC*   4 dye? necessited?] dye? necessited,
TC: dy necessited? *Dob, S*: dye of necessity? *1633+; see note*   5 to death] into . . .
1633+   8 might] *? Bur*: may *S, 1633+*   afflictions] affliction *TC, Dob*   misery]
myseries *S, 1633+*   11 taught *ed.*: tought *W*   amongst] *? Bur*: amonge *Dob,*
1633+   Valiants] valiant'st *TCC*: valiant *Dob, Gallants 1633+*   12 reputation]
Reputations *S, 1633+*   14–15 a brave . . . resolution *Bur*: a braue, and a fiery *(blank)*
W: a very braue, and a very clyminge *Σ: see note*   15 is indeed] indeede is *Dob, S*:
is *1633+*   16 an earthly, and] and earthly and *TC, Dob*: earthlie, and *S*: earthly, and
indeed *1633+*   groveling] very . . . *TC, Dob, S, 1633+*   17 these *Σ*: their *W*,
? Bur: those *Dob*   thirst] thrist *S*: thrust *1633+*

deathes, and would at every lashe leap into the Sea. Why
do
they take weapons from condemnd men, but to barr them
of
that ease which Cowards affect, a speedy death? Truly this   20
life is a tempest, and a warfare; and he that dares dye to
escape the anguishes of it, seemes to me but so valiant,
as he which dares hang himselfe, least he be prest to the
warrs. I have seene one in that extremity of melancholy,
which was then become madnes, strive to make his owne   25
breathe an instrument to stop his breathe, and labor to
choke himselfe: but alas he was mad. And we knew
another,
that languished under the oppression of a poore disgrace
so
much, that he tooke more paines to dye, then would have
servd to have nourish'd life and spirit inough to have   30
outlivd his disgrace; what foole will call this cowardlines,
valor, or this basenes, humility? And lastly of those men
which dye that Allegoricall death of entring into Religion,
how few are found fitt for any shew of valiancy, but only
of soft and supple metall, made only for cowardly
solitarynes.   35

---

18 lashe] task *Bur*: loose *Dob*, *S*, *1633*+   19–20 of that] from that *TC*: from the *Dob*
21 and he] he *Bur*   that] *? Bur*: which *S*, *1633*+   22 anguishes] anguishe *TC*, *S*,
1633+   to me but] to be *TCD*: to mee to bee *TCC*, *Dob*, *S*   23 which] omit *TC*:
that *Dob*   be] showld be *TC*, *Dob*   24 melancholy] modestie *W* (*b.c.*)   25 was
then become] then was ... *TC*: then was *Dob*   strive] omit *Dob*, *S*, *1633*+   26 stop]
stay *S*, *1633*+   27 we knew] I knewe *TCD*: I knowe *TCC*: omit *Dob*   29–8 so
much] omit *TC*, *Dob*   30 have nourish'd] nourish *Bur*   31 will] wowld *TC*
32 those] *? Bur*: these *TCC*, *S*, *1633*+   33 which] that *TC*, *Dob*   that] *? Bur*:
the *S*, *1633*+   34 fitt] fitter *TC*   35 of] *? Bur*: a *S*, *1633*+

PARADOX VI

That the guifts of the body are better then those of the mind or of Fortune

I say agayne that the body makes the mind. Not that
it created it a mind, but formes it a good or bad mind.
And this mind may be confounded with Soule, without any
violence or injustice to Reason or philosophy, then our
Soule (me seemes) is enhabled by our body, not this by
that.   5
My body licenceth my Soule to see the Worlds beutyes
through myne eyes, to heare pleasant things through myne
eares, and affords it apt Organs for conveyance of all
perceiveable delights. But alas my Soule cannot make any
part,
that is not of it selfe disposed to see or heare: though   10
without doubt she be as able and as willing to see behind
as before. Now yf my Soule would say, that she enhables
my
parts to tast these pleasures, but is her selfe only
delighted with those riche sweetnesses which her inward
eye
and senses apprehend, she should dissemble, for I feele her   15
often solaced with beutyes which she sees through myne eyes,
and Musicke which through myne eares she heares. This
perfection then my body hath, that it can impart to my
mind all

(Paradox XI. *1633a*   *Title: those*] the guyfts *TC*   or of Fortune] *? Bur:* or
Fortune *TCD, S; TCC deletes* of: *omit 1633+*   1 that the] the *Bur*   2 created
it a mind] creates *TC, Dob*   bad] *? Bur:* a bad *Dob, 1633+*   4 then *Σ:* when *W*   our]
the *S, 1633+*   5 me seemes] mee thinks *Bur:* it seemes *S, 1633+*   our] the *TC,*
Dob   that] yt *S, 1633+*   7–8 through myne eares] thorough . . . *1633a*   8
conveyance] *? Bur:* the . . . *S, 1633a and b:* the convenience *1652*   9 delights]
delight 1633+   Soule *Σ:* Mind *W*   10–11 to see . . . doubt] *omit Bur*   11
doubt *ed.:* dout *W: omit S*   12–13 my parts] *? Bur:* any part *Dob, S, 1633+*   14
which] that *TC, Dob*   eye] Eyes *S, 1633+*   15 feele *Σ:* see *W, 1633+*   16
with . . . myne] *omit Bur*   17 Musicke] *? Bur:* with . . . *Dob, S, 1633+*   17–18
This . . . hath] The perfection then of my body hath this *Bur*   18 to my] to the *Bur*

her pleasures, and my mind hath this maime, that she can
neyther teach my indisposd parts her facultyes, nor to the   20
parts best disposd shew that beuty of Angels or Musicke

of

Spheares, wherof she boasts the contemplation. Are

Chastity,

Temperance, or Fortitude guifts of the mind? I appeale to
phisicians whether the cause of these be not in the body.
Healthe is a guifte of the body, and patience in sicknes of   25
the mind; then who will say this patience, is as good a
happines as health, when we must be extreamly miserable

to have

this happines? And for nourishing of Civil Societies and
mutual Love amongst men, which is one cheife end why

we

are men, I say the beuty, proportion, and presence of the   30
body hath a more masculine force in begetting this Love
then the vertues of the mind. For it strikes us sodainly,
and possesseth us immediatly, when to know these vertues,
requyres sound judgment in him which shall discerne, and
a long triall and conversation betweene them. And even at   35
last, alas how much of our faythe and beleefe, shall we
be driven to bestow, to assure our selves that these
vertues are not counterfayted? For it is the same to be and
to seeme vertuous. Because he that hath no vertu can

19 her] his S, 1633+   hath this maime]...mayne Bur: hath still many TCD, Dob,
S, 1633+: still hath many TCC; see note   19–20 can neyther Bur, TCC, Dob, S,
1633+: neyther W: cannot TCD   20 my...parts] my...part 1633b, 1652: any...
part Bur   21 parts best disposed] best disposed part Dob, S: best espoused parts 1633+
that] it 1633+   or Musicke] of...TC, Dob, S, 1633+   23 or] omit TC, Dob: and
S, 1633+   24 phisicians] the...TC   cause] causes Bur   of these] heerof TC,
Dob   25 a guifte] ? S: the...1633+   sicknes of] sickn/ a guift of S: sicknesse the
gift of 1633+   26 this] ? Bur: ? S: that 1633+   27 extreamly] omit Bur
have] purchase S, 1633+   29 mutual] naturall Bur   one] our TC, Dob, S, 1633+
29–30 end why we are men] end why men are Bur: end and why...TCD; end is inserted:
...wee were men TCC: and w/...S: end: while...1633+   30 the beuty] ? Bur:
this...S, 1633+   proportion, and presence] presence, and proportion Dob, S, 1633+
33 immediatly] ? Bur: ymmoderatelie S, 1633+   these] ? Bur: those 1633+   34
sound] ? Bur: some S, 1633+   which] that Dob   and] omit 1633+   35 triall]
tyme S, 1633+   36 alas] ? Bur: omit Dob, S, 1633+   38 not counterfayted]
not counterfeite Bur: no counterfetts Dob   39 to seeme] ? Bur: seeme S, 1633+
because] ? Bur: ...that 1633+

dissemble none. But he that hath a litle may guild, and   40
enamell, yea and transforme much vice into vertu. For
                                        allow
a man to be discreete and flexible to companies which are
great vertues and guifts of the mind, this discretion
wilbe to him the Soule and Elixar of all vertue. So that
touch'd with this even pride shalbe made civil humility,   45
and cowardise, honorable and wise valor. But in things
seene ther is not this danger. For the body which thou
lovst and esteemst fayre is fayre certainly, and yf it
be not faire in perfection, yet it is fayre in the same
degree that thy judgment is good. And in a faire body I   50
do seldome suspect a disproportiond mind, or expect a
good in a deformed. As when I see a goodly house I
assure my selfe of a worthy possessor, and from a ruinous
wytherd building I turne away, because it seemes eyther
stuffd with varlets as a prison, or handled by an unworthy   55
negligent tenant, that so suffreth the wast thereof. And
truly the guifts of fortune which are riches are only
handmayds, yea pandars of the bodyes pleasure, with ther
service we nourish health, and preserve beuty, and we buy
delights. So that vertue which must be lovd for her selfe   60
and respects no further end, is indeede nothing; and
riches whose end is the good of the body, cannot be so
perfectly good, as the end wherto it levells.

40 that] ? *Bur*: which *S, 1633+*   41 enamell] . . . yt *Bur*   and *Σ*: *omit W*
42 flexible to companies] flexible to (*blank*) *S*: *flexible* to *complaints 1633+*: Sociable *Bur*;
see note   43 vertues and guifts] guifts and vertues *Bur*: *vertuous gifts 1633+*
44 vertue] vertues *TC, Dob, S, 1633+*   45 civil] *omit TC, Dob, S, 1633+*   46 honorable
and] *omit Bur*   48 lovst] allowest *Bur*   and yf] if *1633+*   49 not faire in] not in
Bur   it is *Σ*: is it *W*   the same] that *TC, Dob*   51-2 or expect . . . deformed]
omit Bur   or expect a good] or an exceedinge good *TC, Dob*: and as seldome hope for A
good *S, 1633+*; *see note*   52 As] *omit Dob, S, 1633+*   53 and] *omit 1633+*
53-4 a ruinous wytherd building *Bur, Dob, S*: ruinous wythered buildings *W, TC*: a *ruinous
weather-beaten building 1633+*; *see note*   55-6 unworthy negligent *Bur, Dob*: vnthrifty
negligent *W*: vnworthy and negligent *S, 1633+*: vnworthy *TC*   56 that so . . .
therof] *omit Bur*   suffreth] ? *Bur*: suffers *S, 1633+*   58 handmayds *ed.*: hand
mayds *W*   of] to *Bur*   pleasure] pleasures *TC, S*   59 and preserve *Σ*: we . . .
W   beuty] *dainty 1633+*   we buy] buy *Bur*   60 lovd] beloued *TC*   her selfe]
? *Bur*: it selfe *Dob, S, 1633+*   61 further *ed.*: furder *W*: farther *TCD*   63
perfectly good] good perfectly *TC*

PARADOX VII

That a wise man is knowne by much Laughinge

Ride si sapis o puella ride; yf thou beest wise laugh.
For since the powers of discourse, and reason, and laughter,
be equally proper to only man, why shall not he be most wise
which hath most use of laughing, as well as he which hath
most of reasoning and discoursing. I allwayes did and shall   5
understand that Adage,
            per risum multum possis cognoscere stultum,
that by much laughing thou mayst know ther is a foole, not
that the laughers are fooles, but that amongst them ther is
some foole at whome wise men laugh. Which mov'd
                                          Erasmus to   10
put this as the first argument in the mouthe of his Folly,
that she made beholders laughe. For fooles are the most
laughd at, and laugh least themselves of any. And Nature
saw this faculty to be so necessary in man, that she hath
beene content that by more causes we should be importun'd   15
to laughe then to the exercise of any other power. For
things in themselves utterly contrary begett this effect.
For we laugh both at witty and absurd things. At both
which sorts I have seene men laugh so long and so
ernestly, that at last they have wept that they could laugh
                                              no   20
more. And therfore the poet having describ'd the quietnes
of a wise retired man, sayth in one what we have sayd

(Paradox X. *1633a*)   2 discourse, and reason] discourse, reason *Bur, 1633b, 1652*
3 to only man] to non bytt man *Bur*: onely to Man *TC, Dob*: vnto man onlie *S, 1633+*
shall] should *Bur, Dob, S*   be] be onely *1633+*   4 which . . . which] that . . . that
TC, Dob   5 most] . . . vse *TC, Dob*   7 risum multum possis] . . . poteris *S*:
multum risum poteris *Bur, Dob*   9 laughers] lawghinge *TC*   amongst] *? Bur*:
among *1633+*   10 at . . . laugh] that wyse men lawgh at *TC*: which wise men laugh
at *Dob*   11 the first] *? Bur*: his . . . *S, 1633+*   Folly *ed.*: folly *W*   12
beholders] the . . . *Bur*   12–13 the most . . . least] *? Bur*: most . . . least *TC*: most
. . . the least *Dob*: the most . . . the least *S, 1633+*   15 content] contented *Dob*
16 to the exercise *S, 1633+*: by . . . *W*: *? Bur*: to any *TC, Dob*; *see note*   19 sorts]
sort *S*: *omit Dob*   22 we have *Σ*: we had *W, S*: we before had *W (b.c.)*: hee *Bur*

before in many lines,
>   *Quid facit Canius tuus? ridet.*

We have receaved that even the extremity of laughing, yea   25
of weeping allso hath beene accoumpted wisdome: and
Democritus and *Heraclitus* the lovers of these extremes have
beene called lovers of wisdome; Now amongst our wise
>   men, I
dowbt not, but many would be found, who would laughe
>   at
Heraclitus his weepinge, none which would weepe at   30
Democritus laughing. At the hearing of Comedies or other
witty reports, I have noted some, which not understanding
the jeasts, have yet chosen this as the best meanes to
seeme wise and understanding, to laugh when their
companions laughe, and I have presumd them ignorant,
>   whom I   35
have seene unmovd. A foole if he come into a Princes
Court, and see a gay man leaning at the wall, so glistering
and so painted in many colors that he is hardly discernd
from one of the pictures in the Arras hangings, his body
like an Ironbound chest girt in, and thicke ribd with   40
broad gold laces, may and commonly doth envy him, but
>   alas
shall a wise man, which may not only not envy this fellow,
but not pity him, do nothing at this monster? Yes: let him

23 before ... lines] in many lynes, before *TC, Dob*: before what we had said before in
many lynes *S*   24 *Canius*] Camus *TC*: *Canis S*   25 that even the] that even,
that *S*: that the *TC*: that *Dob*   26 hath] haue *Dob*   and] And that *1633+*   28
called lovers] called the lovers *Bur, TCC*: accounted louers *Dob*   amongst] ? *Bur*: among
1633+   29 who] that *Dob*   30 hic] *omit Dob, 1633+*   none] but ... *TC,
Dob*   which would] that wowld *TC, Dob*: which *Bur, S, 1633+*   31 *Democritus*
laughing] Democritus his laughing *Bur*: the lawghinge of Democritus *TC, Dob*   or] and
Bur   32 noted] knowne *Dob*   which] who *Dob, S*   33 the jeasts] ieasts *TC,
Dob, S: iests*, etc. *1633+*   have yet] yet haue *TC, Dob*   as] *omit Dob*   34 wise and
understanding] vnderstanding and wise *Dob*   35 laughe] laughed *Bur*   36
into] to *TC, Dob*   37 glistering] glitteringe *TC*   38 and so] and *Bur*: so *TC,
Dob*   39 hangings] hanginge *TC, Dob, 1633+*; *see note*   39–41 his body ...
laces] *omit Bur*   40 thicke] thicker *TC*   41 commonly doth] doth commonly
Dob   42 which] that *TC, Dob*   42–3 may not only not envy this fellow, but not
pity him, do nothing at this monster] ... him, do nothing *Bur*: may, not, onely enuye but
not pitty this monster doe nothinge *TCD*: may not, not only enuy but not pittie this monster
doe nothing *TCC*: may not only not envy but pitty this monster, doe nothinge *Dob*: may not
onlie not envye but not pitty this *Monster* doe nothinge *S, 1633+*

laugh. And if one of these hott colerique firebrands,
which nourish themselves by quarelling and kindling
                                        others   45
spitt upon a foole but one sparke of disgrace, he like a
thatchd house quickly burning, may be angry. But the
                                        wise
man as cold as the Salamander, may not only not be angry
with him, but not be sory for him. Therfore let him
                                        laughe.
So shall he be knowne a man, because he can laughe: 50
a wiseman that he knowes at what to laughe; and a valiant
man, that he dares laughe. For who laughs is justly
reputed more wise then at whome it is laughed. And
                                        hence I
thinke proceeds that which in these later formall times I
have much noted. That now when our superstitious civility   55
of manners is become but a mutuall tickling flattery of
one another, allmost every man affects an humor of
jeasting, and is content to deject, and deforme himselfe,
                                        yea to
become foole, to none other end that I can spy, but to give
his wise companions occasion to laughe, and to shew
                                        themselves   60
wise. Which promptnes of laughing is so great in wise
                                        men,
that I thinke all wise men (yf any wise men do read this
paradox) will laugh both at it and me.

44 hott colerique] chollerick hott *TC*   46 but] *omit S, 1633+*   48 the] a *Dob*
50 shall he] *? Bur*: hee shalbe *S, 1633+*   knowne] ... to be *TC, Dob* because he can] that
can *TC*: that he can *Dob*   51 that *Σ*: for *W*   at what *Σ*: what *W*: when *Bur*
52 man *Σ*: *omit W*   52–3 For who ... laughed] *omit Bur*   52 who] he which *S*:
hee that *1633+*   54 these *Σ*: the *W*   later formall] latter ... *Dob*: formall later
TCD   56 become but] become *1633+*: growne and become but *TC, Dob*   56–
7 of one] one of *Bur*: from one *TC, Dob*   57 allmost *ed.*: all most *W*   man] one
TC, Dob   affects] *? Bur*: affecteth *1633+*   58 to deject, and deforme *Σ*: ... to
deforme *W*: to be *deiect*, and to *deforme 1633+*   58–9 to become] *? Bur*: to become a
TC, Dob: become *1633+*   59 none] *? Bur*: noe *TCC, Dob, 1633+*   that *Σ*: which
W   spy] espie *TC, Dob*   60 companions] *? Bur*: companion *TC, 1633+*   to
shew themselves *Σ*: shew ... *W*: shewe himselfe *Dob*   61 wise. Which promptnes]
in *promptnesse 1633+*   in] amongst *Bur*   62 any wise men] wise men *Bur*: any wyse
man *TC, Dob, 1633b, 1652*

PARADOX VIII

That good is more common then evill

I HAVE not beene so pitifully tired with any vanity,
as with sely old mens exclayming agaynst our tymes and
extolling ther owne. Alas they betray themselves. For yf
the
tymes be chang'd, ther manners have chang'd them, but
ther
Senses are to pleasure, as sickmens tasts to Liquors. For   5
indeed no new thing is done in the world. All things are
what and as they weare; and good is as ever it was, most
plenteous, and must of necessity be more common then
evill,
because it hath this for Nature and end, and perfection to
be common. It makes love to all creatures and all affect it.   10
So that in the worlds early infancy, ther was a tyme when
nothing was evill; but if this world shall suffer dotage in
the extremest crookednes therof, ther shalbe no time
when
nothing shalbe good. It dares appeare and spred and
glister
in the world, but evill buryes it selfe in Night and   15
darknes; and is supprest and chastis'd, when good is
cherished
and rewarded. And as Embroderers, Lapidaryes, and other
Artisans can by all things adorne ther works, for by adding

A leaf is missing in S; the last two-thirds of this Paradox after It dares appeare (*l. 14*) *is missing.*
   (Paradox IV. *1633a*)   2 our] theys *TC, Dob, S, 1633+*   5 pleasure] *?* Bur:
pleasures *S, 1633+*   tasts] *?* Bur: taste *TC, Dob*: ... are *1633+*   7 most] more
TC, Dob, S, 1633+   8–10 then ... common] *omit TCC*   9 and end] end
Bur, Dob: *omit S, 1633+*   10 creatures and all] natures, and all *Dob*: Natures All *S*:
Natures, all, all *1633+*   13 crookednes] degree and crokednes *Bur*   14 appeare
and spred] appeare, spred *Bur*   16 supprest and chastis'd] chastised and suppressed
Dob, 1633+   17 other] ... like *Bur*   18 works] work *Bur, TC, Dob; see note*
for] and *TC*

better things they better them so much, by equall things
they double ther goodnes, and by worse they encrease ther   20
Shew, and Lustre, and eminency, So good doth not only
prostitute her owne amiablenes to all, but refuseth no ayd,
no, not of her utter contrary evill, that she may be more
common to us. For evill manners are parents of good
                                                          Lawes.
And in every evill ther is an excellency, which in common   25
speech, we call good. For the fashions of habits, for our
movings in gestures, for phrases in our speech, we say
they weare good as long as they weare usd, that is as long
as they weare common: and we eate, we walke, we sleepe
                                                          only
when it is, or seemes good to do so. All faire, all   30
proffitable, all vertuous is good. And these three things I
                                                          thinke
embrace all things but ther utter contraryes, of which allso
foule may be riche and vertuous, poore may be vertuous
                                                          and
faire, vicious may be faire and riche. So that Good hath
this good meanes to be common, that some subjects she
                                                          can   35
possesse intyrely, and in subjects poysond with evill, she
can humbly stoope to accompany the evill. And of
                                                  indifferent

---

19–21 they better . . . eminency] they adorne them so much by equalls they double there
goodness and by worse they encrease theire lustre and eminency *Bur*: better theyr shew
lustre and emminencie *TC*: they better the shewe and lustre and eminency *Dob*: the better
they shew in *Lush* and in *Eminency* *1633*+; *see note*   21 only] *omit Bur*
22 prostitute her owne amiablenes *TC*: . . . owne *(blank)* *W*: . . . her amiableness *Bur*:
prostrate her amiablenes *Dob, 1633*+   refuseth] refuses *Dob, 1633*+   ayd] ende *TC*,
Dob, 1633+   23 utter] owne *TCC*: *omit Bur*   more] the . . . *1633*+   24 us. For
ed.: vs, for *W*   25–6 And in . . . good *Σ*: *omit W*; *see note*   26 For *Σ*: So for *W*   the fashions of] our fashions in
TC, Dob, 1633+: *omit Bur*   the fashion of our *TC*   26–7 our movings] our meouinge *TC, 1633*+: the movinge
Dob   27 for] *omit Bur*   our *Σ*: *omit W*   28 weare good] are . . . *TC*   as
long] so long *Bur*; *see note*   29 we walke, we sleepe only] walke sleep onely *Bur*: in common speech
walke only *Dob, 1633*+   30 seemes *Σ*: seeme *W*   31 vertuous] vertues
TCC: vertue *TCD*   33 foule] faire *TC, Dob, 1633*+   33–4 and faire] and
riche *W* *(b.c.)*   35 good] *omit TC*   36–7 poysond with evill . . . accompany
the evill] accompanied with evil *Bur*; *see note*

many things are become perfectly good only by beeing
common;
as Customes by use are made binding Lawes; but I
remember
nothing that is therfore ill because it is common but
women; 40
of whom allso they which are most common are the best of
that
occupation they profes.

PARADOX IX

That by Discord things increase

Nullos esse Deos, inane caelum
Affirmat Selius, probatque, quod se
Factum, dum negat haec, videt beatum.

So I assever this the more boldly, because while I
maintaine it, and feele the contrary repugnances and adverse 5
fightings of the Elements in my body, my body increaseth;
and whilst I differ from common opinions, by this discord
the number of my Paradoxes encreaseth. All the riche
benefitts which we can faine in concord is but an even
conservation of things; in which evennes we may expect no 10
change nor motion; therfore no encrease or augmentation,
which is a member of motion. And yf this unity and peace
can give increase to things, how mightily is Discord and
warr to this purpose, which are indeed the only ordinary

38 many things] things many *TC*: things, many things *Dob, 1633+*   are] *omit Bur*
perfectly] precisely *Bur*: *omit TC*   only by] by only *Bur*: by *TC, Dob, 1633+*   41 which]
that *TC, Dob, 1633+*   42 they profes] Σ: which . . . *W*

A leaf is missing in S; the first ten lines up to expect *are missing.*
     (Paradox III. *1633a*)   1-3 *Nullos . . . beatum; see note*   2 Selius] *Coelius*
1633+   3 *dum negat haec, videt Bur*: . . . *vidit W*: vidit dum negat haec *TC, Dob,*
1633+   4 while] whylst *TC*   6 fightings] fightinge *TC*   7 whilst] whyle
TC, Dob   9 which] *omit 1633+*   faine] frame to our selues *TC, Dob, 1633+*
10 conservation] consideration *TC*   may] can *1633+*   11 nor] ? *Bur*: no *Dob,*
S, 1633+   13 to] of *Bur*   mightily] mighty *Dob, S*   14 this] that *TC,*
Dob, S, 1633+   which are] for these are *Bur*   only ordinary] only *Bur*: ordinary *TCC*

parents of peace. Discord is never so barren that it   15
affords no fruit, for the fall of one State is at worst
the increase of another; because it is as impossible to
find a discommodity without any advantage as corruption
without generation. But it is the nature and office of
Concord to preserve only; which property when it leaves,   20
it differs from it selfe, which is the greatest Discord
of all. All Victoryes and Emperyes gain'd by warr, and
all judiciall decidings of doubts in peace, I claime
chilldren of Discord. And who can deny that Controversies
                                                             in
religion are growne greater by Discord; and not the   25
controversies only but even Religion it selfe. For in a
troubled misery men are allwayes more religious then in
a secure peace. The number of good men (the only
charitable harborrers of Concord) we see is thin, and dayly
                                                           melts
and waynes; but of bad and discording men it is infinit   30
and growes hourely. We are acertaind of all disputable
doubts, only by arguing, and differing in opinion, and yf
formal disputation which is but a painted, counterfait,
and dissembled Discord, can worke us this benefitt, what
shall not a full and maine discord accomplish? Truly,   35
methinks I owe a devotion, yea a Sacrifice to Discord for
casting that ball upon *Ide*, and for all that busines of
Troy; whom ruind I admyre more then *Rome* or *Babilon* or
Quinzay. Nor are removd corners fullfilld only with her

---

16 no fruit Σ: no fruites *W*: not fruites *W* (*b.c.*)   State] ? *Bur*: Estate *S*, *1633*+   at] at
the *Dob*, *1633*+   17 the] an *Bur*   increase] increasinge *TC*: encreaser *Dob*, *S*,
1633+   as impossible] as much impossybylyty *Bur*   18 any] *omit Dob*, *S*, *1633*+   as]
as to finde *TC*, *Dob*, *S*, *1633*+   20 property Σ: properly *W*   23 decidings Σ:
deciding *W*, *S*   I] I doe *S*, *1633*+   24 that] but *Dob*, *S*, *1633*+   26
controversies only] controuersie *TC*, *Dob*, *S*, *1633*+   even] ... the *TC*, *Dob*: *omit*
S, *1633*+   27 misery] Ministery *TC*   29 harborrers] nourishers *TC*, *Dob*, *S*,
1633+   thin, *ed.*: thin; *W*   30 waynes; *ed.*: waynes, *W*   bad and discording men]
bad discording men *Bur*: bad discording *TC*, *Dob*, *S*, *1633*+   34 us] *omit Bur*   35
not] *omit Bur*   36 owe *ed.*: ow *W*   36–7 for casting] forecastinge *S*, *1633a*
37 upon] on *TC*   *Ide*] ? *Bur*: Ida *S*, *1633*+   38 ruind] envied *Bur*   *Rome* or *Babilon*]
Babylon, *Rome S*, *1633*+   39 Nor are removd corners] remoued corners not *Dob*, *S*,
1633+; *see note*   fullfilld only] only fulfilled *Bur*, *TC*, *S*, *1633*+: only filled *Dob*

fame, but with Cityes and thrones planted by her fugitives. 40
Lastly betweene cowardise and despayre valor is
                                        ingendred,
and so the Discord of extreames begetts all vertues; but
of the like things ther is no issue without miracle.
            Uxor pessima, pessimus maritus,
            Miror tam malé convenire vobis.   45
He wonders that betweene two so like ther could be any
discord, yet for all this discord perchance ther was nere the
lesse increase.

PARADOX X

That it is possible to find some vertue in some women

I AM not of that sear'd impudency that I dare defend
women, or pronounce them good: yet when we see
                                        phisitians
allow some vertu in every poyson, alas why should we
except women? Since, certainly they are good for phisick:
at least, so, as wine is good for a fever. And though they   5
be the occasioners of most Sins, they are allso the
punishers and revengers of the same Sins. For I have
                                        seldome
seene one which consumes his substance or body upon them,
excape diseases or beggery. And this is ther justice. And
if *Suum cuique dare*, be the fullfilling of all civil   10
justice, they are most just: for they deny that which is

40 thrones] townes *Bur*   41 ingendred] gendred *TCC, Dob, S, 1633+*   43 of the
Σ: of *W*: on the *Bur*   miracle] a . . . *1633+*   44 *pessimus maritus*] maritus pessimus
TC   45 *vobis*] omit *TC, Dob, S, 1633+*   46 two] any *Bur*   47 yet . . .
perchance] yet perchance for all this discord *Bur, Dob, S, 1633+*

(Paradox VI. *1633a*)   Title: *women*] woman *Dob, S*   1 AM *ed.*: ame *W*
sear'd] lewd *Dob*   impudency] ? *Bur*: *Impudence 1633+*   2 when we see] since *Bur*:
wee see *1633+*   4 except] . . . only *Bur*   5 at least, so] omit *Dob, S*   wine]
some . . . *Dob, S, 1633+*   fever] . . . to increase it *Bur*   6 occasioners] occasions *W*
(*b.c.*)   most] many *1633+*   6–7 they are allso . . . revengers] yet they . . . *TCC*:
yet are they . . . revengers also *Dob, S*   8 which] who *Dob, S*   substance or body]
substance and *body 1633+*: body and substance *Dob, S*   9 or] and *Dob, S*   11 for]
for that *Dob, S*

thers to no man.

Tanquam non liceat, nulla puella negat.

And who may doubt of great wisdome in them, that doth
but
observe with how much labor and cunning our Justices
and   15
other dispencers of the lawes to entrap them, and study
how zealously our Preachers dehort men from them, only
by urging ther Subteltyes and policies, and wisdome which
are in them, yea in the worst and most prostitute sorte
of them. Or who can deny them a good measure of fortitude,   20
if he consider how many valiant men they have
overthrowne,
and beeing them selves overthrowne, how much and how
patiently they beare? And though they be all most
intemperat,
I care not: for I undertooke to furnish them with some
vertu, not all. Necessity which makes even bad things
good,   25
prevayles allso for them: and we must say of them as of
some sharpe punishing lawes; If men were free from
infirmityes, they were needlesse: but they are both good
scourges
for bad men. These or none must serve for reasons: and it
is my great happines that Examples prove not rules, for to   30
confirme this opinion the World yields not one Example.

15 Justices] Iusticers *S, 1633+*   16 other dispencers] *Dispersers S*   entrap] embrace
TC: imbrace *1633+*: entrace *Dob, S*   17 our] your *Dob*   18 Subteltyes and policies]
subtilties *Bur*: pollicies subtiltyes *Dob, S*   19–20 yea ... sorte of them] *omit 1633+*
20 Or] And *Dob, S*   21 many] *omit 1633+*   22 and beeing ... overthrowne]
omit S   23 though] although *Bur*   all] omit *TC, Dob, S, 1633+*   25 vertu]
vertues *Dob, S*   all] with all *TC, Dob, S, 1633+*   makes even] even makes *Bur*   26
and] for *TC, Dob, S, 1633+*   27 some *Σ*: *omit W*   punishing] pinching *TC, 1633+*:
and pinchinge *Dob, S*   28–9 but ... men] *omit 1633+*   30 great] greatest
TC   31 opinion *Σ*: *omit W*: rule *Dob, S*   yields *Σ*: affords *W*

PROBLEMS

PROBLEM I

Why are Courtiers sooner Atheists then men of other Condition?

Is it because, as phisitians contemplating Nature and
finding many abstruse things subject to the search of
reason, thinke therefore that all is so: So they seeing mens
destinyes made at Court, necks put out and in joynt there,
warrs, peace, life, death derived from thence, climb no   5
higher? Or doth a familiarity of greatnesse, and dayly
Acquayntance and conversation with it, breede a contempt
of all greatnesse? Or because they see that Opinion, and
neede of one another, and feare, makes the degrees of
Servants Lords and Kings, doe they thinke that God   10
likewise, for such Reasons hath bin mans creature?
Perchance it is because they see Vice prosper best there, Or

PROBLEMS. *Text from O'F unless otherwise stated. Readings are given from the following
representative witnesses: O'F, Dob; Ash 826, R; TC (TCD with TCC), S 962; O 2; S; 1633+
(1633a and b and 1652). When a Problem is not found in one of these the omission is noted.*

This Problem is omitted in 1633a and b.

(Problem XVI. *1652*)   Title: *sooner Atheists* Σ: Atheists sooner *O'F, S 962*
men of other Condition Dob, Ash 826, S: . . . Conditions *O'F, 1652:* . . . meaner condition *TC,
S 962:* other men *O 2*   1 Is it] It is *TCC, S 962, O 2, S*   2 abstruse] obstruse
TC, S 962   3 thinke] thinks *1652*   that all is so] that all alsoe is *Ash 826:* that alsoe is
O 2   they] these *Ash 826, hi* (these) *R*   4 made at] made a *Ash 826:* mad at *1652*
necks put] neck *1652*   joynt] of . . . *Ash 826:* ioine *S*   5 warrs] warre *Ash 826,
1652, bellum* (war) *R*   death] and . . . *Ash 826, TC, 1652*   6 of *Ash 826, TC, S 962:*
with *O'F, Dob, O 2, S, 1652, cum* (with) *R*   6–7 and . . . it] *omit O 2*   6 dayly]
a . . . *Ash 826, S 962, S*   7 Acquayntance and conversation] conversation and acquain-
tance *Ash 826, 1652*   8 of all greatnesse *Ash 826, TC, S 962, 1652, omnis majestatis*
(of all greatness) *R:* of greatness *O'F, Dob, O 2:* therof *S*   they] that . . . *O 2, 1652*   and]
or *1652*   9 of one another] of another *Ash 826, TCD:* one of another *O 2*   makes]
make *Ash 826:* maketh *O 2*   10 doe they] doth he *Dob, O 2, S*   10–11 that God
likewise *Ash 826, TC, S 962, 1652:* likewise that God *O'F, Dob, O 2, S*   11 Reasons
Ash 826, TC, S 962: Reason *1652:* Evasions *O'F, Dob, O 2, S: omit R*   creature] Creator
Ash 826, TC, S 962, 1652; see note   12 Or *Ash 826, TC, S 962, O 2:* And *O'F, Dob, S,
1652: Fortasse* (perhaps) *R*

burdend with Sinne, doe they not for theyr ease endevour
to put off the feare and knowledge of God, as facinorous
men deny Magistracy? Or are therefore most Atheists in   15
that place, because it is the foole that hath sayd in his
heart there is no God?

PROBLEM II

*Why doth Sir Walter Ralegh write the Historie of
these times?*

BECAUSE being told at his arraignment that a witnesse
accusing himself had the strength of twoe, hee
thinks by writing the ills of his time to bee beleeved.
Or is it because hee would re-enjoye those times by the
meditation of them? Or because if hee should undertake   5
higher times, hee doth not thinke that hee can come any
nearer to the beginning of the world?

---

13 for theyr ease *Ash 826, TC, S 962, 1652: ipsos levandos* (for releaving themselves) *R: omit*
O'F, Dob, O 2, S   15 therefore most *Ash 826, TCD*: they . . . *TCC, S 962*: they
most *O'F, Dob, S*: the most *1652*: there more *O 2: plures* (more) *R*   15–16 in that
place] *omit Ash 826*   16 hath sayd] saith *TC, S 962*: said *1652*.

Copy-text TCD.

This Problem occurs in Tan; it is not found in R, 1633+.

   Title: *Why . . . times] Why was Sir Walter Raleigh thought the fittest Man to write the
History of these Tymes S, Tan   Why doth . . . write] Why did . . . write O'F, Dob: Why
. . . writt S 962: Why . . . did write O 2   Walter Ralegh Σ: W.R. TC, S 962: W. K.
Ash 826   these] his Ash 826: omit S 962   1 BECAUSE] . . . that Dob, S: Was it . . .
that Tan   2 strength] force O'F   2–3 hee thinks . . . time] hee . . . time, thinks O 2:
He may seeme . . . owne tyme S, Tan   3 ills] storye Ash 826: euills O 2   time]
times O'F   4 would] might Tan: migh S   those] these Ash 826   6 that] omit O'F,
O 2, S   can come] cometh Ash 826   7 nearer to Σ: neare to TC, S 962: nearer
Ash 826   world?] O'F, Dob, S, Tan read: world, Or because, like a Bird in a Cage, hee
takes his tunes from every passenger that last whistled. Or because hee thinkes not that the
best Eccho that repeates most of the Sentence, but that which repeats lesse, more playnly.   10
9 passenger Σ: one O'F   10 Eccho that] . . . which S, Tan   repeats] repeateth
Dob*

PROBLEM III

Why doe Great Men choose of all dependants to preferre theyr Bawds?

IT is not because they are got neerest theyr Secrets, for they whome they bring were neerer. Nor because
commonly
they and theyr Bawds have lyen in one belly, for then they should love theyr Brethren as well. Nor because they are witnesses of theyr weaknesse, for they are weake ones.
Eyther   5
it is because they have a double hold and obligation upon theyr Masters for providing them Surgery and remedy
after,
as well as pleasure before, and bringing them such stuff,
as
they shall always neede this service, Or because they may bee receav'd and entertaynd every where, and Lords fling   10
off none but such as they may destroy by it, Or perchance wee deceave our selves and every Lord having many, and
of
necessity some rising, wee marke onely these.

This Problem is omitted in 1633a and b.

(Problem XV. *1652*)   Title: *choose of all dependants Ash 826, TC, S 962*: of all dependants chuse *Dob, S, 1652*: of all theyr dependants choose *O'F, O 2*   preferre] preserue *S, 1652, promovent* (promote) *R*   theyr Bawds] Bawdes *S*: their little Pimps *1652*   2 were] are *S 962, O 2*: come *S, 1652*   3 lyen] laine *O 2, 1652*   4 Brethren] brothers *1652*   5 witnesses] witness *TC, S 962, O 2, S*   6 it is] is yt *Ash 826, S 962, S*   and obligation] *omit Ash 826*   7 for] by *TC*: *omit Ash 826*   8 them] . . . alwais *S, 1652*   9 this] their *S, 1652*   10 receav'd and entertaynd] entertained, and receiued *TC, S 962*   11 off *TC, S 962, O 2, 1652*: of *O'F, Dob, Ash 826, S* may] *omit TC, S 962*   destroy *Σ*: vndoe *O'F*   13 these] those *TC, S 962*

PROBLEM IV

Why doth not Gold soyle the fingers?

DOTH it direct all the Venim to the heart? Or is it
because Bribing should not bee discoverd? Or because that
should passe purely for which pure things are given, as
Love, Honour, Justice, and Heaven? Or doth it seldome come
in Innocent hands, but in such as for former fowlenesse   5
you cannot discerne this?

PROBLEM V

Why dye none for love now?

BECAUSE woemen are become easyer? Or because these
later times have provided mankind of more new meanes for
the destroying themselves and one another: Poxe
                                    Gunpowder,
young marriages and Controversyes in Religion? Or is there
in truth no precedent or example of it? Or perchance some   5
doe dye, but are therefore not worthy the remembering or
speaking of.

This Problem is omitted in 1633a and b.
    (Problem XIV. *1652*)   2 Bribing] bribings *Dob, TC, S 962*: bribery *Ash 826*   3
passe] pay *1652*   4 Honour *ed.*: honour *O'F*   Heaven? *ed.*: Heauen *O'F*   5 in
. . . in] in . . . into *O 2*: into . . . into *1652*   Innocent *Ash 826, TC, S 962, 1652*:
Innocents *O'F, Dob, O 2, S*   fowlenesse] foulnesses *TC, S 962*

This Problem is omitted in 1633a and b.
    (Problem XII. *1652*)   2 later] latter *Ash 826, S 962, O 2, S*: *nostra tempora* (our
times) *R*   3 the destroying themselves and one another *Ash 826, TC, S 962*: . . . of
themselves . . . *1652*: *ad nostram, et aliorum destructionem* (destruction to themselves and of
others) *R*: . . . of themselues *Dob, S*: destroying themselues, as *O'F, O 2*   another: *colon
supplied ed.*   4 young] newe *Ash 826*: *praematura* (premature) *R*   and] *omit Ash 826*
5 truth] history *Ash 826*: true History *1652*   precedent *Ash 826, 1652*: *omit R*: president *Σ*
or example *Σ*: and . . . *O'F*   it? Or *Ash 826, TC, S 962, 1652*: it? But *O'F, Dob, O 2, S*
6 doe dye] dye *Ash 826*: die so *1652*   therefore not] nott therefore *O 2, 1652*: not then *Ash
826*   worthy] worth *Ash 826*   remembering *Σ*: remembrance *O'F, O 2*   or] nor *TCD,
S 962*: of *O 2*

PROBLEM VI

Why doe young Laymen so much study Divinity?

Is it because others, tending busily Church
preferment, neglect the study? Or had the church of *Rome*
shutt
up all our wayes till the Lutherans broke downe theyr
uttermost stubborne dores and the Calvinists pick'd
theyr inwardest and subtillest locks? Surely the Devill   5
cannot bee such a foole to hope that hee shall make this
study contemptible by making it common, Nor, as the
Dwellers by the river *Ougus* are sayd (by drawing infinite
ditches to sprinkle theyr barren country) to have
exhausted and intercepted the maine channell, and so lost
theyr   10
more profitable course to the sea: so wee by providing
every ones selfe divinity enough for his owne use, should
neglect our teachers and fathers. Hee cannot hope for
better Heresyes then hee hath had, nor was his kingdome
ever so much advanced by debating religion (though with   15
some Aspersions of Errour) as by a dull and stupid
security in which many grosse things are swallowed.

Possibly

This Problem is omitted in R.
  (Problem V. *1633a*)   *Title: Laymen . . . study*] Lawe men study so much *Ash 826*
1–2 Church preferment *TC, S 962, O 2*: the . . . *Dob*: the . . . preferments *O'F*: to . . .
preferments *Ash 826*: Churches . . . *S, 1633*+   2 the study *Ash 826, TC, S 962*:
study *O'F, Dob, O 2, S, 1633*+   3 Lutherans] Latherans *Ash 826*   3–4 theyr
uttermost *TCC, S 962, S, 1633*+: . . . outermost *O'F, Dob, TCD*: the . . . *Ash 826*: all
there *O 2*   5 inwardest *Σ*: inward *O'F*: inwards *O 2*   subtillest] subtile *Ash 826*
6 to hope that hee shall make this *Dob, TC, S 962, S, 1633*+: to hope hee . . . *Ash 826*: as
to hope to make that *O'F*: as to thinke hee canne . . . *O 2*   7 Nor] nor that *TC, S 962*,
S, 1633+   8 *Ougus Dob, O 2*: Ogus *O'F*: Ongus *Ash 826, TC, S 962*: oriyns *S*: *Origus*
1633+; *see note*   9 ditches] dikes *Ash 826*   10 intercepted] interrupted *Ash 826*
the maine channell] . . . Channells *TCD*: there . . . *O 2, S, 1633*+   so] thereby *Ash 826*:
omit Dob   13 our] their *TC, S 962*   14 Heresyes] hereby *Ash 826*   16 of]
and *TC, S 962*   stupid] sluggish *TC, S 962*   17 Possibly] Possible *1633*+

out of such an Ambition as wee now have to speake
playnly
and fellowly of Lords and Kings wee thinke also to
acquaynt our selves with Gods secrets. Or perchance when　20
wee study it by mingling humane respects, it is not
divinity.

PROBLEM VII

Why hath the common opinion affoorded woemen Soules?

It is agreed that wee have not so much from them as
any part of eyther of our mortall soules of sence or
growth; And wee denye soules to others equall to them in
all but Speeche, for which they are beholding onely to
theyr bodily instruments, for perchance an Apes heart or　5
a Gotes or a Foxes or a Serpents, would speake just so
if it were in the brest and could move the tongue and
jawes.
Have they so many Advantages and meanes to hurt us (for
even theyr loving destroyes us) that wee dare not displease
them, but give them what they will, and so, when some call　10
them Angels, some Goddesses, and the Peputian Heretikes
made them Bishops, wee descend so much with the
streame to

---

18 now have] haue now *1633*+ : haue *O 2*　　19 fellowly of Lords and Kings *Ash 826*: . . .
Kings, and Lords *TC, S 962*: fellowly with . . . *Dob*: fellowlike with . . . *O'F, S, 1633*+:
fellow like of . . . *O 2*　　21 it is not] is not *Ash 826*: itt is *O 2*

(Problem VI. *1633a*)　　2 any part of eyther of our *TC, S 962*: . . . eyther our *O'F,
Dob, S, 1633*+: either part of our *Ash 826*: any parte of our *O 2*　of sence] as sense *Ash 826*
or] and *O'F (b.c.)*　　4 Speeche] in . . . *O 2, S, 1633*+　onely] *omit S, 1633*+　　5
perchance] perhaps *Ash 826, O 2*　　Apes *Ash 826, TC, S 962, simiae* (ape's) *R*: Oxes
O'F, Dob, S, 1633+: Oxe *O 2*　　6 or a Foxes] a Foxes *TC, S 962*　　7 if . . . jawes]
if yt could moue the tongue and iawes and were in the breast *Ash 826*　the tongue *Σ*: that
tongue *O'F, Dob, 1633*+　　8 many] much *O'F (b.c.)*: *omit Ash 826*　Advantages and
meanes] meanes and advantages *Ash 826*: aduantages *O 2*　　9 even] euer *Dob, O 2, S,
1633*+　destroyes] destroy *Ash 826*: destroyed *1633*+　　11 the] they, like *TC*: they
like the *S 962*　Peputian *ed.*: Puputian *O'F*: Preputian *Dob, Ash 826*: Terputiani *R*:
Alpuleyan *TC, S 962*: Pupulian *S*: Palpulian *1633*+: puritane *O 2*; *see note*　　12 made]
make *Ash 826, S, 1633a, faciant* (make) *R*　to] as to *Dob, Ash 826, O 2, S*

allow them soules. Or doe wee somwhat, in this dignifying
them, flatter Princes and greate Personages that are so
much governd by them? Or doe wee, in that easynesse and   15
prodigality wherein wee dayly loose our owne soules, allow
soules to wee care not whome, and so labour to perswade
out selves that sith a woman hath a soule, a soule is no
greate matter? Or doe wee but lend them soules and that
for use, since they for our sakes give theyr soules agayne,   20
and theyr bodyes to boote? Or Perchance because the
                                                        Devill
who doth most mischeefe is all soule, for conveniency and
proportion because they would come neere him wee allow
                                                         them
some soule, And so as the *Romans* naturalized some
Provinces in revenge, and made them *Romans* onely for the   25
burden of the common wealth: so wee have given woemen
                                                      soules,
onely to make them capable of damnation.

13 allow] make *Ash 826* somwhat] *omit Ash 826*   this *Σ*: thus *O'F, Dob*   14
them *Dob, Ash 826, TC, S 962*: of . . . *O'F, S, 1633+, earum* (of them) *R: omit O 2*   that]
whoe *Ash 826, qui* (who) *R*   15 easynesse] ease *Ash 826*   16 wherein *Σ*:
wherewith O'F   16–17 allow soules] *omit S, 1633+*   17 to wee care not whome] wee
care not to whom *TCD*: . . . not to whom *TCC*: . . . care to whom *Ash 826*   and so] and
O 2: soe *S, 1633+*   19–20 but lend . . . and that for use *Ash 826*: but lend . . . and
for vse *TC, S 962*: lend . . . but for vse *O'F. Dob, O 2, S, 1633+*   20 sakes] soule
O'F (b.c.): soules *O 2*: sake *S*   21 theyr] *omit Ash 826*   because] *omit Ash 826*   22
who doth most mischeefe is all soule *Ash 826, TC, S 962: qui pessime semper agit, pura puta
est anima* (who always acts worst, is perfectly pure soul) *R*: who is all soule doth most mischeefe
O'F, Dob, S, 1633+: whoe is all soule and doth most mischiefe *O 2*   for
conveniency *Ash 826, TC, S 962*: for convenience *O'F*: and for convenience *Dob, O 2
S, 1633+*   23 would *Σ*: should *O'F: omit Ash 826*   neere] nearest *Ash 826, proximae*
(nearest) *R: neerer 1633+*   24 some soule *Ash 826, TCC, S 962*: some soules *O'F,
Dob, S, 1633+*: soule *TCD*: soules *O 2*   25–6 for the burden *Ash 826, TC, S 962, O 2,
S, 1633+*: for burden *Dob*: because they should beare the burden *O'F: ut reipublicae onera
ferrent* (so that they should carry the burdens of the republic) *R*

PROBLEM VIII

Why are the fayrest falsest?

I MEANE not of false Alchimy beauty, for then the
question should bee inverted why are the *falsest fayrest?*
It is not onely because they are much sollicited and sought
for, so is Gold, yet it is not so comminge, And this suite
to them should teach them theyr valew and make them more   5
reserved. Nor is it because delicatest bloud hath best
spirits, for what is that to the flesh? Perchance such
constitutions have the best witts, and there is no other
proportionable subject for woemens witts but deceipt.
Doth the mind so follow the temper of the body that   10
because these complections are aptest to change, the mind is
therefore so too? Or as Bells of the purest mettall
retayne the tinkling and sound longest: so the memory of
the last pleasure lasts longer in these, and disposes
them to the next? But sure, it is not in the complection,   15
for those that doe but thinke themselves fayre are
presently enclined to this multiplicity of loves, which
beeing but fayre in conceipt are false indeed, And so
perchance when they are borne to this beauty, or have
made it
or have dreamt it they easily beleeve all Addresses and   20
Applications of every man, out of a sence of theyr owne

    (Problem VII. *1633a*)   2 are] are not *Ash 826*   4 for Σ: for, for *O'F*   is
Gold] as gold *TC, S 962*   yet it] and yet that *Ash 826*: yet *TCC*   comminge *Ash 826, TC,*
S 962: common *O'F, Dob, S, O 2, 1633+*; *see note*   5 should] might *Ash 826*   6
delicatest . . . best *Ash 826, TC, S 962*: the delicatest . . . the best *O'F, Dob, O 2, S, 1633+*
7 what is] what's *TC, S 962*   8–9 other proportionable *Ash 826, aliud . . . proportionale*
(other proportionable) *R*: other proportionall *TC, S 962*: proportionable *O'F, Dob, O 2, S,*
1633+   9 woemens] womans *TCD, S 962*   witts] witt *TC, S 962, S, 1633+*   10
temper *Ash 826, TC, S 962*: temperature *O'F, Dob, O 2, S, 1633+*, *temperiem* (temperature)
R   11 these] their *S*: those *1633+*   12 too] *omit S, 1633+*   the] *omit Ash*
826   13 the *Ash 826, TC, S 962, O 2*: theyr *O'F, Dob, S, 1633+*   longest] lardge *S*:
largest *1633b, 1652*   14 longer] longest *Ash 826, O 2*   disposes] disposeth *O 2, S,*
1633+: that disposeth *Ash 826*: dispossesses *TCD*: dispossesse *TCC*   16 that] which
TCC, S 962, O 2,   17 this] *omit Ash 826*   which] and *Ash 826*   21 out] and
Dob, TC, S 962, O 2

worthinesse, to bee directed to them, which others lesse
worthy in theyr owne thoughts, apprehend not or
discredit. But I thinke the true reason is, that beeing like
Gold in many propertyes, (as that All snatch at them, That   25
all corruption is by them, That the worst possesse them,
That they care not how deepe wee digg for them, and That
by the Law of Nature *Occupanti conceditur*) they would bee
also like in this, That as Gold to make it selfe of use
admitts Allay; so they that they may bee tractable and   30
malleable and currant have for theyr Allay Falshood.

PROBLEM IX

Why have Bastards best Fortune?

BECAUSE Fortune her selfe is a whore? But such are
not most indulgent to theyr children. The old naturall
reason (that these meetings in stolne love are most
vehement, and so contribute more spirit then the easy
and lawfull) might governe mee, but that I see now that   5
Mistresses are become domestique and in ordinary, and
they and wives wayte but by turnes, and agree as well as
if they liv'd in the Arke. The old Morall reason (That
Bastards inherit wickednesse from theyr parents, and
so are in a better way of preferment by having a stocke   10

24 like] liker *TC, S 962*   25–6 That all corruption is by them *Ash 826, TC, S 962,
O 2: quod omnis corruptio ex illis* (because all corruption is from them) *R: omit O'F, Dob, S,
1633+*   26 That] but *S, 1633+*   28 *Occupanti conceditur*] *Occupandi . . .
TC, S 962, S, 1633+*: . . . *concedatur R*   29 also like *Ash 826, TC, S 962*: like also *Dob,
S, 1633+*: like it also *O'F, O 2*   it selfe] yt *Ash 826, TC, S 962*; *see note*   30 tractable
and] tractable, *S, 1633+*   31 malleable] mutable *Dob, O 2, S, 1633+*   malleable
and currant] currant and malleable and abide the test *Ash 826: malleabiles, examini respondentes,
et admissibiles* (malleable, responding to the test, and admitted) *R*   for] to *Dob, O 2, S, 1633+*

The first nineteen lines up to and including equivalent *are omitted in 1633a.*
    (Problem I. *1633a*)   Title: best *Σ*: the . . . *O'F, Dob   Fortune*] fortunes *Ash 826,
TCC, S 962, S*   1 But] *omit Ash 826*   2 most] the . . . *TC, S 962   children*]
issue *1633b, 1652*   3 that these meetings] . . . meetinge *Ash 826*: but those . . . *1633b*:
but those meeting *1652   most *Σ*: more *O'F, Dob*   4–5 and so . . . lawfull] *omit Ash
826*   5 lawfull) might] lawfull *(blank)* might *TC, S 962   governe*] moue *Ash 826*
5–6 I see now that Mistresses are become *Ash 826, TCC, S 962*: I see nowe Mistresses . . .
TCD, S: now I see *Mistresses . . . 1633b, 1652*: I see that Mistresses are now become *O'F,
Dob*: . . . are growne *O 2*   7 by *Σ*: in *O'F*   7–8 as if they liv'd] as though . . .
O 2: . . . had lived *S*: as they had *lived 1633b, 1652*   10 of] to *1633b, 1652*

before hand then those that must build all theyr
fortune upon the poore weake stocke of originall sinne)
might prevayle with mee, but that since wee are fallen
into such times as now the world might spare the Devill
because wee could bee badd enough without him, I see
                                                                men   15
scorne to bee wicked by example or to bee beholden to
others for theyr damnation. It seemes reasonable that
sith Lawes robb them of Succession and civill benefits
they should have some thing else equivalent, As Nature,
which is Lawes paterne, having denyed woemen constancy   20
to One, hath provided them with cunning to allure many,
And so Bastards *de jure* should have better witts and
abilities. But (besides that by experience wee see many
fooles amongst them) wee should take from them one of
theyr cheefest helpes to preferment if wee should deny   25
them to bee fooles. And that (which is onely left) that
woemen choose worthyer persons then theyr husbands, is
false *de facto*. Eyther then it must bee that the church
having remoovd them from all place in the publike
                                                            service
of God, they have thereby better meanes then others to   30
bee wicked, and so fortunate, Or else because the two
greatest powers in the world the Divell and Princes
concurre to theyr greatnesse, the one giving Bastardy, the
other Legitimation, as Nature frames and conserves

11 before] after *Ash 826*   that] which *TC, S 962*   must] *omit S, 1633b, 1652*   12 poore
weake] poore, and weake *TC, S 962, 1633b, 1652*   stocke] helpe *Ash 826, auxilium* (assist-
ance] *R*   13 fallen] now . . . *Ash 826*   14 might] could *Ash 826*   15 wee
Ash 826, TC, S 962: sumus (we are) *R*: it *O'F, Dob, O 2*: she *S, 1633b, 1652*   17 seemes]
seeme *Ash 826*   18 Lawes robb *Σ*: Lawe robbs *O'F, Dob*   Succession *ed.*: Succession,
O'F: successions *TC, S 962*   and *Ash 826, Dob, TC, S 962, O 2*: and other *O'F*: in *S,
1633b, 1652*   benefits] . . . and *O'F (b.c.)*   21 with] *omit Ash 826, O 2*: that *Dob
22 de jure* should] should *de iure Ash 826*   23 abilities *Ash 826, TC, S 962, O 2*:
experience *O'F, Dob, S, 1633+*   besides that by experience] beside that *Ash 826*: beside
that experience *TCC*   24 amongst] among *Ash 826*: *omit S*   25 cheefest] best *Ash
826*: chief *TC, S 962*   if] and *1633+*   27 persons *Ash 826, TC, S 962*: men *O'F,
Dob, O 2, S, 1633+: adulteros* (adulterers) *R*   28–31 Eyther . . . fortunate] *omit R*
29 having remoovd] remoueing *Ash 826*   place] places *Ash 826*   30 thereby *Ash 826,
TC, S 962, O 2: omit O'F, Dob, S, 1633+*   then others] *omit Ash 826*   31 else because]
because *Ash 826*: else *O 2*   32 the world] this world *Dob, O 2, 1633+, hujus mundi* (this
world) *R*   33 the one] that one *TC, S 962*   33–4 the other *Σ*: and . . . *O'F*

greate Bodyes of Contraryes. Or perchance it is because   35
they abound most at Court, which is the forge where
fortunes are made, or at least the shopp where they are
sold.

Why Venus starre onely doth cast a Shadowe?

Is it because it is neerer the earth? But they whose
profession it is to see that nothing bee donne in heaven
without theyr consent (as *Kepler* sayes in himselfe of all
Astrologers) have bidd *Mercury* to bee nearer. Is it
because the workes of *Venus* neede shadowing covering and   5
disguising? But those of *Mercury* neede it more. For
Eloquence, his occupation, is all shadowes and colours. Let
our life bee a sea, and then our reason, and even passions,
are wind enough to carry us whither wee should goe, but
Eloquence is a storme and tempest that miscarryes us. And   10
who doubts that Eloquence (which must perswade people to
take a yoake of Soveraignty and then beg and make lawes
to tye them faster, and then give monny to the Invention,
repayr and strengthen it) needes more shadowes and
colourings then to perswade any man or woman to that
which is   15

---

35 perchance it is] it is *S*: the cause is *1633*+   36 most] *omit Ash 826, R*   37 at
least *Σ: omit O'F*   are sold] be sold *1633*+

(Problem VIII. *1633a*)   Title: *Venus starre onely doth Dob, TC, S, 1633*+:...
doth only *S 962, O 2*: doth Venus starre onely *O'F*: doth only Venus Star *Ash 826*   1
Is it] *omit Ash 826*: It is *S 962*   neerer] neere *Ash 826*   3 Kepler *Dob, O 2: Kepter
Ash 826*: Repler *S 962*: Re *TC, S, 1633*+: *Ripler, O'F, see note*   sayes] sayth *Ash 826*   all]
omit TC, S 962, S, 1633+   5 neede] want *TC, S 962, S, 1633*+   covering *Σ: and
... Ash 826: omit O'F*   6 neede] needs *TC, S 962, S, 1633a*   7 Eloquence, his
occupation, *Σ:* Eloquences occupation *O'F, O 2*   shadowes] shaddowe *TC, S 962,
S, 1633*+   9 whither] whether *Dob, S 962, 1633*+   10 that miscarryes] which
miscarryeth *Ash 826*   us] *omit TC, S 962, 1633*+   11 that *Σ:* but ... *O'F:* but
Ash 826   which] that *Ash 826*   12 and then beg *Σ: omit O'F*   lawes] *Lawper
Ash 826: leges et instituta* (laws and statutes) *R*   13 them] themselves *Ash 826*   monny
... Invention] more money in subventions *Ash 826; see note*   14 repayr and strengthen
TC, S 962, O 2, S, 1633+: to ... *Ash 826:* ... strengthening *Dob:* repayring and strengthn-
ing *O'F*   15 colourings *Dob, TC, S 962, S:* colours *O'F, coloribus* (colours) *R:*
coloureinge *Ash 826, O 2, 1633*+   which] *omit Ash 826*

naturall, And *Venus* markets are so naturall, that when wee
sollicite the best way (which is by marriage) our
perswasions worke not so much to drawe a woman to us, as
agaynst
her nature, to drawe her from all others besides, And so
when wee goe agaynst nature and from *Venus* workes (for   20
Marriage is chastity) wee neede shadowes and colours, but
not
else. In *Senecas* time it was a course and *un-Romane* and
a contemptible thing, even in a matron, not to have had a
love besides her husband, which though the Lawe required
not at theyr hands, yet they did it Zealously, out of the   25
counsell of the custome and fashion, which was Venery
of Supererogation.

    Et te spectator plus quam delectat Adulter,
sayth *Martiall*: And *Horace*, because many lights would not
shewe him enough, created many Images of the same
Object,   30
by waynscotting his chamber with looking glasses. So then
Venus flyes not light so much as *Mercury*, who creeping
into our understanding in our darkenesse, were defeated if
hee were perceaved. Then eyther this Shadowe confesseth
that same darke Melancholly repentence which
accompanyes   35
it. Or that so vyolent fires neede some shadowy refreshing
and intermission, Or else Light signifying both day

16 markets] workes *Ash 826, opera* (works) *R*   17 sollicite] . . . them *Ash 826*: *ea
sollicitamus* (we solicit them) *R*   by] *omit Ash 826*   19 her nature] nature *Ash 826*
others] other *TC, S 962, 1633+*: *omit Ash 826*   20 workes] worke *TC, S 962, S, 1633+*
22 else. In *Senecas* time] *Ash 826, R read*: else. Is it because her workes are workes of darkenesse?
Childish and vnrefined times might thinke so. Ours doe them professedly ynough; so longe
agoe as in *Senecaes* tyme; *see note*   and *un-Romane Dob, Ash 826, TCD*: an . . . *TCC,
S 962, 1633+*: vnromane *O'F*: and vn=oo=mane *S*: vnnaturall *O 2*   22–3 and a] and
Dob, Ash 826, O 2   23 had *Σ*: *omit O'F, Dob*   24 love *Σ*: louer *O'F*   besides]
beside *1633+*   her] a *Ash 826*   which] . . . because *Ash 826*   required] . . . yt *Ash 826*
25–6 out of the counsell] and out *Ash 826*   26 the] *omit O 2, 1633+*   29 And *Σ*:
omit O'F, Dob   would] could *Ash 826*   31 then] that *S 962, 1633+*   33 in]
omit TC, S 962, 1633+   were] would be *TC, S 962, S, 1633+*   34 perceaved. Then
eyther] *Ash 826, R read*: perceaued; and of her dareinge to appeare, it is one Argument that
her place is nearer the sunne then his, and one of her names *Lucifera*. Either then; *see note*
35 same] some *Ash 826, quandam* (some) *R*   which] *omit Ash 826, R*   36 it] *omit TC,
S 962, S, 1633+*   neede]neede *TC, S 962, S, 1633+*   36–7 refreshing and
intermission] refreshings and intermissions *Ash 826*

and youth, and shadowe both Night and Age, Shee
pronounceth, by this, that shee professeth both all times and
persons.   40

PROBLEM XI

Why is Venus Starre multinominous called both Hesperus and Vesper?

THE Moone hath as many names, but not as shee is a
starre, but as shee hath divers governments. But *Venus*
is multinominous, to give example to her prostitute
disciples who so often, eyther to renew or refresh
themselves towards Lovers, or to disguise themselves from   5
Magistrates, are to take new names. It may bee shee takes
many names, after her many functions. For as shee is
supreme Monarch of all Love at large (which is lust) so is
shee joyned in Commission by all *Mythologists* with *Juno,*
Dyana, and all others, for marriage. It may bee, because   10
of the divers names of her Affections, shee assumes
divers names to her selfe. For her affections have more
names then any Vice *scilicet*: Pollution, Fornication,
Adultery, Lay Incest, Church Incest, Rape, Sodomy,
Mastupration, Masturbation, and a thousand others.   15
Perchance her divers names shew her Applyablenesse to
                                                                divers
men. For *Neptune* distilld and wept her into Love, the

38 shadowe]. . . signifyinge *Ash 826*   39 professeth] possesseth *Dob, Ash 826,*
O 2, possidere (possesses) *R; see note*   39–40 both . . . persons] all times and all persons
Ash 826, omnia tempora et omnes personas (all times and all persons) *R*: both all persons, and
times *TC, S 962, S, 1633+*

(Problem IX. *1633a*)   Title: called *Σ*: omit *O'F   Hesperus Σ*: Hesper *O'F*   4
renew or *TC, S 962, S, 1633+*: . . . and *O'F*: (*blank*) and *Dob*: reuiue and *O 2*   7 many
names] newe . . . *TC, S 962, S, 1633+*: names *O 2*   8 Love] loues *Dob*: Sunns *TC,*
S 962, S, 1633+   8–9 is shee *Σ*: shee is *O'F*   9 by all *Mythologists*] . . .
Mythology *Dob*: with all Mythologicks *TC, S 962, S, 1633+*   11–12 of her Affections,
shee assumes divers names] *omit TC, S 962, 1633+; see note*   13 *scilicet 1633+*: sclt
S: sc: *O'F, Dob*: vizt: *TC, O 2*: viz: *S 962*   15 Mastupration] Mascupration *TC,*
S 962, S, 1633a   16 shew] shewed *TC, S 962, S, 1633+*   17 wept her into] wett
her in *TC, S 962, S, 1633+*

sunne warmd and melted her, *Mercury* perswaded and swore
her; *Jupiters* authority securd, and *Vulcan* hammerd her.
As *Hesperus* shee presents you with her *Bonum Utile*,   20
because it is wholesomest in the morning, as *Vesper*, with
her *Bonum Delectabile* because it is pleasantest in the
Evening. And because Industrious men rise and endure,
with the Sunne, theyr civill businesse, this starr calls
them up a little before, and rememberes them agayne a   25
little after for hir businesse. For certaynly
                Venit Hesperus, Ite Capellae,
was spoken to Lovers in the persons of Goates.

PROBLEM XI. *Ash 826 corrected from R*

*Why is venus star multinominous and called both
Hesperus and vesper?*

THE moone hath as many names, but not as shee is a
star, but as shee hath diverse governments, as in Kings
titles, yoᵂ see Dukes Earles and Lordes names. *Lactantius*
thinkeinge to avile this star hath advantaged her more
then any of her Idolaters, hee sayth shee first invented   5
Artem meritriciam and then certainly shee is antienter
then any of the vitious gods, and I beleyve then the
Inventer of Musicke, for before *Jubal* invented *psalterium
et citharam*, his mother had invented the takeinge of
another husband: If *Venus* did this then is shee   10
multinominous to gyve example to her prostitute disciples,
                                                  Whoe
so often [either] to renewe or refresh them[selves] towards
lovers, or to disguyse themselves from the Magistrates

---

18 warmd and melted] warmes, and melts *TC*, *S 962*, *1633*+   19 securd] ... her *O 2*
21 wholesomest] pleasantest *O'F* (*b.c.*): helsome *S 962*   23 endure] endevour *TC*,
S 962   24 theyr] in ... *TC*, *S 962*, *S*, *1633*+   businesse] businesses *TC*, *S 962*,
S, *1633*+   25 agayne Σ: omit *O'F*, *O 2*   28 persons] presence *TC*: presentes *S 962*

2 star, (*stella,*) *R*: star *Ash 826*   governments, *ed.*: gouernments *Ash 826*   3 names.
(*nomina.*) *R*: names? *Ash 826*   *Lactantius*] ... *Firmianus R*   6 antienter] vitiouser *Ash
826* (*b.c.*)   12 [either] *aut R*: omit *Ash 826*   them[selves] *ed.*: them *Ash 826*; *see note*

take new names. Yt may bee shee takes many names for
             her
many functions, for as shee is the supreme Monarch of all 15
Love at large (which is Lust) whose affections have more
names then any other vice (pollution, fornication,
Adultery, Lay incest, Church incest, rape, Sodomy,
mastupration, masturbation, and the other Ten Thousand)
               so is
shee joyned in Commission by all *Mythologists* with *Juno* 20
and *Diana* and others for maryage. Perchaunce her diverse
names shewe her applyablenesse to diverse men, for
Neptune distild and wept her into love, the sun warmed and
melted her; *Vulcan* blew and hamered her, *Mercury*
perswaded and swore her, and *Jupiters* authority secured her; 25
but why especially had shee the names of *Hesperus* and
Vesper? Beleive not this to bee the reason that they include
all times and by riseinge and fallinge are Emblems of
all fortunes; but because the world hath accepted this
for the *summum bonum*, it is reason[able that it should] 30
receave all the Degrees of *bonum* except those which doe
utterly contradicte yt and destroy yt as *bonum honestum*
seemes to doe. Therefore as *Hesperus* shee presents yo^w
with *bonum utile*, because it is holsomest in the
morninge, and as *Vesperus* with *bonum delectabile* because [it 35
is pleasantest in the evening]. And because industrious
men rise and indure with the sun about their Civill
businesse, this star calls them up a litle before, and
remembers them agayne after the sun for her businesse.
For Certainly that verse   40
    Venit Hesperus Ite capellae.
spake to lovers in the person of goates.

14 names. Yt *ed.*: names; yt *Ash 826* 15 functions, (*functionum,*) *R*: functions *Ash 826*
22–3 men, . . . love, *ed.*: men (. . . loue) *Ash 826* 24 blew and hamered her,
(*conflavit et malleavit,*) *R*: bloud and hamered her *Ash 826* 27 Beleive *ed.*: beleiue
Ash 826 this (*hanc*) *R*: that *Ash 826* they include (*includant*) *R*: they .2. include *Ash*
826 29 fortunes; *ed.*: fortunes, *Ash 826* 30–1 it is reason[able that it should]
receave (*rationi consentaneum videtur, ut . . . recipiat*) *R*: it is reason it receaue *Ash 826*
35–6 [it is pleasantest in the evening] *vespertino tempore maxime delectat R*: it is then
pleasantest *Ash 826* 36–42 And because . . . of goates] *omit R: see note* 38 businesse,
ed.: businesse *Ash 826* 40 For *ed.*: for *Ash 826*

PROBLEM XII

Why is there more variety of Greene, then of other Collours?

Is it because it is the figure of youth, wherein
Nature would provide as many Greenes as youth hath
Affections? And soe present a Sea-greene, for profuse
wasters in Voyages: A Grass-Greene for suddaine newe
men
Ennobled from Grasiers. And a Goose-greene for such   5
Polititians, as pretend to preserve the Capitoll. Or ells
prophetically foreseing an Age wherein they shall All
hunte: And for such as misdemeane themselves a
Willowe Greene: For, Magistrats must aswell have *Fasces*
borne
before them, to Chastise the small offences as *Secures*   10
to Cutt off the Great.

Copy-text TCD.

(Problem IV. *1633a*)   1 Is it] It is *TCC*, *S 962*, *S*, *1633+*   2 would] could
O'F, Dob, O 2   Greenes] *Greene 1633+*   3 Affections? And *ed.*: Affections, and
TCD   7 shall All *O 2*, *S*, *1633+*: shall *TC*, *S 962*: should All *O'F, Dob*   9–11
For ... the Great] *O'F, Dob read*: Or because shee would bee able to shewe and furnish
Greene Merchants, Greene Lawyers, Greene Captaynes, Greene Privy Counsellors, and
Greene Prelats properly.   9 *Fasces O 2*, *S*, *1633+*: Maces *TC*, *S 962*; *see note*

PROBLEM XII. *Ash 826 text corrected from R*

Why is there more variety of greene then any other colour?

THAT there is more of that colour then any is reasonable. Because consisting of two parts white and one halfe parte blacke, and the two lower grosser Elements, [than which the other two,] though probably greater, when they are condensed and colourable are   5
not so great. And beside all proper greene, how much greene is translatitiously applyed to almost every thinge? *Ronsard* and all his Countrymen since are inraged with greene eyes; wee when wee wish them red, prayse verdure in Lips, so in sauces and meats, therefore   10
wee tast greene. And *.A. Gellius* could heare greene for he sayes the Letter .H. was added to make *viridem sonum*. And *Petrarch* sayth of his last age, that he was *giunto al verde*, whether his Metaphor rose from the grave, or the snuffe of a Candle, Lett his angry Commentators agree.   15
That therfore of which there is most and is most communicable and most applyable to diverse thinges must
bee
most diverse and various. Or else nature to bee at once liberall and thrifty, would thus delight us with variety of objects and yet still afford us the cherishing and   20
refocillation of that colour. Except since greene was to figure youth, Nature would provide as many greenes as youth hath affections. And so present a sea greene for profuse wasters in voyages. A grasse greene for sodaine

---

1 any *ed.*: any it *Ash 826*   4 Elements, *ed.*: Elements *Ash 826*   [than which the other two,] *quibus reliqua duo R*: omit *Ash 826*; *see note*   though (*quamvis*) *R*: thought *Ash 826*   5 greater, *ed.*: greater; *Ash 826*   7 translatitiously *ed.*: translatiously *Ash 826*; *see note*   8 Ronsard (*Ronsardus*) *R*: Konsard *Ash 826*   9 eyes; *ed.*: eyes, *Ash 826*   red, *ed.*: red; *Ash 826*   12 H *R*: G *Ash 826*; *see note*   13–14 *giunto al verde, ed.*: gionto al verde *Ash 826*; *see note*   15 agree. *ed.*: agree, *Ash 826*   18 various. *ed.*: Or various or *Ash 826*

new men innobled from grasiers. And a goose greene for   25
Polititians, which pretend to preserve the Capitoll Et.c.
Or else profetically foreseeinge an age when all men should
hunt, Shee would be able to furnish greene merchants,
greene Lawery, greene Captaynes, greene privy Counsellers,
and greene Prelates properly.   30

PROBLEM XIII

Why doth the Poxe so much affect to undermine the nose?

Paracelsus perchance sayth true, that every disease
hath his exaltation in some certayne part, but why this in
the nose? Is there so much mercy in this disease that it
provides that one should not smell his owne stinke? Or
hath it but the common fortune that beeing begot and
                                                      bredd   5
in the obscurest and secretest corner, because therefore
his Serpentine crawlings, and Insinuations bee not
suspected nor seene, hee comes sooner to great place, and
                                                   is abler
to destroy the worthyest Member then a disease better
borne. Perchance as mise defeat Elephants by gnawing   10
theyr Proboscis, which is theyr nose, this wretched
Indian Vermine practises to doe the same upon us. Or as

27 Or *ed.*: or *Ash 826*   28 be *ed.*: to *Ash 826*

This Problem is omitted in 1633a and b.

(Problem XI. *1652*)   1 sayth] sayes *TC, S 962*   2 certayne part] part *O'F*
(*b.c.*), *Ash 826*: part Certaine *S, 1652*: certaine place *TC, S 962*   3 mercy] more *TC,*
S 962   it *Σ*: *omit O'F*   4 that] so ... *Ash 826*   his] their *TC, S 962*: that *S*   5
fortune] *omit TC, S 962*   6 the] *omit O 2, 1652*   obscurest and *Σ*: *omit O'F*: abstrusest
and *O 2*   corner *Ash 826, TC, S 962*: loco (place) *R*: corners *O'F, Dob, O 2, S*: places *1652*
7 crawlings, and Insinuations *Ash 826, TC*: crawlinge, ... *S 962*: *itinera, et ... insinuationes*
(journeys, and ... windings) *R*: crawling, and Insinuation *O'F, Dob, O 2, S, 1652*   bee not
Ash 826, TC, S 962: should not bee *O'F, Dob, O 2, S, 1652*   8 sooner to *Ash 826, TC,*
S 962: ... into *O'F, Dob, O 2, S*: soonest into *1652*   abler] ablest *O 2*: able *S*: more able
1652   9 worthyest Member] best ... *Ash 826*: ... members *TC, S 962,* ... *membra*
(members) *R*   12 practises] practizeth *O 2, S, 1652*   upon] on *Ash 826, O 2*   as]
else *Ash 826*: *potius* (rather) *R*

the Ancient furious custome and connivence of some

Lawes

(that one might cutt off theyr noses whome hee
deprehended in Adultery) was but a type of this, and now

thatt   15

more charitable Lawes have taken away all revenge from
particular hands, this common Magistrate and executioner
is come to doe the same office invisibly. Or by
withdrawing this conspicuous part the nose, it warnes from
adventuring on that coast (for it is as good a marke to   20
take in a flagg, as to hang out one.) Possibly heate,
which is more potent and active then cold, thought her
selfe injurd, and the harmony of the world out of tune,
when cold was able to shewe the high wayes with noses in
Muscovy except shee found the meanes to doe the same in   25
other countryes. But because, by consent of all there
is an Analogy and proportion, and Affection betweene
the nose, and that part where this disease is first
contracted, (And therefore *Heliogabalus* chose not his
Minions in the Bath but by the nose, And *Albertus* had a   30
knavish meaning when hee preferrd great noses, and the
Licentious Poet was *Naso Poeta*) I thinke this reason is
neerest truth, That the Nose is most compassionate with
that part. Except this bee neerer, That it is reasonable
that this disease should in particular men affect the   35

13 furious Σ: and . . . *O'F*: *omit O 2*   connivence] conniuencye *O 2, S, 1652*   14 theyr
noses *Ash 826, TC, S 962*: . . . nose *O'F, Dob, S,1652*: his nose *O 2*: *nasum illis* (nose from
them) *R*   14–15 hee deprehended] they . . . *Ash 826, deprehendebant* (they . . .) *R*
15 now thatt *Ash 826, TC, S 962*: thatt now *O'F, Dob, O 2, S, 1652*   16 have]
having *S, 1652*   17 and executioner Σı omit *O'F*   19 part] . . . of *Ash
826, S* warnes] . . . others *Ash 826*: *alij admoneantur* (others are warned) *R*: . . . us *1652*
20 adventuring] all . . . *1652*   on] vpon *TC, S 962, O 2, S, 1652*   that] the *Ash 826,
O 2*   21 in] *omit Ash 826*   out one] out *Ash 826*: one out *1652*   22 and
active] *omit Ash 826*   24 shewe] straw *Ash 826*   high wayes with noses *Ash 826, TC,
S 962*: *omnes vias nasis* (all ways with noses) *R*: high way to noses *O'F, Dob, O 2, S, 1652*
25 *Muscovy*] *Muscovia 1652*   the meanes] some . . . *Ash 826*: meanes *Dob*   26 But]
Or *1652*   consent *Ash 826, TC, S 962*: the . . . *O'F, Dob, O 2, S, 1652*   27 is] in *TCD,
S 962*   and proportion] an . . . *Ash 826*: proportion *S, 1652*   30 Minions]
Minion *TC, S 962*   a] some *Ash 826*   31 when hee preferrd] in preferring
Ash 826, praeferendo (in preferring) *R*   32 was Σ: was called *O'F*   33 most]
more *Dob, S*,   34 that] this *S, 1652*   part. *ed.*: part, *O'F*   neerer, *ed.*: neerer *O'F*
35 should in particular men *Ash 826*: should in particular *TC, S 962*: in particular men should
O'F, Dob, O 2: in particular should *S, 1652*

most eminent and conspicuous part, which amongst men in generall doth affect to take hold of the most eminent and conspicuous men.

Why are new Officers least oppressing?

MUST the old Proverbe that Old doggs bite sorest bee true in all kind of doggs? Mee thinkes the fresh memory they have of the monny they parted with for the place should hasten them for the reimbursing. And perchance they doe but seeme easyer to theyr Suitors, who, as all other 5 Patients, doe account all change of payne ease. But if it bee so, it is eyther because the suddayne sence and contentment of the honour of the place, retards and remitts the rage of theyr profits, and so, having stayed theyr stomacks, they can forbeare the second course a while, 10 Or having overcome the steepest part of the hill and clamberd above competitions and oppositions, they dare loyter and take breath. Perchance beeing come from places where they tasted no gayne, a little seemes much to them at first (for it is long before a Christian conscience 15 overtakes, or strayes into an Officers heart). It may bee that out of the generall disease of all men not to love the Memory of a predecessor, they seeke to disgrace them

36 conspicuous *Ash 826, TC, S 962, conspicuam* (conspicuous) *R*: perspicuous *O'F, Dob, O 2, S, 1652*   amongst men *TC, S 962*: among men *Ash 826, inter homines* (among men) *R*: in men *O'F, Dob, O 2*: omit *S, 1652*   37–8 and conspicuous] and most ... *TCC, S 962*: Conspicuous *S*: and perspicuous *O 2*

This Problem is omitted in R.

(Problem X. *1633a*)   3 they have *Ash 826, TC, S 962, S, 1633+*: omit *O'F, Dob*: that ... *O 2*   the monny] mony *Ash 826*   5 theyr] the *Ash 826*   6 ease] easie *TC, S 962, O 2, S, 1633+*   7 it is eyther] eyther it is *Ash 826*: ytt is *O 2*   9 profits] profitt *Ash 826*   11 part] and thornyest place *Ash 826*   12 oppositions] ..., and attendances *Ash 826*   14 gayne] gaynes *Ash 826*   to them] omit *Ash 826, O 2*   16 overtakes, or strayes] ouertake and stray *Ash 826*: ... straines *S*   heart] conscyence *Ash 826*   17 the] a *TC, S 962*   18 a] omit *TC, S 962*

by such easynesse, and so make good first Impressions, that so having drawne much water to theyr myll they may   20 after grind at ease. For if from the rules of good horsemanshipp they thought it wholsomest to jett out in a moderate pace, they should also take up towards theyr Journyes end, not mend theyr pace continually, and gallop
                                                                        to
theyr Inne dore the grave. Except perchance theyr   25 conscience at that time so touch them, that they thinke it a
                                                                        an
Injury and damage both to him that must sell, and to him that must buy the office after theyr death, and a kind of dilapidation, if they, by continewing honest, should discredit the place and bring it to a lower rent and   30 undervalew.

PROBLEM XV

Why Puritans make long Sermons?

IT needes not for perspicuousnesse, For God knowes they are playne enough. Nor doe all of them use the
                                                                        long
Sembriefe Accent, some of them have Crotchets enough.

---

19 so] *omit* TC, S 962, S, 1633+   21 after] afterwards *Ash 826, 1633+* from] in *Ash 826*
22 wholsomest] wholsome TC, S 962, S, 1633+: fittest O 2   jett] sett *Ash 826, O 2*
23 theyr] the *Ash 826*   24 not mend ... and gallop TC, S 962, 1633+: ... to Gallop
S: and not continue nor mend their pace, nor gallop *Ash 826*: and mend ... O'F, Dob, O 2
24–5 to theyr Inne dore Dob, TC, S 962: towards ... O'F, O 2: to the ... *Ash 826*: ... *Inns
Dore S, 1633+*   25–6 theyr conscience at that time] ... of that time Dob: at that
tyme their Conscyence *Ash 826*   27 to him ... to him Σ: to them ... O'F: ... him
Ash 826   30 discredit the place and bring it to] bring the place to O'F (b.c.)   rent and]
... or TC, S 962, 1633+

This Problem occurs in A 25; it is omitted in R.

(Problem II. *1633a*)   Title: *Why Dob*, TC, S 962, O 2, S, *1633+*: Why doe O'F
which inserts doe, *Ash 826, A 25   long*] longest *A 25*, TC, S 962   1 knowes] knoweth
Ash 826   2–3 the long Sembriefe Accent TC, S 962: ... semibreife time *Ash 826,
A 25*: long Semibreefe Accents O'F, S: longe Sem-breife Accents Dob, O 2: *Sembriefe-Accents
1633+; see note*   3 some *Ash 826, A 25*, TC, S 962: for ... O'F, Dob, O 2, S, *1633+*

It may bee they pretend not to rise like glorious Tapers
or Torches, but like long thinne wretched and sick watch   5
candles, which languish and are in a dimme consumption
from the first Minute, yet spend more tyme in theyr
glimmeringe, yea in theyr snuff and stinke, then others in
theyr more profitable glory. I have thought sometimes
that out of conscience they allow large measure to course   10
ware, And sometimes that usurping in that place a liberty
to speake freely of Kings and all, they think themselves
Kings then and would raigne as long as they could.
But now I thinke they doe it out of a Zealous Imagination
that it is theyr duty to preache on till theyr Auditory   15
wake agayne.

PROBLEM XVI

Why are Statesmen most Incredible?

ARE they all wise enough to follow theyr excellent
Patterne *Tiberius*, who brought the Senate to bee diligent
and industrious to beleeve him, were it never so opposite
and diametricall, that it destroyd theyr very ends, to

4 pretend *Ash 826, A 25, TC, S 962*: intend *O'F, Dob, O 2, S, 1633+*   5 or *Ash 826,*
A 25, TCC, S 962: and *O'F, Dob, TCD, O 2, S, 1633+*   long *Σ: omit O'F, Dob, 1633+*
and] *omit 1633+*   watch] watchinge *S, 1633+*: wax *O 2*   6 languish and *Σ: omit*
O'F   dimme] divine *TC, S 962, 1633+*   7–8 yet ... glimmeringe *Ash 826, A 25*:
omit *Σ; see note*   8 snuff *Σ*: very ... *O'F, Dob*   stinke, then others in *A 25*: ... doe
in *Ash 826*: thinke then the ... *TC, S 962*: stinke when others are in *O'F, Dob, O 2, S,*
1633+   10 large] longe *Ash 826, S, 1633+*   11 sometimes] sometime *TC,*
S 962   in that place a liberty] ... place, libertie *A 25*: a liberty in that place *Ash 826*
12–13 Kings and all, they thinke themselves Kings then and would *Ash 826, A 25, TC,*
S 962: Kings, they would *O'F, Dob, O 2, S, 1633+*   14 thinke] ... that *TC, S 962*   a
Zealous Imagination] Religion and ... *Ash 826, A 25*: zelouse ... *S 962*   15–16 that
... wake *Σ*: that, hauing brought theyr Auditory a sleepe, it is theyr duty to preache on till
they wake *O'F*   16 agayne] *omit 1633+*

This Problem is omitted in R, O 2, 1633a and b.

(Problem XVII. *1652*)   Title: *Incredible*] Incredulous *O'F (b.c.), TC, S 962, S,*
1652; see note   1 all *Σ: omit O'F, Dob*   3 to beleeve] not ... *Ash 826*   were it
never] ... ever *TC, S 962*: And is it *Ash 826*   4 and *Σ*: or *O'F, 1652*   that *Σ*: as
... *O'F*   destroyd] destroyes *Ash 826*   theyr *Σ, O'F (b.c.)*: his *O'F; see note*

bee beleeved? As *Asinius Gallus* had almost deceaved this   5
man by beleeving him, And the Mayour and Aldermen of
London Richard the Third. Or are the businesses
about which these men are conversant so conjecturall,
and so subject to unsuspected Interventions, that
they are therefore forcd to speake oraculously, multiformly,   10
whisperingly, generally (and thereby escapingly) in
the language of Almanack makers, for weather? Or are
                                                              those
(as they call them) *Arcana Imperii*, as, by whome the Prince
provokes his lust, and by whome hee vents it, Of what
                                                              cloth
his socks are, and such, so deepe and so unreveald, as any   15
error in them is inexcusable? If these were the reasons,
they would not onely serve for State businesse, But why
will they tell true what a clocke it is and what weather,
but abstayne from truth of it, if it disconduce to theyr
ends, as witches which will not name Jesus, though it   20
bee in a curse? Eyther they knowe little out of theyr owne
elements, or a custome in one matter begets a habit in
all; or, the lower sort Imitate the Lords, they theyr
Princes, these theyr Prince; Or else they beleeve one
another, And so never heare truth. Or they abstayne from   25
the little channell of truth, least at last they should
find the fountayne it selfe, God.

---

5 deceaved] destroyd *O'F* (*b.c.*)1 defeated *Ash 826*   5-6 this man by] his man *Ash 826*
6 Mayour] Mayor *TC*: Maior *Dob, Ash 826, S 962, S*: Major *1652*   7 Richard] in . . .
S, 1652   the businesses] businesses *Dob, S, 1652*: buisines *TC, S 962*   8
about which *Σ*: whereabout *O'F*   9 and] omit *TC, S 962, S, 1652*   10 they are
therefore *Σ*: therefore they are *O'F*   oraculously] Graculously *TC, S 962*
multiformly *Σ*: multiformily *O'F*: omit *S 962, 1652*   11 and thereby] therby *Ash 826*:
and therefore *1652*   escapingly] escapably *Ash 826*   12 weather *Σ*: weathers *O'F*
14 Of] and *Ash 826*   15 such, *Σ*: . . . like, *O'F*   16 inexcusable] excusable *Ash
826*   17 not] omit *Ash 826*   State businesse] . . . businesses *Dob, Ash 826*: estate . . .
TC, S 962: estate of busynes *S*   18 tell] not . . . *1652*   19 truth of it, if it] truth
though it *Ash 826*   disconduce] . . . not *TC*: Conduce not *S, 1652*   21 out of *Σ*:
but in *O'F*   22 elements] Element *Ash 826*   a habit] an . . . *1652*   23 the
Lords] lords *S 962, 1652*   24 these theyr Prince *Σ*: omit *O'F*   27 it selfe *Σ*:
omit *O'F*

PROBLEM XVII

*Why doth Johannes Salisburiensis writing de Nugis
Curialium handle the Providence and
Omnipotency of God?*

THOUGH the Stoicks charge theyr Adversaryes who putt
free will, and make us all wicked, (since nothing, naturally,
desyres that which is ill,) to make our life a madness, And
They charge the Stoicks who putting providence and
necessity, doe yet admitt Lawes and rewards, paynes and   5
endevours, that they make all but a jest and a toye: yet I
thinke this Churchman did not so, because hee thought hee
knewe how both these might consist together. Because
beeing of the family of *Thomas of Becket* (who was a greate
Courtier), As hee put hunting and gaming and
                                                wantonnesse   10
for the toyes of a Lay-Courtier: hee ment such meditations
as those for the toyes of Clergy Courtiers, for the
worthyest Mistery may bee annihilated, as the heavyest
                                                  mettall
may bee beate so thinne that you may blowe it away. But
those times admitted no Jesting agaynst the church, And   15
for the other Courtiers: hee could not taxe nor accuse
them, that in theyr sportfull life they overreached to
those too high contemplations, for they never thinke on
them. Nor could hee reproche them by this, that all which
they doe are toyes, for they are wicked seriously. Eyther   20

This Problem is omitted in R, TC, O 2, S, 1633+.

    Title: *Salisburiensis Dob, S 962*: Salisburiens: *Ash 826*: Sarisburiensis *O'F*   1 putt]
... downe *O'F* (*b.c.*): ... off *S 962* (*b.c.*)   3 desyres *Σ*: denyes *O'F*   make] ... all
Ash 826   4 charge] change *Ash 826*   putting] ... downe and *O'F* (*b.c.*)   5
paynes] and ... *Ash 826*   6 endevours, *ed.*: endevours) *O'F*: indeavour *Ash 826*
8 these *Σ*: those *O'F*   together. *ed.*: together, *O'F*   9 *of Becket*] Beckett *Dob, S 962*
11 for] of *Ash 826*   12 as] of *O'F* (*b.c.*)   Courtiers, *ed.*: Courtiers *O'F*   14
that] *omit Ash 826*   18 too *Σ*: *omit O'F*   19 reproche them] reproach *Dob, S 962*
all *Σ*: all things *O'F*   20 wicked seriously *Ash 826*: seriously wicked *O'F*: wickedly
serious *Dob, S 962*

therefore hee ment to insinuate and convey his doctrine
by disguising it amongst toyes, of which (in things
inclineable to good) hee thought them onely capable. Or
                                                    else
hee put a tricke of logike, which is reason, (and they are
men of passion) upon them, That by drawing them into a   25
doubting and disputing of some particular Attributes of
God, they might, before they were aware, implicitely
confesse that there was one.

PROBLEM XVIII

Why doe women delight soe much in feathers?

THEY thinke that feathers imitate wings, and soe
shewe their restlesness, and instability. As they are in
matter, soe would they also bee in name: like
Embroiderers, Painters, and such Artificers of curious
                                                    vanities,
which *Varro* and the vulgar Edition call *Plumarios*. Or   5
els they love Feathers, upon the same reason which
moves them to love the unworthiest men, which is that
they may bee thereby excuseable in their inconstancy
and often chaunge.

21 therefore] then *Ash 826*   his] this *Ash 826*   22 amongst] among *Dob:* with *Ash 826*

Copy-text TCD.

The Problem is omitted in O 2 and 1633a and b.

(Problem XIII. *1652*).   Title: *soe*] omit *1652*   1 and] omit *TCC*   2
instability. As *ed.*: instability, as *TCD*   3 would they also bee] . . . be alsoe *S*: they
would be *1652*   5 *Varro . . . Plumarios ed.*: the vulgar Edition call Pluminarios *TC*,
S 962: the vulgar Edytion call Pluminaries *S*: the vulgar call *Pluminaries 1652*; *see note*   6
love] have *1652*   7 to love the] the more *S*   9 chaunge] changing *1652*

PROBLEM XVIII *text in O'F, Dob, Ash 826, and R*

Why doe Woemen delight so much in Feathers?

To say *Similis Simili* is too round, and it is obvious
to every one. And it is besides the scope of my reason in
my Problemes, which extends onely *ad verisimile*, not to an
expresse and undenyable truth, as this reason is. It must
bee confest that some men also love feathers, but they   5
are courtiers or souldiers, men (though perfectly
contrary in theyr courses, yet) concurring in a desire of
pursuing woemen, and assimilating themselves unto them,
Nor is there any thing so proper to woemen which is not
sometimes intruded upon by them, For Princes usurpe upon   10
falshood, Officers upon Scraping, the Clergy upon
Brawlings, These *de jure* belong to woemen, who beeing
communicable creatures, and having no good, must
                                              communicate
theyr ill. Eyther they thinke that feathers imitate
wings, and so shewe theyr restlesnesse and Instability   15
Or by wearing or bearing feathers they would have a
title to a roome in that verse, where *Petrarch* reckons
up to *Boccace* what things have bannished Vertue.
            La Gola il sonno e l'otiose piume.
For *Petrarch* is no where so superfluous to repeate agayne   20
that which hee had already sayd in this word *sonno*. Nor
could hee have calld the featherbedds Idle bedds, For
idle Bedds have not donne so much agaynst vertue as
they, (for *Gregory the 13.* grewe learned in his bedd).

Title: delight so much Dob, Ash 826: so much delight *O'F*   1 it is] too *O'F (b.c.)*: . . .
to *Ash 826*   2–3 reason . . . extends] . . . extend *Dob*: Reasons . . . extend *Ash 826*,
rationum . . . extendunt (reasons . . . extend) *R*   3–4 an expresse and *Ash 826*: expresse
and *Dob*: expresse an *O'F*   6 are] are eyther *Ash 826, sunt vel . . . vel* (are either . . .)
R   though] thought *Ash 826*   15 so *Dob, Ash 826*: omit *O'F*   16 or bearing
Dob, Ash 826: of *O'F*   17 a] that *O'F (b.c.)*   19 *sonno e ed.: sonno et O'F, Ash 826*:
somno, & R: somno et Dob   l'otiose] l'ociose R   piume] piums Ash 826   21 this] his *Dob,
Ash 826   sonno]* Somno *Dob, R*   24 *the 13. Ash 826*: 13 *R*: the 3d *O'F*: 3. *Dob; see note*

Therefore by feathers hee expresseth some inseperable   25
companion of Woemen, or woemen them selves. Perchance
                                                          as
they are, in matter, they would bee also, in name, like
Embroyderers, Paynters, and such Artificers of
curious Vanityes, which *Varro* and the vulgar edition call
Plumarios (for I dare not thinke them of so good   30
conscience and humility that they confesse that they
                                                   deserve
to bee *Emplumadas* the punishment which the Spanish
                                                   Justice
inflicts upon looser woemen). Or else they love
feathers upon the same reason which makes them to love
                                                   the
unworthyest men, which is, that they may bee thereby   35
excusable in theyr Inconstancy and often change. Or by
this they have utterly excluded themselves from entring
into any definition of man. For as before they found
Aristotles definition *Animal rationale* peremptory
agaynst them: So now they have shutt up that of *Plato* or   40
Speusippus, Animal bipes implume.

PROBLEM XIX

Why did the Devill reserve Jesuits for these latter times?

DID hee knowe our Age would denye the Devills
possessions, and therefore provided by these to possesse
                                                   men

---

27 bee also] also bee *Ash 826*   29–30 call *Plumarios*] calls plumaries *Ash 826*   31 confesse
that *Dob, Ash 826*: confesse *O'F*   32 *Emplumadas R: Enplamadas Ash 826*: *Emplumados*
O'F: Emplumades Dob; see note   34 makes] moues *Dob*   to love *Dob, Ash 826*: loue
O'F   39 peremptory *Dob*: peremptry *O'F*: to bee peremptory *Ash 826*   41 *Speusippus*
(Speusippi) R: Pseusippus O'F, Dob: Leucippus Ash 826; see note

This Problem is omitted in TC, O 2, and S.

   (Problem III. *1633a*)   Title: *for*] to *Ash 826*: till *1633+*   latter Σ: later *O'F*   times]
dayes 1633+   I knowe] . . . that *Dob, 1633+*   2 possessions] possessings
Ash 826: possessing *1633+*   provided Σ: proceede *O'F*

and Kingdomes? Or, to end the disputation of Schoolemen,
why the Devill could not make Lyce in Egipt, and
                                                              whether
those things which hee presented there might bee true,   5
hath hee sent us a true and reall plague worse then those
Ten? Or in ostentation of the greatnesse of his Kingdome
(which even disunion cannot shake) doth hee send these
which disagree with all the rest? Or knowing that our
                                                              times
should discover the Indyes, and abolish theyr Idolatry,   10
doth hee send these to give them another for it? Or
peradventure they have bin in the Romane church this
                                                              1000
yeares though wee have called them by other names.

5 which] omit S 962, 1633+   6 those Σ: all ... O'F   8 disunion] diuision
1633+   these] them Ash 826: vs ... 1633+   12 this 1000] these thousand Dob,
1633+

DUBIA

A Defence of Womens Inconstancy

THAT *Women are inconstant*, I with any man confes, But
that *Inconstancie* is a bad Qualitye I against any man will
maintayne; for every thinge, as it is one better then
another, soe is yt fuller of Chaunge. The Heavens
themselves
Continually turne, the Starrs move, the Moone changeth,   5
fyer whirleth, Ayre flyeth, water ebbs, and flowes, the
Face of the earth altereth her lookes, tyme stayes not,
the colour, that hath most light will take most dyes;
Soe in Men they that have the most reasonn are the most
alterable in there dessignes, and the darkest and most   10
Ignorant do seldomest change. Therfore Women
changing more
then menn have alsoe more reason, they cannot be
Immutable
like stockes, like stones, like the earths dull Center.
Gould that lyeth still rusteth, water Corupteth, and Ayre
that moveth not poysoneth. Then why should that which is   15
the perfectyon of other things be Imputed to women as

Copy-text S.

*S is the only manuscript to contain the full text; extracts, ll. 5–7, 3–4, 8–12, 14–17, 72–6,
77–83, 89–91, 87–8 are found in Pud. The full text is found in 1633+. Readings are recorded
from Pud and 1633+.*

(Paradox I. *1633a*)   1 inconstant *1633+*: *vnconstant S*   3 for] And *Pud*
4 is yt *1633+*, *Pud*: yt is *S*   of *1633+*, *Pud*: *omit S*   6 flyeth] shifteth *Pud*   7
her] his *Pud*   8 hath] is *1633+*   take *1633+*, *Pud*: ... the *S*   9 Soe] set
1633+ (b.c.)   the ... the] *omit Pud*   10 alterable] intolerable *1633a*: inalterable
1633b, 1652   10–11 and most Ignorant] or most ... *1633+*: or ignorantest *Pud*
11 seldomest] most seldomly *Pud*   Women *1633+*, *Pud*: Womens *S*   14 lyeth]
lyes *Pud*   water Corupteth] standing water corrupts *Pud*   and] *omit 1633+*

greatest Imperfectyon? Because thereby they deceive men?
Are not your witts pleased with those Jeasts which cozen
your Expectatyonn? You can call it pleasure to be beguyled
in Tryfles, and in the most excellent Toye in the world   20
you call it Treacherie. I would you had your Mistresses
soe Constant that they wold never Change, noe not soe much
As their *Smocks*, then should you see what a sluttish virtue
Constancy were. *Inconstancy* is A most Commendable and
cleanly qualitie; and *Women* in this quality are farr more   25
absolute then the *Heavens*, then the *Starrs*, then *Moone*, or any
thing beneath it, for longe observation hath pickt certainty
out of this *Mutability*. The learned are soe well
acquainted with the *Starrs* Signes and *Plannets*, that they
                                                          make
them but *Characters* to read the meaning of the heaven in   30
his owne forhead. Everie symple fellowe can bespeake the
Change of the Moone a great while before hand. But I wold
fayne have the learnedst man soe skilfull as to tell when
the symplest *woman* meaneth to *varie*. Learninge affords
                                                           no
rules to knowe, much lesse knowledge to rule the minde of   35
A Woman. For as *Philosophie* teacheth us, that light things
doe alwais tend upwards, and heavy things declyne
                                                    downwards,
Experience teacheth us otherwise, That the disposition of
a Light *Woman* is to fall downe; the Nature of *Woamen*
                                                         being
contrary to all art and Nature. Women are like Flyes
                                                    which 40
feed Amongst us at our Table, or Fleas suckinge our verie
blood, who leave not our most retyred places free from
their Familiaritie. Yet for all their fellowship will they
never be tamed, nor Commanded by us. *Women* are like the
                                                          Sunn

17 greatest] their ... *Pud*   19 beguyled] beguild *1633a*   20 Tryfles] troubles
1633+   23 a] *omit 1633+*   24 were *ed.*: weare *S*   26 then *Moone*]
Moone *1633+*   28 this] their *1633+*   37 downwards] downeward *1633+*
40 and *1633+*: or *S*   41 Amongst] among *1633+*   44 nor *1633+*: or *S*

which is vyolently carryed one way, yet hath a proper   45
Course Contrary. Soe though they (by the Mastery of
                                            some
over-ruleinge Churlish husbands) are forced to his Bias,
yet have they a motyon of their owne, which their
                                            Husbands
never knowe of. It is the nature of Nice and fastydious
myndes to know things only to be weary of them. Women
                                            by   50
their sly-changablenes, and pleasing doublenes, prevent
even the Mislike of those, for they can never be soe well
knowne, but that their is still more unknowne. Every
                                            Woman
is *A Science*, for he that plodds upon a woman all his life
longe shall at length fynd him selfe short of the knowledge   55
of her. They are borne to take downe the pryde of *witt*,
                                            and
Ambytion of wisdome makinge fooles wise in the
                                            Adventuringe
to wynn them, wise men fooles with conceipt of looseing
their labour, wittie men starke madd beinge Confownded
with their uncertaintyes. *Philosophers* wright against   60
them for spyght, not desert, that havinge attayned to
some knowledge in all other things, in them only, Thay
know *nothing but are merely Ignorant*. Active and
experienced men rayle against them because they love in
their live-lesse and decrepite Age, when all goodnes leaves
                                            them.   65
These Envyous Lybellers Ballad against them because
having nothinge in them selves able to deserve their love
they maliciously discommend all they cannot obtayne;
thinking to make men beleve they Know much because
                                            they
are able to dispraise Much, and rage against *Inconstancy*   70
when they were never Admytted into soe much favor as to

be forsakenn. In myne opynion such men are happie that
women are *Inconstant* for soe they may chance to be
　　　　　　　　　　　　　　　　　　beloved
of some Excellent Woman (when it comes to their turne)
out of their Inconstancy, and Mutability, though not out　　75
of their owne desert. And what reason is their to clogg
any woman with one Mann be hee never soe singular?
　　　　　　　　　　　　　　　　Women
had rather (and it is far better, and more *Judiciall*) to
Injoy all the virtues in severall men, then but some of
them in one, for otherwise they loose their tast like　　80
divers sorts of Meat minced together in one dish. And
to have all Excelencyes in one Man (if it were possible)
is Confusyon, not diversitie. Now who can deny but such
as are obstinately bent to undervalewe their worth are
those that have not Sowle enough to Comprehend their　　85
Excellencye, Women beinge the most excellent Creatures,
　　　　　　　　　　　　　　　　　　　in
that Man is able to subject all things ells, and to growe
wise in every thinge, but still persists a Foole in *Woman*.
The greatest Scholler if he once take a wife is fownd soe
unlearned, that he must begin his hornbooke, and all is by　　90
Inconstancie. *To Conclude* therefore this name of
Inconstancie which hath bene soe much poysoned with
　　　　　　　　　　　　　　　Slanders ought
to be Chaunged into *variety*, For the which the world is
　　　　　　　　　　　　　　　　　　soe
delightfull, And a woman for that the most delightfull
thinge in the World.　　　　　　　　　　　　　　　95

72 such men are happie] yt is good for some men *Pud*　　73 are] bee so *Pud*　they may]
the may *Pud*: may they *1633+*　　74 Woman] Women *1633a and b*　　75 their]
hi$r *Pud*　　79 but some] all *Pud*　　80 for] *omit Pud*　they] the *Pud*　tast *1633+*,
Pud: tasts *S*　　81 Meat *1633+*, *Pud*: Meats *S*　　82 if] though *Pud*　　83 is
Confusyon, not diversitie *Pud*: is as Regular is Confusyon, not diversitie *S*: is *Confusion* and
Diuersity 1633+; *see note*　　86 excellent] excellentest *1633a and b*　　87 Man is]
Raeson beeing *Pud*　　88 persists] *omit Pud*　*Woman*] themm *Pud*　　90 is]
omit Pud　　92 bene soe much] so much beene *1633+*　　93 *variety 1633+*:
varieties S　　94 that the *1633+*: that she is the *S*　　95 the] this *1633+*

PARADOX XII

That Virginity is a Vertue

I CALL not that *Virginity a vertue*, which resideth
onely in the *Bodies integrity*; much lesse if it be with a
purpose of perpetuall keeping it: for then it is a most
inhumane vice—But I call that *Virginity a vertue* which
is willing and desirous to yeeld it selfe upon honest and   5
lawfull terms, when just reason requireth; and untill then,
is kept with a modest chastity of Body and Mind. Some
perchance will say that *Virginity* is in us by *Nature*, and
therefore no *vertue*. True, as it is in us by *Nature*, it is
neither a *Vertue* nor *Vice*, and is onely in the body: (as in   10
Infants, Children, and such as are incapable of parting
from it) But that *Virginity* which is in Man or Woman of
perfect age, is not in them by *Nature*: *Nature* is the
greatest enemy to it, and with most subtile allurements
seeks the over-throw of it, continually beating against   15
it with her *Engines*, and giving such forcible assaults
to it, that it is a strong and more then ordinary *vertue*
to hold out till marriage. *Ethick* Philosophy saith, *That
no Vertue is corrupted, or is taken away by that which is
good*: Hereupon some may say, that *Virginity* is therfore no   20
vertue, being taken away by marriage. *Virginity* is no
otherwise taken away by marriage, then is the light of the
                                                        starres
by a greater light (the light of the Sun): or as a lesse
Title is taken away by a greater: (an Esquire by being
created an Earle) yet *Virginity* is a *vertue*, and hath her   25
Throne in the middle: The extreams are, in *Excesse*, to
violate it before marriage; in *Defect*, not to marry. In ripe

This Paradox is found only in 1652.

(Paradox XII. 1652)   12 or *ed.*: or or *1652*   23 Sun): *ed.*: Sun:) *1652*
26 *Excesse, ed.*: *Excesse*; *1652*   27 *Defect ed.*: defect *1652*

years as soon as reason perswades and opportunity admits,
These extreams are equally removed from the mean: The
excesse proceeds from *Lust,* the defect from *Peevishnesse,*   30
Pride and *Stupidity.* There is an old Proverb, That, *they that
dy maids, must lead Apes in Hell.* An Ape is a ridiculous and
an unprofitable Beast, whose flesh is not good for meat, nor
its back for burden, nor is it commodious to keep an house:
and perchance for the unprofitablenesse of this Beast did   35
this proverb come up: For surely nothing is more
                                                      unprofitable
in the Commonwealth of *Nature,* then they that dy old
                                                           maids,
because they refuse to be used to that end for which they
were only made. The Ape bringeth forth her young, for the
most part by twins; that which she loves best, she killeth   40
by pressing it too hard: so foolish maids soothing
                                                      themselves
with a false conceit of *vertue,* in fond obstinacie, live and
die maids; and so not onely kill in themselves the *vertue* of
Virginity, and of a *Vertue* make it a *Vice,* but they also
accuse their parents in condemning marriage. If this   45
application hold not touch, yet there may be an excellent
one gathered from an Apes tender love to Conies in keeping
them from the Weasel and Ferret. From this similitude of
an Ape and an old Maid did the foresaid proverb first arise.
But alas, there are some old Maids that are *Virgins* much   50
against their wills, and fain would change their *Virgin-life*
for a *Married*: such if they never have had any offer
of fit Husbands, are in some sort excusable, and their
willingnesse, their desire to marry, and their forbearance
                                                              from
all dishonest, and unlawfull copulation, may be a kind of   55
inclination to *vertue,* although not *Vertue* it selfe. This
Vertue of *Virginity* (though it be small and fruitlesse) it
is an extraordinary, and no common *Vertue.* All other
                                                        Vertues
lodge in the *Will* (it is the *Will* that makes them vertues.)

But it is the unwillingnesse to keep it, the desire to 60
forsake it, that makes this a *vertue*. As in the naturall
generation and formation made of the seed in the womb of a
woman, the body is joynted and organized about the
28 day,
and so it begins to be no more an *Embrion*, but capable as a
matter prepared to its form to receive the soule, which 65
faileth not to insinuate and innest it selfe into the body
about
the fortieth day; about the third month it hath motion and
sense: Even so *Virginity* is an *Embrion*, an unfashioned
lump, till it attain to a certain time, which is about twelve
years of age in women, fourteen in men, and then it 70
beginneth to have the soule of *Love* infused into it, and to
become a *vertue*: There is also a certain limited time
when it
ceaseth to be a *vertue*, which in men is about fourty, in
women about thirty years of age: yea, the losse of so much
time makes their *Virginity* a *Vice*, were not their endeavour 75
wholly bent, and their desires altogether fixt upon
marriage:
In Harvest time do we not account it a great vice of sloath
and negligence in a Husband-man, to overslip a week or
ten
dayes after his fruits are fully ripe; May we not much more
account it a more heynous vice, for a *Virgin* to let her 80
Fruit (*in potentia*) consume and rot to nothing, and to let
the *vertue* of her *Virginity* degenerate into *Vice*, (for
Virginity ever kept is ever lost.) Avarice is the greatest
deadly
sin next Pride: it takes more pleasure in hoording
Treasure
then in making use of it, and will neither let the possessor 85
nor others take benefit by it during the Misers life; yet it
remains intire, and when the Miser dies must come to som

87 must *ed.*: most *1652*.

body. *Virginity* ever kept, is a vice far wors then Avarice,
it will neither let the possessor nor others take benefit
by it, nor can it be bequeathed to any: with long keeping   90
it decayes and withers, and becomes corrupt and nothing
worth. Thus seeing that *Virginity* becomes a vice in
defect, by exceeding a limited time; I counsell all female
Virgins to make choyce of some *Paracelsian* for their
Physitian, to prevent the death of that *Vertue*: The   95
Paracelsians (curing like by like) say, That if the lives of
living Creatures could be taken down, they would make us
immortall. By this Rule, female *Virgins* by a discreet
marriage should swallow down into their *Virginity* another
Virginity, and devour such a life and spirit into their womb,   100
that it might make them, as it were, immortall here on earth,
besides their perfect immortality in heaven: And that
Vertue which otherwise would putrifie and corrupt, shall
                                                                then
be compleat; and shall be recorded in Heaven, and enrolled
here on Earth; and the name of *Virgin* shal be exchanged   105
for a farre more honorable name, *A Wife.*

The Desciption of a Scot at first sight

AT his first appeering in *Charterhouse* an olive
colourd velvet suite owned him, which since became
                                                          Mouse-
colour. A payre of unscoured stockings Gules. One
                                                      indifferent
Shooe. His Band of *Edenborough* and his cuffs of *London*,
                                                              both
strangers to his shirt: A white feather in a hatt that had   5
bin sodd. One onely cloake for the rayne, which yet hee

Copy-text O'F.

*This Character is found in Group II (S 962); Group III (B, Dob, O'F); S; and 1652. Readings of
B are not recorded.*

   Title: The Σ: omit O'F: A S 962   Description] Character 1652   first] the ... 1652
1 Charterhouse] the ... Dob, 1652   2 since] suite S 962   3 colour Σ: dunne
O'F   4 and his] his S 962: and 1652   6 which] omit S 962

made serve him for all weathers. A barren halfe Acre of
face, in middst whereof an eminent nose advanced
himselfe,
like the new mount at *Wansted* overlooking his beard, and
all the wild country thereaboutes. Hee was tended enough,   10
but not well, for they were certayne dumb creeping
followers, yet they made way for theyr Master theyr Laird.
At the first presentment his Breeches were his Sumpter,
and his pockets, Trunks, clokebaggs, Portmantaus and All.
Hee then grewe a knight wright, and there is extant of his   15
ware at 100, 150 and 200^{lb} price. Immediately upon this
hee shifted his suite, so did his whore, and to a Beare-
bayting they went, whither I follewd them not, but *Tom
Thorney* did.

Character of a Dunce

Is a Soule drownd in a lump of flesh, Or a peece of
earth that *Prometheus* put not halfe his proportion of fire
into. A thing that hath neyther Edge of desire, nor feeling
of Affection in it. The most dangerous creature for
confirming an Atheist, who would strayt sweare his Soule
were   5
nothing but the bare Temperature of his Body. Hee
sleepes
as hee goes, and his thoughts seldome reache an inch

---

8 in middst] in the midst *S 962*: Amidst *S, 1652*   himselfe Σ: it selfe *O'F, S 962*
10 tended Σ: attended *O'F*   12 followers] fellowes *S 962*   yet Σ: and yet *O'F*   theyr
Laird] the Leard *S, 1652*   13 his Sumpter] the . . . *S 962*   14 and his] his *S 962*
pockets] Packets *1652*   16 at] at a *Dob, S*   100, 150 and 200^{lb}] 100^{lb}. 150^{lb}. and
200^{lb} *S, 1652*   upon] after *1652*   17 shifted] shifteth *1652*   18 whither] whether
Dob, S 962, S

Copy-text O'F.

*This Character is found in Group II (S 962); Group III (B, Dob, O'F); S; 1652; and in all
editions of Overbury's Characters from the eleventh editon in 1622 on. Readings of B are not
recorded.*

Title: *Character of*] omit *Dob, S 962*: The true Caracter of *S, 1622, 1652*   1 Is] He
hath *S, 1622, 1652*   Or] or is *S, 1622, 1652*   3 hath] hath not *S 962*   5 strayt]
omit *1622*   were Σ: was *O'F*   6 bare Σ: omit *O'F*: very bare *S*   7 an inch Σ: any *O'F*

further then his eyes. The most part of the facultyes of
his soule lye fallow, or are like the restive Jades that
no spurr can drive forwards towards the pursuite of any   10
worthy designes. One of the most unprofitablest of Gods
creatures, beeing, as hee is, cleane put besides its right
use, made up for the Cart and the Flayle and by mischance
intangled amongst bookes and papers. A man cannot tell
possibly what Hee is now good for, save to move up and   15
downe and fill roome, or to serve as *animatum Instrumentum*
for others to worke withall in base employments, or to bee
a foyle for better witts, or to serve (as, they say,
Monsters doe) to set out the variety of Nature and
Ornament of the Universe. Hee is meere nothing of him
                                        selfe,   20
neyther eates, nor drinkes, nor goes, nor lookes, nor
spitts, but by imitation, for all which hee hath sett
formes and fashions, which hee never varyes, but sticks to
                                        with
the like plodding constancy that a Myllhorse followes his
trace. Both the Muses and the Graces are his hard   25
Mistresses, though hee dayly invocate them: Though hee
sacrifice *Hecatombs*, they looke asquint. You shall note him
                                        oft
(besides his dull eye, and louting head, and a certayne
                                        clammy
benumbd pace,) by a fayre displayd beard, a night Capp
                                        and
a gowne whose very wrinkles proclayme him the true
                                        Genius   30

9 or *Σ*: and *O'F*   restive *Σ*: reasty *O'F*, *S 962*   10 no spurr can] we
spurr & *S 962*   forwards *Σ*: forward *O'F*, *Dob*   11 designes] design *1652*   most
unprofitablest] vnprofitablest *Dob*: most unprofitable *1622, 1652*   Gods] all gods *S 962*,
1652   12 hee is] he is a thinge *S, 1622, 1652*   12–13 cleane . . . use *Σ*: *omit*
O'F   12 cleane put *Dob*, *S 962*, *S*: put cleane *1622, 1652*   its *Dob*: it *S 962*, *S*: his
1622, 1652   13 up] fitt *S, 1622, 1652*   by mischance *Σ*: unfortunately *O'F*: by
chance *S 962*   14 amongst . . . papers] amonge . . . prayers *S 962*   15 possibly]
possible *S, 1652*   save] saueinge *S 962*   18 a] *omit S, 1622*   19 doe] dogg
S 962   and] or *S 962*   21 nor lookes] *omit 1622, 1652*   23 formes] frames
S 962   26 invocate] intreate *S 962*   27 looke] still . . . *S, 1622, 1652*   oft] *omit*
S 962   28 louting] dull *S 962*   29–30 night Capp . . . gowne] gowne & a night
Capp *S 962*   30 him *Σ*: him to bee *O'F*   true] very . . . *S 962*

of formality. But of all others his discorse and
Compositions best speake him, Both of them are much of
                                                    one stuff
and fashion. Hee speakes just what his booke or last
companion sayd unto him, without varying a whitt, and
                                                    very
seldome understands him selfe. You may knowe by his
                                            discorse 35
where hee was last, for what hee heard or read yesterday
hee now dischargeth his memory or note booke of, not his
understanding, for it never came there. What hee hath hee
flings abroad at all adventures, without accomodating it to
time, place, persons, or occasions. Hee commonly looseth   40
him selfe in his tale, then flutters up and downe windlesse
without recovery, and whatsoever next presents it selfe his
heavy conceit seizeth upon, and goeth along with, however
Heterogeneall to his matter in hand. His jeasts are eyther
old fledd *Proverbs* or leane starvd hackny *Apothegmes*, or   45
poore verball quipps, out worne by serving men, tapsters,
and milkemayds, even layd aside by Balladers. Hee assents
                                                    to
all men that bring any shaddow of reason, and you may
                                                    make
him, when hee speakes most dogmatically, with one breath
                                                    to
averr pure contradictions. His Compositions differ onely   50
Terminorum positione from dreames, nothing but rude
                                            heapes
of immateriall incoherent drossy rubbish stuff
                                            promiscuously
thrust up together, Enough to infuse dulnesse and
barrennesse of conceit into him that is so prodigall of his

32 speake] speaks *S 962*   33–4 booke . . . companion] Bookes . . . company *S, 1622, 1652*:
looks . . . Companoine *S 962*   34 a] one *S, 1622, 1652*   36 heard or read] read or
heard *1652*   37 dischargeth *Σ*: discharges *O'F, Dob*   or] and *S 962*   40 time,
place] place, time *S 962*   41 then] and *S, 1622, 1652*   windlesse *Σ*: wind lesse *O'F*
49 with] even . . . *S, 1622, 1652*   50 averr *Σ*: answere *O'F*   pure] *omit S 962*: poore
1622   54 barrennesse] blockisnes *S 962*   into] to *S 962*

eares as to give the hearing, Enough to make a mans   55
memory ake with suffering such durty stuff cast into it, as
unwelcome to any true conceit as sluttish morsells, or
wallowish potions to any stomack, which whilst hee
                                                   emptyes
himselfe of it sticks in his teeth, nor can hee bee
delivered without sweats and sighs and hems and Coughs,   60
enough to shake his Grandams teeth out of her head. His
hearers spitt, and scratch and yawne and stampe and turne
like a sick man from side to side, from sitting to leaning,
from one elbowe to another, and deserve as much pitty
                                                   during
theyr Torture as a man in a fitt of a Tertian Fever, or a   65
selfe-lashing Penitentiary. In a word, ripp him quite
asunder and examine every shread of him—you shall find
him to bee just Nothing but the subject of Nothing, the
Object of contempt. Yet such as hee is you must take him,
for there is no hope hee should ever become better.   70

An Essaie of Valour

I AM of opynion that nothinge is so potent eyther to
procure, or merrit Love, As Valour. And I am glad I
                                                   am soe,
for therby I shall doe my selfe much ease because Valour
never needs much wytt to mayntaine yt. To speake of yt in
ytselfe, It is a Qualitie, which he that hath shall have   5

58 any] A nyce S, *1622, 1652*   whilst] whiles S, *1622, 1652*   60 sweats] sweat
1622, 1652   hems] Humms *1652*   61–2 His hearers . . . turne] Heel . . . turn *1652:*
He spits, and scratches and spawles, and turnes *1622*   63 a sick man] sick men S, *1622,*
1652   from side . . . leaning] *omit* S, *1622, 1652*   64 deserve] deserues *1622*
65 theyr] his *1622:* this *1652*   65–6 a man in a fitt of a . . . Fever . . . a . . .
Penitentiary] Men in fytts of . . . Fevers . . . Penetentiaries S, *1622, 1652*   67 shread]
threade S *962*   68 but . . . Nothing] *omit* S *962*

Copy-text S.

*This Essay occurs in S, 1652, and in editions of Overbury's Characters from the eleventh edition
in 1622 on. The bulk of the text also occurs as ' "Valour Anatomized in a Fancie", by Sir Philip
Sidney, 1581' in Cottoni posthuma, 1651. The text in Cotton, which is designated 1651, omits
the opening 25 lines up to and including* like to ytt, *for and also omits the concluding sentence
ll. 117–19,* But now . . . fewe words.

least need of, soe the beaste league betweene *Princes* is a
mutuall Feare of each other. It teacheth A Man to valewe
his *Reputation* as his life and cheifly to hould the lye
unsufferable, though beinge alone, he fyndes noe hurt it
doth him. It leaves it self to others *Censures*, for he that   10
braggs of his owne Valour diswades others from
                                                    beleiving yt.
It feareth A sword no more then an Ague. It alwaies makes
good the owner, for though he be generally held A Foole, he
shall seldome heare soe much by word of Mouth, And that
Inlargeth him more then anie spectacles, for yt maketh a   15
lyttle Fellowe to be called a tall Mann. It yeilds the wall
to none but A *Woman*, whose weaknes is her prerogative
                                                           or A
man seconded with A woman as an Usher which alwais goes
before his betters. It makes a man become the witnes of his
owne words, and stands to Whatsoever he hath said, and   20
thinketh it a Reproach to Commyt his revylinge to the Lawe.
It furnisheth youth with Actyon, and Age with discourse,
And both by futures, for A mann must never boast him
                                                       selfe in
the present Tense. And to come nearer home, Nothinge
                                                        drawes
a Woman like to ytt, for Valour towards Men, is an
                                                    Embleme   25
of Abilitie towards women, a good qualitie signifyinge A
better. Nothing is more behovefull for that sex, for, from
yt they receive protection and are free from the daunger of
yt. Nothing makes a shorter Cutt to obtayninge, for A Man
of Armes is alwais void of *Ceremony*, which is the wall that   30
stands betweene *Piramus* and *Thisbe*, that is Man, and
Woamen, for their is no pryde in Women but that which

    9 unsufferable] insufferable *1622*   11 Valour] omit *1622*   12 sword] word
1652   16 to] *omit 1652*   20 stands] stand *1622, 1652*   Whatsoever] what ever
1622, 1652   21 to] vnto *1622, 1652*   23 never *1622*: ever *S, 1652*   26
Abilitie] an . . . *1622, 1652*   signifyinge] signifies *1622, 1652*   27 better. Nothing]
better. Nothing draws a Woman like to it. Nothing *1651*; *see note*   28–9 are . . . yt
Sparrow: we . . . yt *Σ*: in a free way too, without any danger *1651*; *see note*   29 to]
for *1652*   31 betweene] betwixt *1622, 1651*   32 for *Σ*: for, For *S*

rebounds from our owne basenes (as Cowards growe valiant
upon those that are more Cowards) soe that onely by our
pale askinge we teach them to denye. And by our   35
Shamefac'dnes we put them in mynde to be modest,
                                      wheras indeed
it is Cunninge *Rhethorique* to perswade the hearers, that
they are that already which we wold have them to be. This
kynd of bashfullnes is far from men of Valour, and
espeacially from Souldyers, for such are ever Men (without   40
doubt) forwarde, and Confydent loosinge no tyme, least
they should loose opportunytie, which is the best factor
for A *Lover*. And because they know Woamen are given to
dissemble, they will never believe them when they deny.
Whilome before this Age of witt, and wearinge Blacke
                                            broke   45
in upon us, Their was no way knowne to wyn a Ladye
                                            but by
Tyltinge, Turnyinge, and rydinge through *Forrests*, in which
tyme these slender striplings with little Leggs, were heald
but of strength enough to marrie their Wyddoes, And
                                      even in
our dayes there can be given noe Reason of the Inundatyon   50
of *Servingmen* upon their Mistresses, but only that usuallie
they carry their Masters weapons and his Valour. To be
accounted Handsome, Just, Learned, or welfavored, all this
carryes no danger with it, but it is better to be admytted
to the Tytle of Valiant Acts, at least the venturinge of his   55
Mortalitie, And all women take delight to hold hym safe in
their Armes whoe hath escaped thither through many
                                            daungers.
To speake at once, man hath a priviledge in valour. In

33 from Σ: in S   36 Shamefac'dnes Σ: Shamfastnes S   38 we *1622*: he S,
1652: the world *1651*; *see note*   39 Valour] valorous disposition *1651*   42 best
Σ: *omit* S   45 Whilome] Certainely *1651*   broke] brake *1651*: were broke *1652*
46 no way Σ: now S   47 rydinge through *Forrests*] Riding to seeke Adventures
through dangerous Forrests *1651*   52 Masters] Mistresses *1622*   his] their *1651*
53 accounted] counted *1622*   or] and *1651*   54 danger Σ: dangers S   better] *omit*
1622, *1652*   55 Acts, *comma supplied ed.*   least]...that imports *1651*   his] *omit*
1651   56 take] *omit* *1651*

Clothes and good faces, we but Imitate woamen and
                                          many of
that sex will not think much (As farr as an Answere goes)   60
To dissemble witt too. So then these neat youths, these
Woamen in Menns *Apparrell*, are too neare a Woman to be
beloved of her, they be both of a trade. But bee hee of grym
Aspect, and such an one as a glasse scarse dares take, and
                                          shee will
desyre him for newnesse, and Variety. A skar in A Mans
                                          face   65
is the same that A mole is in A Womans, and A mole in A
Womans, is a Jewell set in white to make it seeme more
whyte. So A skarr in a Man is a Marke of Honor and noe
blemmish, for, Tis a flaw and a blemish in a souldier (to be
without one.) Now as for all things ells, which are to   70
procure Love, As a good face, witt, Clothes, or a good   Body,
Each of them I must Confesse may worke some what for
                                          want
of a better; That is if Valour be not there Rivall. A Good
Face avayles nothinge if it be upon A Coward that is
bashfull, the utmost of yt is to be kissed which rather   75
encreaseth then quencheth Apetite. He that sends her
Guifts, sends her word alsoe that he is A Mann of small
Guifts otherwise, for wooinge by signes and toakens implyes
the Author Dumbe. And if Ovid who writt the Lawe of
                                          Love
were alive (as he is extant) would allowe it as a good   80
diversitie, then Guiftes shold be sent as *Gratuities* not as
Bribes. Witt getteth rather promise then Loue. Witt is not

59 we] we do *1651*   63 a *Σ*ı *omit S*   63–5 bee hee ... desyre *Sparrow*: bee
of grym Aspect and such an one a glasse dares take and shee will desyre *Σ*: but he of
grim aspect, and such a one a lasse dares take, and will desire *1651; see note*   65 new-
nesse] neatness *1652*   66 mole is *1651*: mole *Σ; see note*   66–7 and A mole in A
Womans, is] *omit 1652*   68 So] For *1622, 1652*   69 in *1622, 1651*: for *S*: too in
1652   71 Clothes] good ... *1652*   72 must] *omit 1622, 1652*   Confesse may
worke] needs say) workes *1651*   73 be not there Rivall] corrive not therewith
1651   74 avayles] avayleth *1651*   upon] on *1651*: in *1622, 1652*   Coward *ed.*:
Coward, *S*   75 yt *ed.*: yt, *S*   77 sends] sendeth *1651*   78 Guifts *ed.*:
Guifts, *S*   80 would] and ... *1651*   80–1 as a good ... then *1651*: as good a ...
That *Σ; see note*   81 not *Σ*: but not *S*   82 Witt getteth rather] and Wit
would rather get *1651*

to be seene, And no Woman takes advice of any in her
Lovinge but of ner owne Eyes and her wayting Womans.
Nay which
is worse witt is not to be felt; and soe noe good Bedfellowe.   85
Witt applyed to A Woman makes her dissolve her
simpering
and discover her teeth with Laughter, and this is surely a
Purge for Love, for, the Beginninge of Love is a kind of
foolish Melancholye. As for the Man that makes his Taylor.
his Bawd and hopes to inveigle his love with such a
Coloured   90
Suite, surely the same deeply hazards the losse of her favor
upon every Change of his Clothes. So likewise for the other
that Courts her sylently, with a good Body, let me Certefye
him that his Clothes alwais stand betwixt his Mistress
Eyes, and him, The Comlynes of Clothes depends upon the   95
Comlynes of the body, and soe both upon Opynion.
She that
hath bene seduced by *Apparrell,* let me give her to witt,
that Men alwais put off their Clothes before they goe to
Bed, And let her that hath bene enamord of her servants
bodye understand that if she sawe him in a skynn of Cloth   100
that is in A suite made to the patterne of his Bodye she
wold see slender cause to love him ever after. There are
no Clothes fytt soe well in A womans Eye as a suite of
steele though not of the fashyon. And no Man soe soone
surpriseth a womans Affectyons, as he that is the subject   105
of *whisperings* and hath alwais some twentie storyes of
his owne deeds depending upon him. Mistake me not, I
understand not by *Valour* one that never fights but when

84 and] or *1651*   85 Bedfellowe] fellow *1652*   86 dissolve]... (or
disclose) *1652*   simpering] simperings *1651*   87 Beginninge]... and originall
1651   91 same]... man *1651*   92 for] omit *1651*   93 Certefye] tell *1651*
94–5 alwais ... of Clothes] omit *1622, 1652*   94 alwais stand *ed.*: alwais stands *S*:
stand allwaies *1651*   95 him *1651*: home *S*   depends] depend *1622, 1652*   96
the] his *1622*   97 to witt] to weete *1651*   98 off *Σ*: of *S*   102 see]
discern *1651*   are] is *1622*   103 fytt] sit *1622, 1652*   106 *whisperings*] all ... *1652*:
all whispering *1622*   some] omit *1622, 1652*   107 deeds] Atchievements *1651*

he is backed with Drinke or Anger, or hissed on with
Beholders. Nor one that is Desperate, Nor one that takes   110
away A servingmans weapons, when perchaunce they cost
                                                           him
his quarters wages: Nor yet one that weares a privie Coat
of Defence, and therein is Confydent, for then such as
made Bucklers wold be accounted the *Catalines* of the
Commonwealth. I entend one of an even Resolution
                                                grounded   115
upon reason, which is alwais evenn, havinge his power
restrayned by the Lawe of not doinge wronge. But now I
remember I am for *Valour*, and therefore must be *A Man
of fewe words.*

Newes from the very Country

THAT it is a fripery of Courtiers, Merchants, and
others, which have been in fashion, and are very neere
worne out. That Justices of peace have the felling of
underwoods, but the Lords have the great falls. That
Jesuits are like Apricocks, heretofore here and there   5
one succour'd in a great mans house and cost deare, now
you may have them for nothing in every cottage. That
every great vice is a Pike in a pond that devoures vertues
and lesse vices. That it is wholesomest getting a
stomacke, by walking on your own ground: and the   10
thriftiest laying of it at anothers table. That debtors
are in *London* close prisoners, and here have the libertie

109 with ... with] by ... by *1651*   111 perchaunce] perphaps *1651*   they] it *1622*,
1652   112 yet] *omit 1651*   113 then such *Σ*: such then *S*   114 made]
make *1651*   accounted] counted *1622*   *Catalines*] very scum *1651*   of the] of this *1652*
116 reason, *comma supplied ed.*   evenn, *comma supplied ed.*   118 must] I ... *1652*

Copy-text 1614.

'*Newes*' *occurs in all editions of Overbury's* Characters *from 1614, (1614) on, in* Poems, By
J. D., *1650, (1650), and the bulk of the text was found in the Burley MS from whencei was
printed in L. P. Smith,* The Life and Letters of Sir Henry Wotton, *(Oxford, 1907). Readings
are given from 1614 and 1650.*

    3 felling] selling *1650*   4 That] The *1650*

of the house. That *Atheists* in affliction, like blind
beggers, are forced to aske though they know not of whom.
That there are (God be thanked) not two such acres in all   15
the country, as the *Exchange* and *Westminster-hall*. That
only Christmas Lords know their ends. That weomen are
                                                              not
so tender fruit, but that they doe as well and beare as
well upon beds, as plashed against walls. That our carts
are never worse employed, than when they are wayted on by   20
coaches. That sentences in Authors like haires in an
horse taile, concurre in one roote of beauty and strength,
but being pluckt out one by one, serve onely for springes
and snares. That both want and abundance equally
                                                    advance a
rectified man from the world, as cotton and stones are both   25
good casting for an hawke. That I am sure there is none of
                                                            the
forbidden fruit left, because we doe not all eat thereof.
That our best three pilde mischiefe comes from beyond
                                                            the
sea, and rides post through the country, but his errand
is to Court. That next to no wife and children, your owne   30
wife and children are best pastime, anothers wife and your
children worse, your wife and anothers children worst. That
Statesmen hunt their fortunes, and are often at default:
Favourites course her and are ever in view. That
intemperance is not so unwholesome heere, for none ever
                                                      saw   35
Sparrow sicke of the pox. That here is no trechery nor
fidelitie, but it is because here are no secrets. That
Court motions are up and down, ours circular: theirs like
squibs cannot stay at the highest, nor return to the place
which they rose from, but vanish and weare out in the way,   40
Ours like mill wheels busie without changing place; they
have peremptorie fortunes, we vicissitudes.

21-2 an horse taile] horse tailes *1650*   31 wife and children] *omit 1650*   best] the
best *1650*

COMMENTARY

I. PARADOXES

MSS.: Group II (*A 18, N, S 962, TCC, TCD, Wy*); Group III (*B, Dob, O'F*); *W, Bur*; *O 2, P*; *S*.
Editions: *1633a, 1633b, 1652.*

The manuscripts and editions listed above contain a more or less full collection of the ten Paradoxes which I have accepted as canonical. If a Paradox is not found in one of these witnesses the fact is noted at the beginning of the commentary on that Paradox. Readings from one further manuscript which contains extracts from the text of one Paradox, *Pud*, have been included.

The Westmoreland MS, which contains all ten Paradoxes, has the best text, but it requires the correction of Woodward's copying errors from the other witnesses.

Many of the variants in the text of the Paradoxes are trivial and should be attributed to scribal corruption. In establishing the text the most important witnesses are *W, Bur*, and Groups II and III. I have accepted the agreement of *W, Bur* with Group II as having the highest authority, and the agreement of *W* and *Bur* as having slightly less. The readings of *TCC* and *TCD* are cited to represent Group II; *TC* signifies their agreement. Readings of *Dob* are given to represent Group III as it appears to represent that tradition of the text most faithfully, lacking both the errors of *B* and the sophistications of *O'F*.[1] *O 2, P*, and *S* are of no value in establishing the text, but since *S* is the manuscript nearest to the copy for the first edition, its readings have been included in the apparatus.

The Paradoxes are printed in the order in which they occur in *W*; this is also the order in which they appear in *Bur* and Group II. The numbers in which the Paradoxes occur in the editions is given in the apparatus in order to facilitate reference.

Where notes from Evelyn Simpson's commentary for her projected edition of the *Paradoxes and Problems* are used, they are taken from her typescript and designated 'E. M. S.'.

I. That all things kill themselves (p. 1)

The reading of *W* has been rejected on five occasions, and on two (ll. 5, 21)

---

1 In the 198 instances of disagreement among *B, Dob, O'F* in the text of the Paradoxes, the three manuscripts read differently 4 times, *B, O'F* agree together against *Dob* only 29 times, while *Dob, B* agree against *O'F* 80 times and *Dob, O'F* against *B* in 85 instances. The variations in readings are all trivial.

its peculiar spelling has been altered. In ll. 7–8, 15, 29 all the remaining witnesses agree against it, and in ll. 13, 14 while there is dissention amongst the manuscripts, *W* has no support.

In this Paradox Donne argues that self-destruction not self-preservation is the law of life, using the doctrine of three souls, vegetable, animal, and rational, ultimately derived from Aristotle (mainly in *De anima*, Bk. II. 1, *De plantis*, Bk. I, but also in *Ethica Eudemia*, Bk. II, 1, and *Topica*, Bk. V. 4).

ll. 3–4. *Plants . . . unworthy Soule.* Donne adhered to the doctrine of three souls according to which the lowest soul or soul of growth was found in plants, the soul of motion along with the soul of growth was found in animals, and the rational and immortal soul was found in man alone. In man, when the rational soul is infused by God into the unborn child, it comprehends or swallows up the two preceding souls. Cf.:

> Wee first have soules of growth, and sense, and those,
> When our last soule, our soule immortall came,
> Were swallow'd into it and have no name,
>   'To the Countesse of Salisbury', ll. 52–4

This doctrine occurs repeatedly in Donne's poetry and in his prose works.

ll. 10–12. *And yf between men . . . not to defend it selfe.* The reading of all the witnesses except *Bur*, *it selfe*, is less clear than the reading of *Bur*, *the selfe*. The reading in *Bur* may be an instance of Donne's attempt to clarify his text. The idea of the sentence is developed at greater length in *Biathanatos*, Pt. II, Dist. vi, Sect. 2, 116–17:

> And he which to himselfe denies necessarie things, or exposes himselfe inordinatly to such dangers as men use not to escape, kills himselfe. He that is as sure that this Medicine will recover him, as that this Poyson will destroy him, is as guilty if he forbeare the Physicke, as if he swallow the Poyson. (E.M.S.)

ll. 12–14. *This defence . . . lawles liberty.* Donne expresses the same idea in 'Holy Sonnet' ('Why are wee . . .'), ll. 5–8:

> Why brook'st thou, ignorant horse, subjection?
> Why dost thou bull, and bore so seelily
> Dissemble weaknesse, and by'one mans stroke die,
> Whose whole kinde, you might swallow and feed upon?

ll. 20–2. *Or how shall man . . . kill'd us all.* Cf. *Biathanatos*, Pt. II, Dist. vi, Sect. 3, 118:

> And in the first and worst Homicide committed in Paradise, in which were employed all the persons in the world, which were able to concurre to evill, when though there was but one man, all the Millions which have been and shall be, were massacred at once, and himselfe too . . .

This Paradox is a preliminary sketch of the idea which Donne was later to elaborate in *Biathanatos*, which is described on its title-page as 'A Declaration of that Paradoxe, or Thesis, that *Selfe-homicide* is not so Naturally Sinne, that it may never be otherwise' (E. M. S.).

ll. 26–30. *And if these things . . . the same things.* The argument is that things kill themselves in their perfection for after perfection is reached they are changed, and, being no longer themselves, they therefore cannot kill themselves.

l. 31. *no perfection indures.* The reading of *W* and *Bur* must be correct, for in the context, the reading of the remaining witnesses '. . . *affection* . . .' does not make sense.

ll. 33–6. *Yea the frame . . . out of it nothing is.* If God did not sustain the world it would end or die; this death must be self-induced, for, if God were idle, there is nothing outside the world to kill it. Group III reads *out of nothinge it is*, a scribal error which can be explained as a misinterpretation of the sentence, substituting the doctrine of the creation of the world *ex nihilo* for Donne's witty ending.

II. That women ought to paint themselves (p. 2)

Omitted in *O 2*.

The reading of *W* has been rejected on twelve occasions and on one (l. 38) its peculiar spelling has been altered.

In ll. 1, 15, 41–2, 43 it omits words, and in l. 2 it uses what is now considered to be the participle of a verb where the active form is used by the majority of the witnesses. On two occasions (ll. 21, 33) *W* has readings which differ in number from the readings of the other witnesses. Although in l. 33 it is tempting to accept the reading of *W*, I have rejected it because of the weight of the manuscript evidence against it. On three occasions (ll. 18, 37, 39) *W* disagrees with the other witnesses in minor readings and on two others (ll. 28–9, 36) the disagreement of *W* and the remaining witnesses is discussed in the notes.

In this Paradox Donne defends women's use of paint by attacking the inconsistencies in men's attitudes towards beauty in women and in the beautiful objects of nature and of art.

See also General Introduction, p. xxii.

Donne's attitude on the use of cosmetics is ambivalent, for he accepts it as the lesser of two evils in 'The Primrose', ll. 18–20:

> Since there must reside
> Falshood in woman, I could more abide,
> She were by art, then Nature falsify'd,

and in an Easter sermon he condemned their use:

It is ill, when it is not our own heart, that appears in our words; it is ill too, when it is not our own blood, that appears in our cheekes; It may doe some ill offices of blood, it may tempt, but it gives over, when it should doe a good office of blood, it cannot blush, (*Sermons*, vi. 269) (E. M. S.)

while in a sermon on the Penitential Psalms he condones it:

Certainly the limits of adorning and beautifying the body are not so narrow, so strict, as by some sowre men they are sometimes conceived to be. Differences of Ranks, of Ages, of Nations, of Customes, make great differences in the enlarging, or contracting of these limits, in adorning the body; and that may come neare sin at some time, and in some places, which is not so alwaies, nor every where, (*Sermons*, v. 302).

Donne continues in the sermon to argue that the beauty of Abraham's wife, Sarah, must have been preserved in her great age by 'unctions, and liniments'. (E. M. S.). Finally, compare 'It is not a clear case, if we consider the originall words properly, That *Jesabel did paint*; and yet all translators, and expositors have taken a just occasion, out of the ambiguity of those words, to cry down that abomination of painting', *Sermons*, iii. 104.

l. 3. *shooing*. The reading of *Bur*, *shoaring*, is possibly authorial; 'shore' in the sense of prop or stay is possible. However, according to the *OED*, in the seventeenth century the term was chiefly nautical and was normally used transitively. Other minor peculiar readings of *Bur* which are possibly authorial are *complayne* for *exclaime* (l. 14) and the smoother but less rhetorically effective *what can be a more heynous adultery* for *what a hainous adultery is it* (ll. 17–18).

ll. 6–7. *conceald, offending without witnes*. The agreement of *W, Bur,* with *TC* and *S 962* establishes this as the true reading from which *concealinge* (Group III and *P*) has arisen from the following present participle. *S* further corrupts the reading by the plural *offendinges* which the edition 'improves' to *offendors*. It is not certain whether *Bur* supports *W* in its comma. Apart from *O'F* which has a comma, and *P* which has a semi-colon, the other witnesses have no stop.

l. 10. *jealousy*. Zeal or vehemence of feeling in favour of a person or thing; devotion, eagerness, anxiety to serve, *OED* 2, *obs*.

ll. 11–12. *kissing, the strange and misticall union of Soules*. Cf. 'To Sir Henry Wotton' ('Sir, more then kisses, letters mingle Soules'), and:

. . . in this spirituall love, and this expressing of it, by this kisse, there is a transfusion of the soule too: . . ., (*Sermons*, iii. 320).

The conceit of the soul in the kiss is traced by S. Gasalee from its first recorded appearance, in an epigram attributed to Plato, to its use in the twentieth century in 'The Soul in the Kiss', *Criterion*, ii (1924), 349–59.

l. 13. *Worthy*. The agreement of *W, Bur* with *TC* and *S 962* establishes this reading. The sense of the sentence must be taken with the next. Adultery even with a worthy partner is just cause for complaint, with *ravishers* and *sodain deflowrers* it is *hainous*. It is easier to see why a scribe taking the sentence by itself might 'correct' *worthy* to *unworthy* than to see why, finding *unworthy*, he should correct to make a witty point. *TCC* alters its text by inserting 'vn'.

ll. 28–9. *Is not . . . new painted.* This sentence which is found in *Bur* also occurs in *TC* and *S 962*, but *TC* and *S 962* omit *new*. The omission of this sentence in the majority of the manuscripts and the editions is easy to understand since the preceding sentence also ends in *painted*. It may well have occurred independently in *W* which does not normally agree with Group III, *S, 1633 +*, and *P*.

ll. 29–30. *fruits, and birds, and beasts.* The order in *W* is probably correct as it is supported in part by two independent manuscripts, *Bur* and *P*; like *W*, they keep birds and beasts together.

ll. 31–2. *And do we not . . . durst not regard.* Cf. 'and why do we regard the pictures and images of such terrible things as ferocious beasts and corpses without fear and horror, when the things themselves affect us with these feelings', Giulio Paolo Crasso, *Quaestiones naturales* in *Medici antiqui graeci* (Basel, 1581), cited by Lawn, 131–2.

ll. 32–7. *We repayre . . . is prevented.* I have altered the full stop after *offended* in *W* (l. 36) to a colon. The first two statements are in parallel against the third:

1. We repair our houses because we are made uncomfortable.
2. We mend and wash our clothes because they offend us.
3. But women paint themselves before we have a chance to be offended.

l. 36. *our eye, and other body is offended.* This is a difficult reading which *W* appears to have simplified by dropping *other*; *S 962* follows *W* in reading *our eyes and boddy is offended*. The presence of *other* in the remaining manuscripts points to its having been present in Donne's original. *Other body*, i.e. other parts of the body, our noses, hands, etc. are offended. *Dob* and *B, S*, and *1633 +* by reading *bodies* for *body* and *are* for *is* imply that it is our eyes and those of other bodies which are offended; *O'F* makes this implication clear by inserting *owne*, contrasting *our owne eyes* and *other bodyes*. The reading of *P, our Eyes and our other bodyes*, supports the sense of *W, Bur, TC, S 962* that it is *we* who are offended.

ll. 39–41. *if thou beginst . . . she is not painted.* *Bur* clarifies the quibbling of this sentence by reading 'if thou begin to hate when it falls thou hatest her . . .'. The sense of the sentence with that of the next is 'You loved her when she was painted (though you did not realize that she was painted); if you begin to hate her when her paint comes off, you are hating her for *not* being painted. If you say now that you hated her before (for being painted), then you hated her and loved her at the same time.'

III. That old Men are more Fantastique then younge (p. 4)

The reading in *W* has been rejected on six occasions. In ll. 3, 14, 26, and 28 *W* disagrees with the other witnesses in minor readings, in l. 15 it adds a word to the text, and in ll. 21–2 it omits a word found in the other witnesses.

In this Paradox Donne argues that old men are more fantastic than young men by playing on the various meanings of 'fantastic', and applying more meanings of the word to old men than to young. Basically he accuses them of being unreasonable or of having lost their reason like the lover in the elegy ('Image of her . . .'), ll. 9–16:

> When you are gone, and Reason gone with you,
>   Then Fantasie is Queene and Soule, and all;
> She can present joyes meaner then you do;
>   Convenient, and more proportionall.
> So, if I dreame I have you, I have you,
>   For, all our joyes are but fantasticall.
> And so I scape the paine, for paine is true;
>   And sleepe which locks up sense, doth lock out all.

l. 1. *fantastique.* Imaginative, *OED* 4a, *obs.*

ll. 4–7. *To be fantastique . . . full and perfect.* 'In young men it is a temporary disorder of the humours, full of fancies, in old men whose senses have lost the power to perceive the real world it is natural and therefore complete and permanent.'

l. 13. *conceiting apparell.* 'Inventing apparel'. Conceit = to conceive as a purpose or design, *OED* 6, *obs.*

ll. 14–15. *when we are melancholy . . . when forsaken, tawny.* There is evidence for colour symbolism in costume in Elizabethan drama; see M. C. Linthicum, *Costume in the Drama of Shakespeare and his Contemporaries* (1936), 24–52. For green as the colour of lovers, see *Love's Labour's Lost*, I. ii. 81. Tawny or yellowish tan indicated sadness, generally because the wearer was forsaken. In Lodge's *Euphues Golden Legacie* (*Works* (1883), i. 128) Montanus wears tawny 'to signify that he is forsaken' (E. M. S.).

l. 22. *fantastique.* Existing only in imagination. *OED* 1a, *obs.*

ll. 22–5. *And that ridling . . . most fantastique.* Cf. 'The Storme', ll. 49–50:

> And tremblingly'aske what newes, and doe heare so,
> Like jealous husbands, what they would not know.

ll. 25–8. *Yea that which falls . . . great provision.* Cf. *Essays in Divinity*, 25,

'But as old age is justly charged with this sickness, that though it abound, it ever covets, though it need less then youth did' (E. M. S.). Cf. also 'Old men are covetous by nature', Tilley, M 568.

ll. 28–30. *Is any habit . . . like our elders.* Cf. Erasmus, *The Praise of Folie*, p. 84, on schoolmen: 'at their Actes and Comencementes ye dooe see theim swadled in with so many cappes, coyves, and furde hodes as they weare, for els I thinke plainely theyr heades wolde rive asunder'.

ll. 31–2. *the Sceptique which doubts all.* Cf. *Sermons*, i. 278, 'Those Sceptique philosophers, that doubted of all, though they affirmed nothing, yet they denied nothing neither . . .' (E. M. S.). Cf. also Sir Walter Ralegh's 'The Skeptick' based upon 'the skeptick [who] doth neither affirm neither deny any position; but doubteth of it, and applyeth his Reason against that which is affirmed, or denied, to justifie his non consenting', *Remains of Sir Walter Raleigh* (1657), 123.

IV. That Nature is our worst Guide (p. 6)

Wy omits the last seven lines of text.

The reading of *W* has been rejected on five occasions and on two (ll. 7, 35) its peculiar spelling has been altered. In l. 29 *W* omits a word which is found in other witnesses, in ll. 8, 51, 55 all the witnesses agree against it in minor readings, and in l. 31 the reading of *Bur* and Group II has been adopted over the reading of *W*.

In this Paradox Donne argues that nature is our worst guide in part by using 'nature' in several of its various meanings. Lovejoy and Boas point out that the 'sacred word "nature" is probably the most equivocal in the vocabulary of the European peoples; that the range of connotation of the single term covers conceptions not only distinct but often absolutely antithetic to one another in their implications', A. O. Lovejoy and G. Boas, editors, *Primitivism and Related Ideas in Antiquity* (Baltimore, Md., 1935), 12.

ll. 2–3. *Or if she . . . better guide then we.* Nature's guide, like our guide, is God. Cf. Hooker, *Ecclesiastical Polity*, Bk. I, ch. iii, 4:

. . . it cannot be but nature hath some director of infinite knowledge to guide her in all her ways. Who is the guide of nature, but only the God of nature?

ll. 4–10. *Can she be . . . in her selfe, in us.* 'Nature' here is *natura naturans*, which although created innocent, *in the white integrity*, yet had the propensity to sin. Cf. *Biathanatos*, Pt. I, Dist. i, Sect. 7, 38, 'So that originall sinne is traduced by nature onely, and all actuall sinne issuing from thence, all sinne is naturall.' Donne seems to have based this concept of original sin on Aquinas, *Summa Theologiae*, 1a, 2ae, 81–5.

l. 9. *so.* 'So' in the sense of 'hence' is the correct reading, although *sowe*, the reading of *TCD* supported by *O'F* and *B*, which do not agree with *Dob* (*soe*), is attractive.

ll. 10–14. *If by Nature . . . follow one course.* 'If we identify man's nature as reason, why should not all men act alike?'

l. 11. *our reasonablenes.* The reading of *1633* +, *or reason, noblenesse*, is probably derived from the reading of *S*, *o͂ʳ reason, o͂ʳ noblenes*, which is itself probably derived from a corruption such as that in *B*, *our reason, ableness.* The abbreviation *o͂ʳ* is also found in *W, TCD, S962, O 2* and *P*. Similarly in l. 17 *or soules* (*1633* +) probably arose from the use of the abbreviated form *o͂ʳ* in *W, TCD, S 962, Dob, O 2, P*, and *S*.

l. 12. *wisard.* Philosopher, sage. *OED* A. 1, *obs.*

l. 16. *temperature.* Temperament. *OED* 5b, *obs.*

l. 16. *slimy.* Morally defiled or objectionable; vile, disgusting. *OED*, 3, *trans.* and *fig.*

ll. 18–22. *To say it . . . become nothing.* A parallel construction showing the impossibility of deriving inclination, mind, and soul from the parents either *as All from All* (which would give all to the first child so that *nothing remaynes* for the rest), or *as part from all* (which part *equally imparted to many children, would . . . in few generations become nothing*).

l. 21. *Gavelkind.* A technical legal term from the sixteenth century, often used to denote the custom of dividing a deceased man's property equally among his sons; *OED* 2. *OED* attributes the first example of figurative use of the word to Donne in 1627, in *Sermons*, viii. 84, 'For, *God* shall impart to us all, a mysterious *Gavelkinde*, a mysterious *Equality* of *fulnesse* of *Glory*, to us *all*'.

ll. 22–5. *Or to say it . . . is utter blasphemy.* This sentence argues the theological point that the soul is infused into man by God, not handed on by parents which is the theory of *Traducianism.* Donne's point is that we cannot derive all our nature from our parents by logic or by theology.

l. 28. *complexions.* 'Complexion' = the combination of the four 'humours' of the body in a certain proportion, or the bodily habit attributed to such combinations, *OED* I. 1, *obs.* exc. *hist.*

ll. 33–4. *Nature though we chase . . . returne. Tis true.* Cf. 'Though you cast out nature with a fork it will still return', Tilley, N 50. 'Naturam expelles furca, tamen usque recurret', Horace, *Epistles*, i. 10. 24.

ll. 36–8. *that old* Tu nihil invitâ . . . *against nature.* 'You nothing beyond etc.' or as expanded on *O'F*, *Tu nihil invitâ dices faciesue Minerva* (You will say or do nothing beyond your ability), Horace, *Ars poetica*, l. 385. Donne translated Horace's line not that 'thou shalt', but 'thou wilt . . .' which is correct. Both the Latin and Donne's translation mean that man's not going beyond his ability is a matter of fact, and not a command. Cf. Erasmus, *Enchiridion militis Christiani, Opera Omnia* (1703–6), vol. v, 29c–d, 'fere enim infeliciter evenire, quae tentes invita Minerva' (those things turn out badly which you attempt to do against your nature). This tag is introduced in *Bur, S* and *1633* + as 'That old axiome . . .'. Such an introduction seems likely to have been added by scribes in an attempt at tidying the text; Donne did not as a rule formally introduce Latin tags in his sermons.

ll. 39–40. *We call our bastards . . . our naturall issue.* In the later sixteenth century, 'natural' came to mean a mere blood-kinship not legally recognized, *OED* III. 13c, which attributes the earliest use to Sir John Ferne in *The Blazon of Gentrie* (1586), 90; the term originates in Roman law.

ll. 41–3. *And that poore knowledg . . . Metaphisique, supernaturall.* The singular form 'metaphysic' was superseded by the plural, 'metaphysics', in the seventeenth and eighteenth centuries. 'Metaphysica' was the title applied from the first century AD to thirteen books of Aristotle's which were catalogued after the *Physics* (μετὰ τὰ φυσικά), *Metaphysica*. It was also misinterpreted as meaning 'the science of things transcending what is physical or natural', and down to the seventeenth century metaphysical was often explained by words such as supernatural and transnatural. *OED* 1 and 'metaphysical' 1b.

ll. 45–8. *Lastly by following her . . . they are made.* Cf. 'Acorns were good till bread was found', Tilley, A 21. That acorns were the oldest food of man was a classical commonplace. Donne's use of the idea reflects the hard primitive view of the myth of the Golden Age as found in the Cynic and Epicurean doctrines. In the hard primitive view early man did not live without effort dining on milk and honey in a happy society, but rather existed, little better than the animals, scrambling in the forests for food. Louis I. Bredvold discussed Donne in relation to hard and soft primitivism in 'The Naturalism of Donne in Relation to some Renaissance Traditions', *JEGP* xxii (1923), 471–502.

l. 52. *yee.* I have accepted the reading of *W* which agrees with that of *Dob, P, S, 1633* +, and which is supported by *S 962, O'F, S, O2* reading *you. Bur* and *TC* read *wee*, which goes less well with the imperative 'confes'.

ll. 54–6. *yet confes that . . . would preserve.* Cf. 'Now, *Sanitas naturalis*; Nature abhores sickness . . .', *Sermons*, iii. 55.

V. That only Cowards dare dye (p. 9)

Omitted in *Wy*.

The reading of *W* has been rejected in l. 17, and in ll. 14–15 a phrase which is omitted in *W* has been supplied from the text in *Bur*.

This Paradox appears to have been suggested by Aristotle's *Ethica Eudemia*,

Bk. III, chs. 6, 7, which Donne quoted in *Biathanatos*, Pt. II, Dist. v, Sect. 2, 114:

Of such reasons derived from the rules of Morall vertue, *Aristotle* insinuates two. For observing that this kinde of death caught men by two baits, *Ease* and *Honour*, Against them who would dy to avoide Miserie, (a) Hee teaches *Death to be the greatest misery which can fall upon us* . . . And then, that Honour and Fame might draw none, (b) he sayes, *It is Cowardlinesse, and Dejection, and an argument of an unsufferable and impatient minde.* (E. M. S.)

Cf. also 'It is better to be a coward than foolhardy', Tilley, C 776. See also General Introduction, p. xxiv.

ll. 1–3. *EXTREAMES are* . . . *backward cowardise.* This statement is derived from Aristotle's doctrine that virtue is the mean between two vices. Cf. *Ethica Nichomachea*, Bk. II, ch. 2, 'For the man who flies from and fears everything and does not stand his ground against anything becomes a coward, and the man who fears nothing at all but goes to meet every danger becomes rash; . . . temperance and courage, then, are destroyed by excess and defect, and preserved by the mean.' Donne read Aristotle in Latin translation as can be seen by the fact that all his quotations from his works are in Latin not Greek; see Problem XVIII. Cf. also Horace, *Epistles*, Bk. i. XVIII. 9, 'virtus est medium vitiorum et utrimque reductum' (virtue is a mean between vices, remote from both extremes).

ll. 4–5. *When will* . . . *cannot be avoyded.* 'Necessited' = necessitated, i.e. compelled or forced, *OED*, 1 *trans.* The argument is, 'when will your valiant man die? when he is forced to? Cowards are similar then, they only suffer what they cannot avoid (but they choose death over suffering)'. The reading of *W*, Bur has been accepted. '. . . dye? necessited?' as it is unusual, and its sense makes it appear more likely to have been supplied by Donne than the punctuation of the other manuscripts. Group II reads '. . . dye? necessited,' while Group III and *S* read '. . . dy necessited?' The compositor, who must have had a reading such as that in Group III and *S* in his copy, saw that it was in error and 'corrected' to '. . . dye of necessity?'.

l. 10. Fortiter . . . potest. Martial, *Epigrams*, xi. 56. 16, 'He acts bravely who is miserable and can endure'.

ll. 11–13. *But it is taught* . . . *any misery.* There is an expression of the same idea in a letter from Donne to an unknown friend which is dated as probably 1599–1600, 'Wee have a new fashioned valor to suffer any thing rather then misery . . .', *Prose Works*, 311 (E. M. S.).

l. 11. *Valiants.* 'Valiant' was not commonly used as a substantive. (E. M. S.) The earliest use noted by *OED* is in 1609, Douay Bible, Jer. 46: 9.

ll. 14–16. *And this seemes* . . . *groveling Spiritt.* The reading of Bur has been adopted, 'a brave a fiery sparkling and a clyming resolucion which . . .'. This reading must be correct, not only because it balances the following 'a cowardly, an earthly and a groveling Spiritt', but also because it best explains how the errors of the other witnesses arose. *W* omits 'sparkling, and a climbing resolution', and a blank space of 20 mm was left in the line to indicate that Woodward could not provide a passage of the text. The remaining witnesses omit 'fiery sparkling' and 'resolution' but include 'climbing'. They read nonsense: 'and this seemes a very braue, and a very clyminge which . . .'. In adopting the reading of *Bur* commas have been inserted after 'brave', 'sparkling', and 'resolution', where no punctuation is recorded for *Bur*. Donne satirized the hollow bravery of the gallants or valiants in Satire III. See General Introduction, p. xv.

ll. 15–16. *resolution . . . Spiritt.* 'Resolution' = determination, *OED* IV. 15. 'Spirit' = a tendency, inclination, impulse, *OED* II. 7b.

l. 17. *thirst.* Evelyn Simpson noted in 'More Manuscripts etc.', 415, that all the manuscripts except *S* read *thirst*, while *S* has the archaic form *thrist*. This form misled the compositor who set *thrust*.

ll. 24–7. *I have seene one . . . he was mad.* Cf. *Biathanatos*, Pt. I, Dist. ii, Sect. 3, 51–2, '*Comas* who had been a Captaine of theeves, when he came to the torture of examination, scorning all forraigne and accessorie helps to dye, made his owne breath, the instrument of his death, by stopping and recluding it.' Donne gained his knowledge of Comas from Valerius Maximus, IX. xii, *De mortibus non vulgaribus; externa*, i. See Sparrow's note, *Devotions*, 157 (E. M. S.). It will be noted that Donne introduced this scene by saying 'I have seene one', as if it were an event which he had actually witnessed, but this may imitate the Latin *vidi* or *vidimus*, not always to be taken at face value.

ll. 27–31. *And we knew another . . . his disgrace.* I do not know to whom Donne is referring here. The 'we knew' suggests that the character was contemporary.

ll. 32–5. *And lastly . . . cowardly solitarynes.* Cf. 'Man hath many offices, that appertaine to this world, and whilest he is here, must not withdraw himselfe, from those offices of mutuall society, upon a pretence of zeale, or better seiving God in a retired life', (*Sermons*, ix. 63) and also:

And as that drawes them from their Office of society, by a civill and Allegoricall Death, in departing from the world into a Cloyster, so this throwes you into a naturall, or vnnaturall and violent Death . . ., (*Pseudo-Martyr*, 'Preface', sig. D 3).

VI. That the guifts of the body are better then
those of the mind or of Fortune (p. 11)

Omitted in *Wy*.

The reading of *W* has been rejected on nine occasions, and on three (ll. 11, 58, 61) its spelling has been altered. In ll. 19, 41 *W* omits a word which is found in all the other witnesses, in ll. 4, 9, 15, 49, 55–6, 59, all the remaining manuscripts agree against it in minor readings, and in ll. 53–4, while there is dissension amongst the witnesses, the reading of *W* seems unlikely to be correct.

In this Paradox Donne argues that the gifts of the body are better than those of either the mind or fortune by using, or mis-using, concepts of Renaissance Platonism. The complementary nature of the soul and the body, the necessity of their interdependence, and the idea that the soul should not be honoured at the expense of the body are given in many of Donne's writings, as, for example, 'The Exstasie', ll. 49–56; 'Aire and Angels', ll. 11–14; 'A Litanie', ll. 143–4; *The Second Anniversary*, ll. 157–68; 'To the Countesse of Bedford' ('T"have written then . . .'), ll. 37–60; *Pseudo-Martyr*, Ch. III, Sect. 6, 17.

ll. 1–2. *I SAY agayne . . . good or bad mind.* Donne's argument is not the Platonic concept that the soul is the form of the body, but rather that the body forms the mind. Cf. Bacon, *Essays*, no. XLIV, 'On Deformity', 'Deformed persons are commonly even with nature; for as nature hath done ill by them, so do they by nature . . . Certainly there is a consent between the body and the mind . . . Therefore it is good to consider of deformity, not as a sign, which is more deceivable; but as a cause, which seldom faileth of the effect' and Burton, *Anatomy*, Pt. I, Sect. ii, Memb. 5, Subsect. 1, who wrote that although the soul activates the body, it 'receives a tincture from the body'. Cf. also *Sermons*, iv. 226, and Marvell, 'A Dialogue between the Soul and the Body'.

l. 3. *confounded*. 'Confound' = to mix up or mingle so that the elements become difficult to distinguish or impossible to separate, *OED* 6.

l. 5. *enhabled*. 'Enable' = to give power to; to strengthen, make adequate or proficient, *OED* 3, *obs.* or *arch.*

ll. 6–10. *My body licenceth . . . or heare.* The argument is the Platonic commonplace that the soul sees the beauties of the world through the senses of the body. However, where the Platonic idea continues that the contemplation by the soul of wordly beauties enables the soul to contemplate the idea of beauty, Donne merely says that the body can derive no pleasure from the soul. He argues the dependence of the soul on the body, instead of saying that the soul uses the body to achieve higher things.

l. 6. *licenceth*. 'License' = to give permission to (do something), *OED* 1, now *rare*.

ll. 10–12. *though without doubt . . . behind as before.* 'The soul cannot make the back of our heads see, though she is both willing and able to look before and after'.

l. 19. *my mind hath this maime.* 'Maim' = grave defect, blemish, or disablement, *OED* c, *trans.* and *fig.* Evelyn Simpson pointed out in 'More Manuscripts etc.', 299, this reading of *W* is clearly correct. The scribe of *Bur*, by omitting one minim, had changed *maime* to *mayne*, and this by an easy alteration has given rise to *many* which is found in all the other witnesses.

ll. 22–4. *Are Chastity... in the body.* Donne may have been thinking of Aristotle, 'Temperance and profligacy have to do with those two senses whose objects are alone felt by and give pleasure and pain to brutes as well; and these are the senses of taste and touch', *Ethica Eudemia*, Bk. III, ch. 2, and 'Temperance must be concerned with bodily pleasures, but not all even of these', *Ethica Nicomachea*, Bk. III, ch. 8.

ll. 25–8. *Healthe is a guifte... this happines.* See General Introduction, pp. xxii–xxiii.

ll. 35–50. *And even at last... thy judgment is good.* This is a difficult argument: Donne says that the virtues of the mind can be recognized only by sound judgement in he who judges and by faith and belief, for a little virtue can hide much vice. The attributes of the body, on the other hand, can be seen and hence measured. Yet, he concludes that judging the beauty of the body (as judging that of the mind) is dependent upon good judgement in the beholder.

l. 42. *flexible to companies.* 'Flexible' = able to be 'bent', inclined, or rendered favourable to, *OED* 3a, *obs.* One who is inclined to adapt himself to his company. The reading has caused difficulties both to the scribe of *S* who wrote 'flexible to (*blank*)' and to the compositor who obscured the meaning of the passage by setting *'flexible to complaints'*. *Bur* reads 'Sociable' which may represent an attempt to simplify the passage.

l. 44. *Elixar.* 'Elixir' is used in the alchemical sense; as an elixir 'turns' base metals into gold, so discretion 'turns' vice into vertue, pride into humility, and cowardice into honourable and wise valour.

ll. 50–2. *And in a faire body... in a deformed.* Cf. 'Holy Sonnet' ('What if this present...'), ll. 13–14:

> To wicked spirits are horrid shapes assign'd,
> This beauteous forme assures a pitious minde.

However, cf. Ortensio Lando's Paradosso II, 'Che meglio sia l'esser brutto, che bello' where Lando argues that noble minds frequently occur in deformed bodies, citing as examples, Socrates, Aesop, Zeno, Aristotle, and others, *Paradossi*, 1544, f. 13.

The reading of *W* has been accepted, '... or expect a good ...', despite the fact that it has no support. Groups II and III read '... or an exceedinge good ...'. *S* and the editions read 'hope for' for 'expect' and repeat 'seldome', which is found earlier in the sentence. *Bur* omits the clause.

ll. 53–4. *a ruinous wytherd building.* 'Withered' = weathered, *OED* 4b, *obs*, *rare*. The editions read *weather-beaten*.

The singular form, *building*, as found in *Bur*, Group III, *S*, and the editions has been adopted over the plural buildings of *W* and Group II. The singular number has been accepted as correct because the 'ruinous' building' is contrasted with the 'goodly house' and is ruinous because 'it seemes eyther . . .'.

ll. 60–1. *So that vertue . . . is indeede nothing.* Cf. 'Virtue is its own reward', Tilley, V 81. As an example of this proverb, F. P. Wilson (ed.), *The Oxford Dictionary of English Proverbs* (3rd edn., 1970), cites Sir Thomas Browne, *Religio Medici*, I. xlvii (1881), 74, '*Ipsa sui pretium virtus sibi* (Claudian, *De Mallii Theod. Consul.* v. 1) that Vertue is her own reward is but a cold principle'. Donne's sentence is, like Browne's, a cynical restatement of a common proverb.

VII. That a wise man is knowne by much Laughinge (p. 14)

The first seven lines of text are omitted in *Wy*.

Seven unimportant readings of *W* have been rejected; in ll. 51, 54, 59 all the witnesses agree against it, in ll. 51, 52, 60 it omits a word found in the other witnesses, and in l. 58 it adds a word to the text. In l. 16, where there is dissention among the witnesses, and the reading of *W* has been rejected, the choice of the reading adopted has been discussed in the notes.

This Paradox may have been written in reaction to Ortensio Lando's Paradosso XII, 'Meglio è di piangere, che ridere', where Lando wrote 'Il riso sempre abondon nelle bocche de pazzi, e dal senno uscito' (laughter always abounds in the mouths of madmen and those without sense), *Paradossi*, 1544, f. 46ᵛ.

l. 1. Ride si sapis o puella ride. Martial, *Epigrams*, ii. 41. 1, 'Laugh if you are wise, O girl, laugh'. Martial attributes the line to Ovid but it is not found in his extant works.

ll. 2–5. *For since the powers . . . and discoursing.* Cf. 'Upon Mr Thomas Coryat's *Crudities*', ll. 13–14:

> If man be therefore man, because he can
> Reason, and laugh, thy booke doth halfe make man

and in 'Metempsychosis', ll. 454–6, the ape:

> His organs now so like theirs hee doth finde,
> That why he cannot laugh, and speake his minde,
> He wonders.

Aristotle discusses laughter as the exclusive property of man in *De partibus animalium*, Bk. III, ch. 10.

ll. 5–10. *I allwayes did . . . wise men laugh.* Cf. 'A fool is ever laughing',

Tilley, F 462, which cites *Dal riso molto, conosci lo stolto*, 'By much laughter, thou knowest a fool', Torriano, *Piazza universale di proverbi Italiani or a common place of Italian proverbes and proverbial phrases* (1666), 237, no. 13. Although Donne wrote 'that Adage' to introduce the proverb, it does not occur in Erasmus's *Adagia*.

ll. 10–12. *Which mov'd* Erasmus . . . *beholders laughe.* Cf. *The Praise of Folie*, 7, 'that as soone as I came forth to saie my mynd afore this your so notable assemblie, by and by all your lokes began to clere up: unbendyng the frounyng of your browes, and laughing upon me . . .', Erasmus' work was the greatest and most famous of the paradoxical treatises of the Renaissance, and exercised a strong effect on succeeding attempts at paradoxical writings.

l. 16. *to the exercise.* The passage has caused difficulties amongst the scribes and in all the witnesses except *S* and *1633* + the meaning has been obscured. *W* reads '. . . by the exercise . . .' instead of '. . . to the exercise . . .', and Groups II and III read nonsense: '. . . by more causes wee should bee importuned to laugh then to any of any other power'. No reading is recorded for *Bur.*

ll. 21–4. *And therfore the poet* . . . Quid facit Canius tuus? ridet. 'What is your Canius doing? He is laughing'. The *poet* is Martial, and Donne has adapted his line, 'Vis scire quid agat Canius tuus? ridet,' (Do you want to know what your Canius is doing? He is laughing), *Epigrams*, iii. 20. 21. Canius Rufus, from Gades, is known only through Martial's Epigrams. *Oxford Classical Dictionary*, 2nd edn. (1970), 201. The minims in his name gave difficulties to the scribes, who wrote variously: Camus, Group II; Canis, *S*; Caius, *B*; Cavimus, *O 2*; and Gauimus, *P.*

ll. 27–8. Democritus *and* Heraclitus . . . *lovers of wisdome.* See Karl Deichgräber, 'Bemerkungen zu Diogenes' Bericht über Heraklit', *Philologus*, xciii (1938–9), 12–30. Deichgräber noted that Theophrastus in his 'Notes' had remarked that Heraclitus' arguments appeared to be half-finished, contradictory and jerky—features which denote 'melancholy'. (Aristotle, *Ethica Nicomachea*, Bk. VII, ch. 7. Melancholics are 'keen and excitable people that suffer especially from the impetuous form of inconstance . . .'). The term 'melancholy' has nothing to do with sadness, but writers such as Seneca in *De tranquillitate animi*, xv. 2, and Lucian in *Vitarum auctio*, 14, compared Heraclitus and Democritus and so began the legend of the weeping philosopher. The tradition of Democritus of Abdera as the laughing philosopher goes back to Aelian, *Variae historiae*, iv. 20 (E. M. S.).

ll. 29–31. *many would be found* . . . Democritus *laughing.* Cf. Lando, Paradosso XII, 'Meglio è di piangere, che ridere', where his claims are opposite to those of Donne's, 'Fu sempre molto da più stimata Heraclito perchè pianse, che Democrito per haver riso' (Heraclitus was always more esteemed for his tears than Democritus for his laughing), *Paradossi*, 1544, f. 46ᵛ.

ll. 36–41. *a Princes Court . . . broad gold laces.* There is a resemblance between this passage and Donne's attack on 'gay painted things' in Satire IV, where he describes the rich apparel of the courtiers who have sold their estates to purchase their finery (E. M. S.).

l. 39. *Arras.* A rich tapestry fabric in which figures and scenes are woven in colours, *OED* 1.

l. 39. *hangings.* The reading of the Paradox has been obscured by the faulty punctuation of the editions which read '. . . . so *painted* in many *colours*, that he is hardly discerned, from one of the *pictures* in the *Arras*, hanging his *body* . . .'.

l. 43. *monster.* Something extraordinary or unnatural, *OED* A. 1, *obs.*

l. 48. *as cold as the Salamander.* The Salamander (a lizard-like creature) was thought to be so cold by nature that contact with it could extinguish fire (Aristotle, *Historia animalium*, Bk V, ch. 19; Pliny, *Historia animalium*, X. 86; etc.).

ll. 55–61. *our superstitious civility . . . shew themselves wise.* This appears to be Donne's cynical social comment on 'Than againe, *we* (saieth he [St. Paul 1 Cor. 4: 10]) *are become fooles for Christes sake . . .* he plainely enjoygneth Folie unto us, for a thyng moste necessarie, and right importyng to salvacion? *For who so semeth* (saieth he [1 Cor. 3: 18]) *to be wise amonges you, let him become a foole, to the ende he be wise in deede*', Erasmus, *The Praise of Folie*, 116.

VIII. That good is more common then evill (p. 17)

The last two-thirds of the text, after l. 14, are omitted in *S*.

The reading of *W* has been rejected on six occasions. In l. 30 all the manuscripts agree against it, in ll. 26, 42 *W* adds a word to the text, in ll. 22, 27 *W* omits a word, and in ll. 25–6 it omits a passage of fifteen words.

ll. 1–3. *I HAVE not . . . ther owne.* There is in this sentence a reminiscence of Horace's description of the old man who is always praising past times:

> difficilis, querulus, laudator temporis acti
> Se puero, castigator censorque minorum.

'Peevish, surly, given to praising the days he spent as a boy and to reproving and condemning the young', *Ars poetica*, ll. 173–4 (E. M. S.).

l. 5. *Senses are to pleasure, as sickmens tasts to Liquors.* 'Sense' = capacity for perception and appreciation of, *OED* I. 9. 'Taste' = inclination, liking for, appreciation, *OED* III. 7.

ll. 7–10. *and good is . . . to be common.* Cf. Aquinas, *Summa Theologiae*,

1a 2ae q. 81, art. 2, '... bonum est magis diffusivum sui quam malum' (good spreads itself more than evil does). Cf. also *Sermons*, vi. 236–7, 'Good is as visible as greene', 'Communitie', l. 14, and 'No evill wants his good', *The First Anniversary*, l. 3.

l. 9. *Nature and end, and perfection.* 'Nature' = the essential qualities or properties of a thing, *OED* I. 1. 'End' = aim, purpose, *OED* II. 14. 'Perfection' = completed state, completeness, *OED* 2, *obs.*

ll. 11–14. *So that in the worlds ... shalbe good.* 'Evil is privation—absence of good. It does not exist *per se*, so that as long as the world lasts, there *must* be good'.

l. 12. *if this world shall suffer dotage.* The idea is the commonplace theory of the decay of the world which was most fully stated by Godfrey Goodman in *The Fall of Man*, 1616, and most strongly attacked in George Hakewill's *An Apologie of the Power and Providence of God*, 1627. It occurs repeatedly in Donne's works, as, for example, 'To the Countesse of Huntingdon' ('Man to Gods image ...'), 'Metempsychosis', 'Satire III', 'Satyre V', and in the *Anniversaries*.

ll. 17–18. *And as Embroderers ... adorne ther works.* This sentence contains a thought which Donne was later to expand in his sermons, that good could not only triumph over evil, but could actually make use of it and produce a design in which evil contributes to the perfection of the final pattern. See *Sermons*, vi. 237, 'For, as poisons conduce to Physick, and discord to Musicke, so those two kinds of evill, into which we contract all others, are of good use ...' (E. M. S.).

l. 17. *Lapidaryes.* 'Lapidary' = an artificer who cuts, polishes, or engraves gems or precious stones, *OED* B. 1a.

l. 18. *works.* The reading of *W* has been adopted despite the agreement of *Bur* and Groups II and II against it. The passage immediately following this reading is corrupt in all the witnesses except *W* and *Bur*, and in *W* and *Bur* the passage reads 'them ... ther goodnes ... ther Shew, *etc.*', all of which refer back to the artisans' *works*.

ll. 18–21. *for by adding ... and eminency.* The meaning of this passage has been obscured by the editions, and the passage itself has caused great difficulty amongst the various scribes. The reading of *W* which is supported by *Bur* with the exception that *Bur* reads *adorne* for *better*, *equalls* for *equall things*, and omits *Shew, and* has been accepted. Like Evelyn Simpson in her text, I have preferred the reading of *W* on the sound textual principle that it best explains the divergent readings of *Bur* on the one hand, and those of the remaining witnesses on the other. The passage means that the craftsman can enhance the quality of his *works* not only by adding *better things* or *equall things* (such as precious stones or silken threads) which naturally add to the *goodnes* of the works, but also by adding worse things (such as dull colours or base material) which act as a foil to increase the *Shew, and Lustre, and eminency* (E. M. S.).

l. 21. *eminency*. Height; prominence, elevation above surrounding objects, *OED* I. 1, *obs., rare*. 'Worse' things can be used to raise the relief of a design.

ll. 21–4. *So good doth . . . more common to us*. In the same manner as the artisan uses base materials in his designs, good uses evil in order to spread and raise herself.

l. 22. *amiablenes*. The quality of being lovable, *OED* 1b, *obs*. or *arch*. Woodward apparently had trouble with his copy and left a blank space of 28 mm in the line to indicate that he was omitting something.

l. 22. *ayd*. 'End' the reading of all the witnesses except *W* and *Bur* has increased the obscurity of this section of the text.

l. 24. *evill manners . . . good Lawes*. Cf. Erasmus, *The Praise of Folie*, 44, 'Or to what effect stode Law, seeyng as yet evill maners reigned not, wherupon good lawes (no doubt) were fyrst grounded?' and 'Ill manners (lives) produce good laws', Tilley, M 625.

ll. 24–6. *good Lawes. And in . . . we call good*. The omission of 'And in . . . we call good' in *W* appears to have arisen because of haplography in the repetition of *good Lawes* and *good*. I have retained the full stop after *Lawes* in *W* and have supplied punctuation for the inserted sentence which is found in all the other witnesses.

ll. 25–6. *in every evill . . . we call good*. 'Excellency' = something that excels or takes the highest place, *OED* 1c, *obs*. The word is used like 'excellent' (*OED* 1b, *obs*. or *arch*.) in a bad or neutral sense. The sentence means in every vice there is an excelling, this is called (in common speech) good. There is a pun on 'excellency'. Cf. *Titus Andronicus*, II. iii. 7 'A very excellent piece of villany', *Henry V*, II. ii. 113, 'Hath got the voyce in hell for excellence', also *Othello*, III, iii. 91, and *Antony and Cleopatra*, I. i. 40.

l. 28. *as long . . . as long*. It is not possible to tell from Evelyn Simpson's notes which *as long* reads *so long* in *Bur*.

ll. 33–4. *foule may be . . . faire and riche*. 'Foule' the reading of *W* and *Bur* must be correct. The point that Donne is making is that the contraries of the three categories of the good (fair, profitable, and virtuous) can each have the goodness of the other two; the contrary of fair being foul, of profitable or rich being poor, and of virtuous being vicious.

ll. 36–7. *subjects poysond with evill . . . accompany the evill*. *Bur* reads *subjects accompanied with evil* which is nonsense. This reading has arisen from haplography because of 'evil . . . evil'.

IX. That by Discord things increase (p. 19)

The opening ten lines are omitted in *S*.
The reading of *W* has been rejected on five occasions, ll. 3, 16, 20, 23, 43.

ll. 1–3. *Nullos esse Deos . . . videt beatum.* ' "There are no gods, heaven is empty", Selius declares, and he proves it, because while he denies these things, he sees himself made prosperous', Martial, *Epigrams*, iv. 21. 1–3. Selius finds it a proof that there are no gods, because he, although an atheist, prospers. This argument is fallacious, being an example of the *argumentum ad hominem*. Donne's first sentence is a good example of the same fallacy. Donne referred to this epigram in a sermon preached at Whitehall in 1617 (*Sermons*, i. 228–9) where he makes the point that it is 'a dangerous preterition, not to bring a mans self into Consideration; but to consider no man but himself, to make himself the measure of all, is as dangerous a narrowness. The Epigrammatist describes the Atheist so, That he desires no better argument to prove that there is no God, but that he sees himself, *Dum negat ista beatum*, prosper well enough, though he do not believe this prosperity to proceed from God. What miseries soever fall upon others, affect not him' (E. M. S.).

Selius. Modern texts of Martial read *Segius*, but the majority of fifteenth- and sixteenth-century texts read *Selius* or *Celius*. All the manuscripts of Donne read *Selius*, while 1633 + read *Cœlius*.

videt. The editions and all the manuscripts, with the exception of *Bur* (and *O 2* and *P*), mistakenly read '*vidit*' for '*videt*'; it is difficult to explain this agreement in patent error. Groups II and III manuscripts and the editions compound the error by presenting the words of the line in the wrong order.

ll. 5–6. *and feele . . . my body increaseth.* An allusion to the medical doctrine of the 'four humours' which represented different combinations of the four elements in a man's body. According to this doctrine, which was first suggested by Hippocrates and finally formulated by Galen, and which lasted until the end of the seventeenth century, health resulted from a balance of the humours and ill health was produced by the predominance of one or another of the humours. Donne was correct in stating that the mutual opposition of all four elements was necessary to health (E. M. S.).

l. 9. *faine.* 'Feign' = to conjure up (delusive representations), *OED* II. 4, now *rare*.

ll. 17–19. *impossible . . . generation.* Cf. 'The corruption of one is the generation of another', Tilley, C 667, and 'that worne axiome of *Aristotle; That the corruption of one thing is the generation of an other*', Henrie Cuffe, *The Differences of the Ages of Mans Life . . .*, written 1600, published 1607, 48.

l. 22. *Emperyes.* 'Empery' = absolute dominion, *OED* 1b, *obs*.

ll. 24–6. *And who . . . Religion it selfe.* Cf. Problem VI, ll. 15–17, the devil's kingdom is never 'so much advanced by debating religion (though with some Aspersions of Errour) as by a dull and stupid security in which many grosse things are swallowed'.

l. 29. *harborrers*. 'Harbourer' = one who harbours, shelters, or entertains, *OED*, 1. The word seems less likely to be scribal than the more usual 'nourishers'.

ll. 36–7. *for casting*. *S* and the first edition, *1633a*, obscure the meaning of this passage by reading *forecastinge*.

l. 37. Ide. The reading of the majority of the manuscripts is a common variant of Ida, the mountain where the Apple of Discord was cast and the Judgement of Paris given, thus leading up to the Trojan War.

l. 38. *ruind*. The reading of *Bur* is *envied*; 'envy' = ? to injure, *OED* 2b, *obs.*, *rare*. Cf. 'envy' sb. = active evil, harm, mischief, *OED* 2, *obs*. The verb used in this sense is of rare occurrence, and could be Donne's alteration.

l. 39. Quinzay. Quinsai was described as a most magnificent city, 'the City of Heaven', by Marco Polo in his *Travels*, Bk. II, ch. 64 in sixteenth-century Latin editions, Bk. II. ch. 68 in Ramusis's Italian translation (1583), and Bk. II, ch. 76 in Jule's English translation (1871). It is now called Hang-chou in the modern province of Chê-chiang, but when Polo went there it was still the capital of the southern Sung dynasty. The name appeared in many forms in the various medieval manuscripts of the Travels, but the typical form is *Quinsai*. Jule uses *Kinsay*, see *Quinsai with Other Notes on Marco Polo*, A. C. Moule, 1957.

ll. 39–40. *Nor are removd corners . . . by her fugitives*. 'Removed corners' = distant places.

l. 39. *fullfilld*. 'fulfil' = to spread through the whole extent of, to pervade, *OED* 1c. The reading of *W*, 'fullfilld only', is the only reading that gives the required sense, which is that distant places are filled full not only with the fame of Troy, but also physically in the form of cities and dominions established by fugitives from Troy such as Aeneas in Latium and Brutus in Britain. The meaning of this passage is obscured in Group III, *S* and in *1633* + because of faulty punctuation, a comma or semi-colon after *Quinzay*, and because of the omission of *Nor are*. These witnesses read nonsense, '. . . or Quinzay; remoued corners not only . . .'.

ll. 44–5. Uxor pessima . . . convenire vobis. 'The worst wife, the worst husband, I wonder you agree so badly', Martial, *Epigrams*, viii. 35. 2–3. The *textus receptus* of Martial reads *non bene* not *tam malé*, so Donne may have been quoting from memory. This particular epigram was used by Ben Jonson as the basis of his own 'Epigram XLII' in which he expanded the three lines of

Latin into eighteen English lines by personifying the quarrelling pair as Giles and Joan. Jonson submitted his epigrams to Donne for criticism; see his 'Epigram XCVI' (E. M. S.).

X. That it is possible to find some vertue in some women (p. 21)

The Paradox is omitted in *O 2*.

The reading of *W* has been rejected twice in l. 31, once where it omits a word and once where all the other witnesses agree against it. In l. 1 its peculiar spelling has been altered.

l. 1. *sear'd impudency*. 'Seared' = of the conscience, heart, etc. rendered incapable of feeling, *OED* 2, *fig.* 'Impudency' = shamelessness, immodesty, *OED* 1, *rare*.

ll. 2–3. *phisitians allow some vertu in every poyson*. Cf. Sir Thomas Browne, *Christian Morals*, Pt. I, sect. 28, 'In venomous Natures something may be amicable: Poysons afford Antipoysons: nothing is totally, or altogether uselessly bad', *Works*, ed. Keynes, i. 254. And Donne himself, 'God can extract good out of bad, and Cordials out of Poyson', *Sermons*, iv. 97.

l. 4. *certainly they are good for phisick*. Cf. *Sermons*, iii. 244, 'Now this institution of mariage had three objects: first, *In ustionem*, it was given as a remedy against burning . . . Let him then that takes his wife in this first and lowest sense, *In medicinam*, but as his Physick, yet make her his cordiall Physick, take her to his heart'.

l. 5. *wine is good for a fever*. Cf. 'Therfore men in olde tyme called wyne the greate Tryacle, for they founde that wyne helpeth in two contraryes. For it heteth cold bodyes, and keleth hote bodyes, and moisteth drye bodyes and abateth and dryeth moyste bodyes', Bartholome, *De proprietatibus rerum*, trans, John de Trevisa, 1535, Bk. XVII, ch. 134, f. cclxxxxvi, and copied in *Batman upon Bartholome*, 1582, f. 329. *Bur* reads, 'wine is good for a fever to increase it' which implies that it cures a fever by hastening it towards its crisis.

ll. 10–12. *if* Suum cuique dare . . . *to no man*. *Suum cuique dare* (to give to each his own). Plato, *The Republic*, Bk. I. vi, τὸ τὰ ὀφειλόμενα ἑκάστῳ ἀποδιδόναι δίκαιόν ἐστι (justice is to render to each his due) Polemarchus giving the poet Simonides's definition of justice. Cf. also 'Justice (saith *Cicero*) is a constant and perpetuall will and desire to give to everie one his right', *The French Academie*, Pierre de la Primaudaye, trans. T. B. [owes]., 1586, Bk. I, ch. 37, 370. Cf. also 'Let every Man have his own', Tilley, M 209. The passage is ironical, 'if to give to each his own is just, then women are the most just, for they give what is *theirs* to everybody'.

l. 13. Tanquam . . . negat. 'As if it were not permitted, no girl says no', Martial, *Epigrams*, iv. 71. 4.

l. 16. *entrap*. *W*, *Bur* have what seems to be the correct reading, the point being that lawyers struggle to entrap women, and preachers to persuade men to avoid them because they are so clever. However, *embrace* (or *imbrace*) the reading of Group II and the editions is possible; 'embrace' = to attempt to influence (a juryman, etc.) corruptly and illegally, *OED* v.³, *law*. If *embrace* is the correct reading, it is used as a pun, and lawyers seek both to embrace and corrupt women. The other manuscripts read nonsense—*entrace Dob, O'F, S; intrace B*; and *ontrance P*.

l. 17. *dehort*. To use exhortation to dissuade (a person) from a course or purpose, *OED* 1, now *obs*.

ll. 19–20. *yea . . . sorte of them*. This passage is omitted in *1633* + because of haplography. *1633* + also omit ll. 28–9, *but they are both good scourges for bad men*. The independence of the text in *1633* + from the text in *S* is shown by an omission by haplography which occurs only in *S* (l. 22, *and beeing them selves overthrowne*).

ll. 26–9. *we must say . . . bad men*. Cf. 'Law is the scourge of sin', Tilley, L 107.

ll. 29–31. *These or none . . . the World yields not one Example*. 'These are the *reasons* for considering women to be good. I cannot prove women to be good by example for there is no example of a good woman in the world.'

II. PROBLEMS

MSS.: Group II (*A 18, N, S 962, TCC, TCD, Wy*); Group III (*B, Dob, O'F*); *Ash 826, HMC 26; O 2, P; S; O 1*.
Latin text: *R*.
Editions: *1633a, 1633b, 1652*.

The number of Problems in these witnesses varies from the full nineteen found in Group III, *S 962*, and *Ash 826* through ten in *1633a* and *b* to six in *O 1*. The absence of a Problem from any of the more complete witnesses is noted at the beginning of the commentary on that Problem. Two further manuscripts, *A 25* and *Tan*, which each contain a single Problem have been included.

There is no 'best text' of the Problems. However, *O'F*, which contains the full nineteen Problems, has the most rational system of punctuation of all the witnesses and is consistently spelt. It looks as if it were put together to serve as copy for an edition (see Gardner, *Divine Poems*, p. lxxi). I have used *O'F* as copy-text except in the three Problems that show revision where *O'F* does not contain the final version of the text. For these three Problems, II, XII, XVIII, the copy-text is *TCD*. In using *O'F* as copy-text its peculiar substantive readings are rejected, and recorded in the apparatus.

Although many of the variants in the text of the Problems are trivial and should be attributed to scribal corruption, the texts of four Problems show extensive variation which I attribute to Donne's revising his text. Because of the pattern in which these revised Problems occur in the manuscripts, I have in general, in dealing with all the Problems, regarded the text in *Ash 826* and *R* to be earliest, the text in Group III to be intermediate, and the Group II text to be the latest. In establishing the text I have accepted the agreement of *Ash 826* and *R* with Group II as having the highest authority, because a reading which survives from the first version to the third, although not found in the second, is more likely to be correct. All readings of *Ash 826* and those of *R* which could represent what Donne wrote are given in the apparatus. Group II is represented by *TCC* and *TCD* whose agreement is designated *TC*, and by *S 962* as this manuscript contains the entire nineteen Problems. Group III is represented by *Dob* whose text closely agrees with that of the copy-text. Readings of *O 2* represent *O 2* and *P*, for their text represents a tradition between those of Groups II, and III is therefore useful in establishing the text. Finally, readings are recorded for *S*, whose text, though poor, is close to that of the first edition for the nine Problems which they share.

The Problems are printed in the order in which they occur in *O'F*. The number in which they occur in the editions is given in the apparatus to facilitate reference.

I. Why are Courtiers sooner Atheists then men of other Condition (p. 23)

This Problem is omitted in *1633a* and *b*.

The reading of *O'F* has been rejected on eight occasions. Two readings of *O'F* in the title which are not supported by *Dob* have been rejected. Five Group III readings found in *O'F* and *Dob* in ll. 6, 8, 10–11, 11, 12 have been rejected, and in l. 13 a phrase omitted in *O'F* and *Dob* has been restored to the text.

It is possible that this Problem is levelled against Sir Walter Ralegh and members of his circle. The Problem appears next to the 'Sir Walter Ralegh' Problem in all the manuscripts. Ralegh was charged with being master of a 'School of Atheism' by a Jesuit, Robert Parsons, in 1592 in *An Advertisement Written to a Secretarie of My L. Treasurers of Ingland, by an Inglishe Intelligencer as he passed throughe Germanie towardes Italie* (the work was a condensation of Parsons's *Responsio* which was written in Latin for European circulation under the pseudonym Andreas Philopater). In 1594 a special commission was sent into Dorset to examine both members of Ralegh's circle and Ralegh himself for remarks which he had made on God at a supper party in the summer of 1593 at Cerne Abbas, the home of Sir George Trenchard. The charge of atheism against Ralegh was kept alive throughout the decade and used against him at his trial in 1603. Other members of Ralegh's circle included the fifth Earl of Derby, the ninth Earl of Northumberland, Thomas

Herriot the mathematician, and Lord Hunsdon (E. M. S.). According to
E. A. Strathmann, *Sir Walter Ralegh a Study in Elizabethan Skepticism*
(New York, 1951), 54, 'Ralegh reached a new low in popular esteem after the
death of Essex in 1601, for which the people held him largely responsible',
although he was not guilty. There was also resentment 'of his exercise of
monopolistic privileges and his own "damnably proud" and sometimes arrogant
bearing'. He was the target of a number of verse libels and lampoons, some of
which were written between Essex's death and his own trial.

It is probable that this Problem is directed against Ralegh, for 'Atheism was
rare in the England of this period, and it is difficult to think of any other
members of the Court at the beginning of the seventeenth century to whom
the label of "atheist" could have been affixed with any chance of recognition'
(E. M. S.). It is possible too, that the Problem belongs to the years 1601 to
1603 when Donne felt hostile towards Ralegh. I argue in the commentary
on Problem II that Donne was not an enemy of Ralegh's during either the
1590s or during the years of his imprisonment.

ll. 1–3. *Is it because . . . that all is so.* The danger of the scientist's becoming
an atheist is pointed out in the 'Epistle to the Reader', *The Second Part of the
French Academie*, Pierre de la Primaudaye, trans. T. B., 1594, sig. b, 'And
surely unles we tread in the steps of this worthy king, [David—Ps. 139: 14]
and propound this as the scope of all our travailes in searching out the severall
parts of our bodies, that God our Creatour and gratious preserver may bee
praised, worshipped, and feared thereby, we shall never know our selves aright,
and as we ought to doe, bur rather joyne with the most part of men who not
using their skill in this behalfe as a ladder to climbe up by unto God, sticke
fast in the very matter and forme of their bodies, so that many of them become
meere Naturalists and very Atheists.' The same point is made in Bacon's essay
'Of Atheism', first published as an essay in 1612, a revision of 'De atheismo' in
Meditationes sacrae published with the first edition of the *Essays* in 1597 and
translated the following year.

ll. 3–10. *So they seeing . . . Servants Lords and Kings.* Donne's general dislike
for the court, before his marriage removed him from its sphere, is seen in
Satires IV and V, the verse letter 'To Sir Henry Wotton' ('Sir more then
kisses . . .') and prose letters to Wotton which were preserved in the Burley
MS and which are printed in Simpson, *Prose Works*, 308–15. His hostility
towards the court and courtiers in this and in other Problems is more bitter.
    they. the courtiers.

ll. 10–11. *God likewise . . . mans creature.* 'Creature', the reading of Group
III, *O 2* and *R* (*creaturam*) must be correct for the argument throughout the
Problem is that men, particularly courtiers, deny the power of God. The
change from 'creature' to 'creator' by a scribe who did not understand what he
was copying is easier to accept than a change from 'creator' to 'creature'.

l. 14. *facinorous*. Extremely wicked, grossly criminal, etc. Said both of persons and their actions. Very common in the seventeenth century, *OED obs. exc. arch.*

ll. 16–17. *foole that hath sayd . . . there is no God.* Cf. 'The fool hath said in his heart, *There is* no God', Ps. 14: 1 and 53: 1. Donne also used the passage in *Sermons*, iii. 256, iv. 252, ix. 56, 168.

II. Why doth Sir Walter Ralegh write the Historie of these times (p. 24)

The Problem is found in *Tan*; it does not appear in *R, 1633* +.

This Problem exists in two states. One state (in *O'F, Dob, B, S, Tan*) differs from the other (in *TC, S 962, Ash 826, O 2*) in that it contains two concluding sentences. As I have concluded that the text in *Ash 826* is early, and that in *TC* late with the text in Group III being intermediate, I can only assume that the sentences found in Group III and also in *S* and *Tan* were added to the Problem at some time after its composition, producing a variant state. I do not know whether these sentences were written by Donne. I have, therefore, printed the text found in *TC, S 962, Ash 826, O 2* as the text, using *TCD* as copy-text, and have printed in the apparatus the extra sentences found in *O'F*, etc.

In following *TCD* as copy-text, there is only one alteration—the expansion of 'W. R.' to 'Walter Ralegh' in the title.

This Problem was first printed by Sir Edmund Gosse in his *Life and Letters of John Donne* (1899), ii. 52–3. It had been copied in the eighteenth century (into the manuscript here designated *Tan*) by the then Bishop Sancroft who noted above the text "'Tis one of Dr Donne's problemes (but so bitter, that his son—Jack Donne LL.D. thought not fitt to print it with the Rest;)'. So, the Problem has always been interpreted as a sign of Donne's hostility towards Ralegh. However, twentieth-century studies (R. C. Bald, *TLS*, 24 October 1952; R. E. Bennett, 'John Donne and the Earl of Essex', *MLQ* iii (1942), 603–4; and M. van Wyk Smith, 'John Donne's *Metempsychosis*', Pt. 2, *RES* xxiv (1973), 141–52) show that Donne was not solely pro-Essex and anti-Ralegh, and that he may in fact have sailed both on the Islands and the Cadiz voyages with Ralegh, rather than with Essex. These works point out that some of Donne's early writings, notably 'Cales and Guiana' and 'To Mr R. W.' ('If, as mine is . . .') show sympathy for Ralegh's project in Guiana, and that 'Metempsychosis' shows resemblances to Ralegh's 'Epitaph on the Earl of Salisbury'. Also, Donne's brother-in-law, Sir Nicholas Carey, was a brother of Lady Ralegh; and Henry Percy, the Earl of Northumberland, who was a friend of Ralegh's, was Donne's choice to break the news of his marriage to Anne More to his father-in-law in 1602. Donne, in 1609, sought the secretaryship of the colony in Virginia which Ralegh had founded.

R. C. Bald suggested that Donne's friendship with Ralegh during the 1590s survived the fall of Essex and Ralegh's trial in 1603, and that Donne may have been in touch with Ralegh during his imprisonment (*John Donne: A Life*

(1970), 229). Certainly, Donne was informed of the machinations which occurred during Ralegh's trial by a letter to him, presumed to have been written by Sir Tobie Mathew, which gave an account of the proceedings (*Tobie Mathew Collection* (1660), 279–88). It appears that this Problem is in need of reinterpretation to show that it is not so much motivated by bitterness towards Ralegh, as by cynicism concerning his state.

Title. The manuscripts fall into two groups, those which are in the present tense (*doth . . . write*), *Ash 826* and *TC* and those which are in the past tense *O'F, Dob, B, S 962, O 2, S,* and *Tan.* Of the seven manuscripts which have the title in the past tense, all but two, *S 962* and *O 2,* contain the extra concluding passage which implies that Ralegh's history is contemporary. I would suggest that the 'present tense version' is the original, and that it was possibly written in 1608 or 1609 after Ralegh had produced *The Present State of Thinges as they now stand betweene the three great Kingdomes, Fraunce, England, and Spaine,* a work which prompted Prince Henry, the Prince of Wales, to urge Ralegh to write *The History of the World.* It was probably through Henry's request of Ralegh that the variant title, 'Why was Sir Walter Raleigh thought the fittest Man to write the History of these Tymes' (*S* and *Tan*) arose.

In the 'Preface' to his *History,* Ralegh acknowledged the fact that there was public interest in what he was doing, and strong opinion as to what the public thought he should have been doing: 'I know that it will bee said by many, that I might have beene more pleasing to the Reader, if I had written the Story of mine owne times; having beene permitted to draw water as neare the Well-head as another. To this I answere, that who-so-ever in writing a moderne historie, shall follow truth too neare the heeles, it may happily strike out his teeth', 'Preface', *The History of the World* (1614), sig. E 4.

ll. 1–2. *BECAUSE being told . . . strength of twoe.* The King's Attorney, Sir Edward Coke, addressing the court at Ralegh's trial, in anticipation of the objection that the court had only one witness, Lord Cobham, instead of the two necessary in a treason charge, said '. . . when a man, by his accusation of another, shall, by the same accusation, also condemn himself, and make himself liable to the same fault and punishment: this is more forcible than many witnesses', Ralegh, *Works,* 1829, 'The trial of Sir Walter Ralegh', vol. i, p. 656.

ll. 5–7. *if hee should undertake . . . the world.* Donne seems to be making a joke which is dependent upon Ralegh's being an atheist. The world, to an atheist, *had* no beginning.

l. 6. *higher times.* 'High' = 'far advanced into antiquity'; of early date, ancient. In phr. *high antiquity* is blended the notion of ascending 'up the stream of time', *OED* 12. *OED* attributes the earliest use of the word to Robert Johnson in *The worlde, or an historicall description of the most famous kingdomes and commonweales therein,* 2nd edn. (1603), 28.

ll. 8–10. *Or because . . . more playnly.* This passage is found only in Group III, *S*, and *Tan*, and it seems probable that it was added to the original version, producing a variant form of the Problem.

l. 8. *a Bird in a Cage.* Henry, the Prince of Wales, 'did so far applaud the advice of *Rawly*, as to say *No King but his Father would keep such a Bird in a Cage*', Francis Osborne, *Historical Memoires on the Reigns of Queen Elizabeth, and King James* (1658), 141–2.

ll. 9–10. *hee thinkes not . . . repeats lesse, more playnly.* By inference, 'he thinks that a short work of recent history is better than a complete history that is not clear'.

III. Why doe Greate Men choose of all dependants to preferre theyr Bawds (p. 25)

This Problem is omitted in *1633a* and *b*.

The reading of *O'F* which is not supported by *Dob* has been rejected in the title and in l. 11. Also in l. 11 the spelling of *O'F* has been altered.

Title. preferre. To put forward or advance, in status, rank, or fortune, *OED* I. 1, *trans.*

Title. Bawds. (little Pimps, 1652) 'Bawd' = one employed in pandering to sexual debauchery; . . . masculine, a 'go-between', a pander; since *c.* 1700 only feminine, and applied to a procuress, or a woman keeping a place of prostitution, *OED.* Cf. Ortensio Lando, *Quattro libri*, 1556, 'Per qual cagione si truovano tante ruffiane' (why are so many [female] bawds found), 42.

ll. 1–2. *IT is not . . . were neerer.* 'Bawds are not promoted because they are most intimate with great men, because the women whom they introduce are more intimate than they.'

l. 1. *got.* 'Get' = to gain, reach, arrive at (a place), *OED* II. 25.

Secrets. The word is used as a pun, implying sexual organs as well as secrets. See 'secret' *OED*, adj. 1j.

l. 3. *belly.* The womb, the uterus, *OED* II. 7.

IV. Why doth not Gold soyle the fingers (p. 26)

The Problem is omitted in *1633a* and *b*.

The reading of *O'F*, supported by *Dob*, has been rejected in l. 5.

Title. Why doth not Gold soyle the fingers. Gold, literally, unlike many base metals does not leave a coloured deposit on the skin. See, for example, Scipion Dupleix, *La Curiosité Naturelle; rédigée en questions selon l'ordre alphabétique* (Paris, 1606), trans. into English, as *The Resolver; or Curiosities of Nature* (1635), 314, 'all metals leave a thicke ordure or taint to the hands . . . excepting only gold'.

l. 1. *Doth it direct all the Venim to the heart*. Cf. 'The Bracelet', ll. 112–14:

> Gold is restorative; restore it then.
> Or if with it thou beest loath to depart
> Because 'tis cordiall, would 'twere at thy heart.

Cf. Burton, *Anatomy*, Part 2, Subsect. 4, '*Erastus* concludes their Philosophical stones and potable gold, &c. *to be no better then poyson*'; cited Gardner, *Elegies etc.* 119.

ll. 1–2. *Or is it . . . not bee discoverd. R* reads 'An idcirco manus non inquinat, ut corruptiones, quae ab eo fiunt, non percipiantur' (Or therefore it does not stain the hands, in order that corruptions, which arise from [gold], should not be discovered).

ll. 2–4. *that should pass purely . . . and Heaven*. 'Because pure things, such as love, honour, etc., are given up for gold, then gold should circulate without staining'.

ll. 5–6. *such as for former fowlenesse you cannot discerne this*. 'Gold is found only in hands which are already so stained from previous crimes, that a new stain is not visible.'

V. Why dye none for love now (p. 26)

The Problem is omitted in *1633a* and *b*.

The reading of *O'F* has been rejected on four occasions and once, l.5, its spelling has been altered. In ll. 3, 5, 6 the readings of *O'F* which are not supported by *Dob* have been rejected, while in l. 5 the reading of *O'F* supported by *Dob* is also rejected.

Title. Why dye none for love now. Cf. *As You Like It*, IV, i. 89–103:

> *Orlando*: Then in mine own person, I die.
> *Rosalind*: No, faith, die by attorney. The poor world is almost six thousand
> years old, and in all this time there was not any man died in his
> own person, videlicet, in a love-cause . . . men have died from
> time to time and worms have eaten them, but not for love.

l. 3. *Poxe*. While medical literature has described a disease like syphilis from the time of Hippocrates and throughout the Middle Ages, syphilis reached epidemic proportions only after the discovery by Columbus of America in 1492. It spread extensively following the march to Naples of the French army under Charles VIII in 1494 (hence the name the French disease or *morbus gallicus*). See R. H. Major, *A History of Medicine*, 2 vols. (1954), i. 364–6.

l. 3. *Gunpowder*. The importance of firearms and cannons as weapons of war dates from the Battles of Ravenna (1512), Marignano (1515), and Pavia (1525). See Major, vol i, p. 368.

l. 4. *young marriages*. It is difficult to know to what Donne is referring here. Child marriages were not uncommon in the sixteenth and seventeenth centuries, see *Child Marriages, Divorces, and Ratifications, etc. In the Diocese of Chester*. A.D. *1561–6*, ed. F. J. Furnivall, E.E.T.S. 108, 1897, but it is hard to see how they could be said to destroy. On the other hand, the reference could be to ill-thought-out marriages, as indeed Donne's own marriage can be viewed.

VI. Why doe young Laymen so much study Divinity (p. 27)

This Problem is omitted in *R*.

The reading of *O'F* has been rejected on six occasions; on two, ll. 2 and 3–4 where it is supported by *Dob* and on four, ll. 1–2, 5, 6, 19 where it is not so supported. In l. 8 where only *Dob* and *O 2* have the correct reading and their reading has been adopted, the various variant readings are discussed.

To whom was Donne referring in this Problem? It is possible that he referred to himself, '. . . I had, to the measure of my poore wit and judgement, survayed and digested the whole body of Divinity, controverted betweene ours and the Romane Church', *Pseudo-Martyr*, 'Preface', sig. B 3. Bald suggested (p. 69) that Donne could have begun his study of Cardinal Bellarmine's *Disputationes de controversiis Christianae Fidei, adversus huius temporis haereticos* as early as 1591 and through 1593 when the third volume was published. During this period Donne was a student first at Thavies Inn and then at Lincoln's Inn; this occupation may have given rise to the variant reading found the title in *Ash 826*, 'Lawe men' for 'Laymen'. Jessopp, who probably based his assumption on this very Problem, wrote that during the last few years of Elizabeth's reign and the first few years of James's, a school of theology was growing up both at Oxford and Cambridge which gave rise to the remarkable preachers of the seventeenth century, 'The revival of interest in theology, and the hitherto unheard-of care and discretion in exercising church patronage, soon brought the ablest men to the front; and the stimulus given to the study of divinity, which Donne alludes to in one of his *Problems*, made theology fashionable among all classes', *John Donne Sometime Dean of St. Paul's* (1897), 55.

ll. 8–11. *Dwellers by the river* Ougus . . . *to the sea*. Ougus must be the correct reading, for although the river was usually called the Oxus by its English explorer Anthony Jenkinson, in Jenkinson's map of Russia, which was first printed in Abraham Ortelius's *Theatrum orbis terrarum*, Antwerp, 1570, the river was called the 'Ougus'. Donne possibly read abou tthe Oxus or Ougus in 'The voyage of M. Anthony Jenkinson, made from the citie of *Mosco in Russia, to the citie of Boghar in Bactria in the yere* 1558', *The Principall Navigations, Voiages and Discoveries of the English nation* . . . (Richard Hakluyt, 1589), 347–64. Jenkinson's account of the river (p. 352) reads as follows:

Note that in times past there did fal into this gulfe the great river *Oxus*, which hath his springs in the mountaines of *Paraponisus* in *India*, now commeth not so farre, but falleth into another river called *Ardocke*, which runneth towarde the North, and consumeth himselfe in the ground . . . the water that serveth all that Countrey is drawen by ditches out of the river *Oxus*, unto the great destruction of the said river, for which cause it falleth not into the *Caspian* sea as it hath done in times past, and in short time all that lande is like to be destroyed, and to become a wildernes for want of water, when the river of *Oxus* shall faile.

Cf. 'We read in the *Eastern Histories*, of a navigable River, that afforded all the inhabitants exportation, and importation, and all commerce. But when every particular man, to serve his own curiosity, for the offices of his house, for the pleasures of his gardens, and for the sumptuousnesse of Grots and aqueducts, and such waterworks, drew severall channells, infinite channells out of this great River, they exhausted the maine channell, and brought it to such a shallownesse, as would beare no boats, and so, took from them the great and common commodities that it had afforded them. So if every man think to provide himselfe *Divinity* enough *at home*, for himselfe and his family . . . he frustrates the Ordinance of God, which is, that his sheep should come to his pastures, to take his grasse upon his ground, his instructions at his house at *Church*', *Sermons*, x. 144.

ll. 14–17. *nor was his kingdome . . . things are swallowed*. As Milgate noted in his commentary, this sentence is the crudely stated central idea of 'Satire III', *Satires etc.* 140.

l. 16. *Aspersions*. 'Aspersion' = the sprinkling in of an ingredient, *OED* 3, *obs*.

ll. 17–22. *Possibly . . . it is not divinity*. 'In the manner in which we pretend to be familiar with the king and court, we seek to make ourselves appear familiar with God. When hopes of secular preferrment promote our study of religious matters; it is not divinity.' Cf. Walton's reconstruction of Donne's refusal of the benefice offered to him by Bishop Morton (Bald, 206–7), 'And besides, whereas it is determined by the best of *Casuists*, that *Gods Glory should be the first end, and a maintenance the second motive to embrace that calling*; and though each man may propose to himself both together; yet the first may not be put last without a violation of Conscience, which he that searches the heart will judge. And truly my present condition is such, that if I ask my own Conscience, whether it be reconcileable to that rule, it is at this time so perplexed about it, that I can neither give my self nor you an answer.'

VII. Why hath the common opinion affoorded woemen Soules (p. 28)

The reading of *O'F* has been rejected on thirteen occasions; on six, ll. 2, 7, 13, 19–20, 22, 24, its reading is supported by *Dob*, and on four, ll. 14, 16, 22, 23, it is not so supported. Three rejected readings of *O'F*, ll. 5, 11, 25–6, are discussed in the notes.

Title. Why hath the common opinion affoorded woemen Soules. Cf. 'Women have no souls', Tilley, W 709, and 'To the Countesse of Huntingdon', 1–2:

> Man to Gods image, *Eve,* to mans was made,
> Nor finde wee that God breath'd a soule in her.

As Evelyn Simpson pointed out, *Prose Works*, 141, the question whether women had souls was debated in two Latin theses in 1595, *Disputatio Nova contra Mulieres qua probatur eas Homines non esse* and *Simonis Gedicii Defensio Sexus Muliebris, Opposita disputationi: Mulieres Homines non esse.* She also pointed to a probable reference to the first thesis in Jonson's *Masque of Beautie*:

> Had those, that dwell in error foule,
> And hold that women haue no soule,
> But seen these move; they would have, then
> Said, *Women were the soules of men,*

to which Jonson had appended the note: 'There hath beene such a profane *paradoxe* published' (1616 folio, 910). The whole question as to whether women have souls goes back to the commentary on 1 Cor. 11: 1–12 and 14: 34–5 in the commentaries on the Pauline Epistles which were wrongly attributed to St. Ambrose until about the year 1600 and which since then have passed under the name of Ambrosiaster. Cf.:

For, howsoever some men out of a petulancy and wantonnesse of wit, and out of the extravagancy of Paradoxes, and such singularities, have called the faculties, and abilities of women in question, even in the roote thereof, in the reasonable and immortall soul, yet that one thing alone hath been enough to create a doubt, (almost an assurance in the negative) whether S. *Ambroses* Commentaries upon the Epistles of S. *Paul*, be truly his or no, that in that book there is a doubt made, whether the woman were created according to Gods Image; Therefore, because that doubt is made in that book, the book it self is suspected not to have had so great, so grave, so constant an author as S. *Ambrose* was; No author of gravity, of piety, of conversation in the Scriptures could admit that doubt, whether woman were created in the Image of God, that is, in possession of a reasonable and an immortall soul, (*Sermons*, ix. 190).

See also *Sermons*, iv. 241.

opinion. See J. B. Bamborough, *The Little World of Man* (1952), 37, ' "Opinion" carried with it the idea of "popular prejudice", hearsay and "reputation" in the (unfavourable) Elizabethan sense . . . Since Opinion was an aspect of the Imagination, its characteristic was that it depended purely on the senses, and could judge only by outward show.'

ll. 1–3. *It is agreed ... sence or growth.* Cf. Paradox I, note ll. 3–4. This argument is derived from Aristotle as the translator of *R* indicated, '*Convenit inter Peripateticos aiebat*'. Cf. 'If then, when the sexes are separated, it is the male that has the power of making the sensitive soul, it is impossible for the female to generate an animal from itself alone, for the process in question was seen to involve the male quality', *De generatione animalium*, Bk. II, ch. 5.

ll. 3–4. *wee denye soules ... all but Speeche.* Cf. Paradox VII, note ll. 2–5. Cf. also Hieronimo Garimberto's Problem, 'Qual è la cagione che la natura habbia dato all'huomo la voce, e'l parlare, al resto de gli animali solamente la voce?', *Problemi naturali, e morali* (*Problemi*, 1549), Problem IX, 12.

ll. 4–5. *they are beholding ... bodily instruments.* This is clearly not true, as Donne was aware, but, cf. *The Second Part of The French Academie*, by Pierre de la Primaudaye, trans. T. B[owes], 1594, Bk. II, ch. 13, 89:

> But in men, voyces framed into wordes are signes and significations of the whole soule and minde, both generally and specially, namely of the fantasie and imagination, of reason and judgement, of understanding and memory, of will and affections.

ll. 5–6. *an Apes heart ... or a Serpents.* The reading *Oxes heart* in Group III, *S, O 2* and the editions is clearly wrong because the list consists of animals which typify the evil qualities commonly ascribed to women—the lecherous goat, the cunning fox, the guileful serpent. Apes were associated with the fall of man as a projection of man's own weakness and his inability to resist evil. See H. W. Janson, *Apes and Ape Lore in the Middle Ages and the Renaissance* (1952), 133.

l. 7. *the brest.* i.e. the human breast.

ll. 10–11. *some call ... Goddesses.* Cf. 'What did the *Germans* our Ancestors? they thought there was in that Sex something of Sanctity and foresight ... held most of them for Goddesses', John Selden, *The Reverse or Back-face of the English Janus*, trans. Adam Littleton (pseud. Redman Westcot), 1682, Bk. I, ch. xii, 20.

l. 11. *Peputian Heretikes.* Cf. 'Between the denying of them souls, which S. *Ambrose* is charged to have done, and giving them such souls, as that they may be Priests, as the *Peputian* hereticks did, is a faire way for a moderate man to walk in', (*Sermons*, iii. 242).

The reading in all the witnesses to the Problem is wrong, with that of *O'F, Puputian*, being closest to the correct reading and that of *O 2, puritane*, being a scribal attempt to make sense of a word which the scribe could not understand. Evelyn Simpson noted (*Prose Works*, 142 n.) that C. C. J. Webb had pointed out that the correct reading was *Peputian*, i.e. Montanist; Pepuza in Western Phrygia being one of their centres.

ll. 21–2. *the Devill . . . is all soule.* This was a common belief as Reginald Scot, noted in *The Discoverie of Witchcraft . . . Heerunto is added a treatise upon the nature and substance of spirits and divels*, 1584, ed. Brinsley Nicholson, 1886 ch. 32, 453–4.

ll. 24–6. *the* Romans *naturalized . . . common wealth.* Miriam Griffin has suggested that this statement alludes to Cassius Dio's reference to the infamous Caracallus, M. Aurelius Antoninus, who ruled the Roman empire from AD 211 until his assassination in 217. 'This was the reason he made all the people in his empire Roman citizens; nominally he was honouring them, but his real purpose was to increase his revenues by this means, inasmuch as aliens did not have to pay most of these taxes', *Dion's Roman History*, Bk. lxxviii, 9, 5–6. I do not know how much of Dio's work Donne knew; but much of his history was available in Latin in the latter half of the sixteenth century. In *Sermons*, viii. 324 he refers to the story of Cleander, found in Dio, Bk. lxxiii, 13, 6. Evelyn Simpson discussed Donne's knowledge of Dio's works in 'Introduction' *Sermons*, viii. 29 and in *Prose Works*, 54.

The reading of *O'F* in ll. 25–6 *because they should beare the burden*, along with the reading of *R*, *ut reipublicae onera ferrent*, make it quite clear that the granting of citizenship i mposed the burden of the common wealth upon the new citizens (not that the new citizens should be a burden on the common wealth). This reading of *O'F* looks like the work of a good copy editor, clarifyi ng an ambiguity in th e text.

VIII. Why are the fayrest falsest (p. 30)

The reading of *O'F* has been rejected on eight occasions. Two readings of *O'F*, ll. 4, 29, which are not supported by *Dob*, have been rejected. Four readings found in *O'F* and *Dob* in ll. 6, 8–9, 10, 13 have been rejected, and in ll. 25–6, a phrase omitted in *O'F* and *Dob*, has been restored to the text. In l. 4 the reading of *O'F* and *Dob* is rejected and that adopted is discussed in the notes.

l. 1. *false Alchimy beauty.* 'Alchemy' = glittering dross, *OED* 4 *fig.* The word is used as an adjective meaning 'cosmetic'.

l. 4. *comminge.* 'Coming' = inclined to make or meet advances; ready, eager, complaisant, forward (In good or bad sense), *OED*, ppl. a. 2. This reading is most likely to be correct, as *common* is a likely scribal substitution for the more unusual word. The meaning is, that although gold is as much sought for as women are, it is not inclined to make itself available as women do. The reading of *R* supports this sense, reading *et tamen incorruptum ac intemeratum semper manet* ([gold] nevertheless remains uncorrupted and pure).

ll. 6–7. *delicatest bloud . . . to the flesh.* Cf. Burton, *Anatomy*, Pt. I, Sec. 1,

Mem. 2, Subs. 2, 'Spirit is a most subtle vapour, which is expressed from the blood, and the instrument of the soul, to perform all his actions; a common tie or medium between the body and the soul, as some will have it . . .' and 'The Exstasie', ll. 61–4:

> As our blood labours to beget
> Spirits, as like soules as it can,
> Because such fingers need to knit
> That subtile knot, which makes us man.

The function of the spirit in linking the soul and the body in Elizabethan psychology is discussed in J. B. Bamborough, *The Little World of Man* (1952), 54–7. In Donne's question the link appears ineffective. 'Delicate' = fine or exquisite in quality or nature, *OED* II. 6b.

l. 9. *proportionable.* Suitable appropriate, *OED* 1b, *obs.*

l. 10. *temper.* Temperature (*OED* 4) = temperament (*OED* 3, *obs.*) 'Temper' = the constitution, character, or quality of a substance or body (orig. supposed to depend upon the 'temper' or combination of elements), *OED* II. 4.

l. 11. *complections.* The combination of the four 'humours' of the body in a certain proportion, or the bodily habit attributed to such combination; 'temperament', *OED* I. 1, *obs.* exc. *hist.*

ll. 12–13. *Bells of the purest mettall . . . sound longest.* Cf. Scipion Dupleix, *La Curiosité Naturelle; rédigée en questions selon l'ordre alphabetique* (Paris, 1606) trans. into English as *The Resolver; or Curiosities of Nature* (1635), 94, 'Wherefore is it that Bels of silver are more resounding then those of any other metall whatsoever they bee, aad [*sic*] those of Iron, lesse then any others?'.

l. 15. *complection.* The natural colour, texture, and appearance of the skin, *esp.* of the face, *OED* 4 (used in the modern sense, meaning the attractiveness of a face).

l. 27. *how deepe wee digg for them.* 'Dig' = penetrate in a sexual sense.

l. 28. *the Law of Nature* Occupanti conceditur. 'The law of occupancy is founded upon the law of nature, viz. *Quod terra manens vacua occupanti conceditur.* So as, upon the first coming of the inhabitants of a new country, he who first enters upon such part of it and manures it, gains the property; . . . so that it is the actual possession and manurance of the land which was the first cause of occupancy, and consequently is to be gained by actual entry', *The Law Dictionary, Explaining the Rise, Progress and Present State of the British Law,* T. E. Tomlins, 1835.

ll. 29–30. *Gold . . . admitts Allay.* The ability of gold to be mixed with an alloy appears to have interested Donne. He referred to the resultant alloy both as having greater worth or usefulness:

As gold whilest it is in the mine, in the bowels of the earth, is good for
nothing, and when it is out, and beaten to the thinnesse of leafgold, it is
wasted, and blown away, and quickly comes to nothing; But when it is
tempered with such allay, as it may receive a stamp and impression, then it
is currant and useful, (*Sermons*, iii. 148),

as well as having less value:

The comforts of God are of a precious nature, and they lose their value, by
being mingled with baser comforts, as gold does with allay, (*Sermons*, iii.
271).

it selfe. This reading of the Group III manuscripts supported by *O 2*, *S*
and the editions appears more likely to be correct than the *yt* of *Ash 826* and
Group II.

IX. Why have Bastards best Fortune (p. 31)

The reading of *O'F* has been rejected on twelve occasions. Eight rejected
readings are supported by *Dob, title*, ll. 3, 5–6, 15, 18, 23, 27, 30 and four
are not so supported, ll. 7, 18, 33–4, 37.

The opening nineteen lines of this Problem were omitted in the first edition,
although they are found in all the manuscripts. When the second edition was
published, without licence, the missing lines were restored. The passage which
was most likely to have been offensive to the court was that which *was* printed
in the first edition, not that which was omitted; perhaps the publisher mis-
understood the instructions of Sir Henry Herbert who had granted the licence,
and printed the passage which ought to have been omitted. When he found that
the Bishop of London had ordered an inquiry as to why Herbert had licensed
the book, the publisher, Seyle, hurriedly produced the second edition without
licence, and printed the Problem as a whole (E. M. S.). This Problem is
probably derived from Ortensio Lando's Problem, 'Perchè sono spesse siate
[*sic, for* fiate] i bastardi più ingeniosi che i legittimi non sono', (why bastards
are more ingenious than legitimate children). See General Introduction,
p. xxxvii.

The Problem also appears to owe its opening to Lando's Paradosso XVIII,
'Non è cosa biasmevole l'esser bastardo'; which was translated into English as
'A Paradox, in the defence of Bastardie: Approoving, that the Bastard is more
worthy to be esteemed, then hee that is lawfully borne or Legittimate' in
Thomas Milles, *The Treasurie of Auncient and Moderne Times* ... (1613),
Bk. VII, ch. 43, 723–5. However, there is a considerable difference between
Donne's Paradox and Lando's—Lando argues seriously for the justification of
bastardy, while Donne attacks the court where illegitimacy appears to be no
barrier to success.

ll. 2–5. *The old naturall reason ... easy and lawfull*. Cf. Milles's translation of
Lando's Paradosso XVIII:

The great Priviledges, which I see are duely appertayning to Bastards, and illegitimate Children . . . makes mee undertake the boldnesse, to preferre them before other; and to shew by good reasons, that they are greatly superiour to such, whom we call legittimate and lawfull borne Children . . . Bastards generally, are begot in more heat and vigour of love, with more agreeable conformity of willes, and farre sweeter Union of the spirites, then the most part of our Legittimate Children . . . their conception is performed by stolne opportunities, warie preventions, watchfull discretion, and an infinite number of more ingenious deceipts, and amorous actions, then eyther needeth, or is required, in a setled condition of marriage, free from that fierie feare, which is the sole spurre unto a longing appetite.

ll. 4–5. *the easy and lawfull*) *might.* Donne is contrasting 'meetings in stolne love' with married love-making. The Group II manuscripts leave a blank after 'lawfull' as if they omitted a word such as a repetition of 'meetings'.

l. 6. *in ordinary.* In the ordinary course, as a regular custom, etc., *OED* III. 18, *obs.*

l. 8. *the Arke.* As Frank Manley noted in his edition of Donne's *Anniversaries* the use of the Ark as a symbol of the just man's inner peace was a commonplace derived from St. Ambrose.

ll. 28–30. *church . . . service of God.* Under canon law a man born illegitimately could not become a priest. See Lyndwood's *Provinciale*, eds. J. V. Bullard and C. Bell (1929), 8, and James K. McConica's annotation on Erasmus' dispensation, Erasmus, *Collected Works*, iv (Toronto, 1977), 188–90. I am indebted to McConica for this note.

ll. 31–4. *the two greatest powers . . . Legitimation.* Cf. 'Satire II', ll. 74–6,

> Bastardy'abounds not in Kings titles, nor
> Symonie'and Sodomy in Churchmens lives,
> As these things do in him; by these he thrives.

ll. 34–5. *Nature frames . . . Bodyes of Contraryes.* Cf. 'Yet some have wondered how it is that the Universe, if it be composed of contrary principles—namely, dry and moist, hot and cold—has not long ago perished and been destroyed . . . It may perhaps be that nature has a liking for contraries and evolves harmony out of them and not out of similarities . . . and has devised the original harmony by means of contraries and not similarities', Aristotle, *De mundo*, ch. 5.

X. Why Venus starre onely doth cast a Shadowe (p. 33)

The reading of *O'F* has been rejected on ten occasions, and two omissions that occur only on *O'F*, ll. 5, 12, are restored to the text. Seven rejected readings of *O'F* are not supported by *Dob*, *title* ll. 7, 11, 14, 15, 22, 24, and two rejected readings are so supported, ll. 23, 29. The reading of *O'F* in l. 3 is also rejected and the reading adopted is discussed in the notes. *Ash 826* and *R* agree in two sentences which are not found in the other witnesses.

Title. Why Venus starre onely doth cast a Shadowe. Venus does cast a shadow; Cf. Bartholome, *De proprietatibus rerum* (1535), Bk. VIII, ch. 26, f. cxxvii, Venus 'sendeth from hym selfe clere beames of lyghte. And therfore he maketh shadowe whan the wether is faire and clere'. C. M. Coffin, 'Donne's Astronomy', *TLS* 18 September 1937, noted that the fact that Venus could cast a shadow could be found in Pliny, *Historia naturalia*, Bk. II, ch. 6, in Kepler's 'Optics' ('*Ad Vitellionem paralipomena . . . astronomiae pars optica*'), Frankfurt, 1604, *Opera Omnia*, ed. Frisch, ii. 293, and in his *De stella nova in pede Serpentarii*, Prague, 1606. In *De stella nova*, Kepler wrote that the new star appeared at the time of the morning rising of Venus, when Venus was near the earth and of such a brightness as to be able to cast a shadow, which he, despite his poor vision, could see (Frisch, ii. 619).

l. 3. *as* Kepler *sayes*. Cf. *Ignatius His Conclave*, 7 '*Keppler*, who (as himselfe testifies of himselfe) *ever since* Tycho Braches *death, hath received it into his care, that no new thing should be done in heaven without his knowledge*'. The sentence referred to Kepler's words, 'Tychone iam mortuo equidem haec me cura incessit, ne quid fortasse novi existeret in caelo me inscio' in *De stella tertii honoris in cygno*, 1606 (E. M. S.).

Kepler. The variety of variant readings which the scribes have produced to represent this name is testimony both to the fact that Donne's 'R' and his 'K' were very difficult to distinguish, and also to the general poor quality of the manuscripts of the Problems. The translator of *R* evaded the issue by writing 'At illi, qui sedulò curant, ne quid fiat in coelis, cujus inscii sint, nempe Astrologi . . .' (But they who sedulously take pains that nothing should happen in the heavens without their knowledge, that is, astrologers . . .).

l. 4. *have bidd* Mercury *to bee nearer*. I. A. Shapiro, in a letter headed, 'John Donne the Astronomer: The Date of the Eighth Problem', *TLS* 3 July 1937, pointed out the relative differences in the nearness to the earth of the planets Venus and Mercury according to whether the system of Copernicus and Tycho Brahe was accepted or that of Ptolemy. He also noted that while in the Problem Donne said that Mercury was nearer the earth, in *The Second Anniversary*, ll. 189–206, he held Venus to be nearer, which it is in the Copernican system. Despite Donne's reference to Kepler in the Problem, he is not using the planetary system of Copernicus and Tycho Brahe, but is rather following that of Ptolemy. The additional sentence found in *Ash 826* and *R* (l. 34), which says that Venus is nearer to the sun than Mercury, also indicates that Donne had the Ptolemaic system in mind. However, Donne knew and marked Kepler's *De stella nova*. See Geoffrey Keynes, 'More Books from the Library of John Donne', *Book Collector*, xxvi (1977), 39–45.

l. 6. *those of* Mercury *neede it more.* There is a perpetual undercurrent of allusion to the various meanings of Mercury and Venus. In the first sentence of the problem the reference is to the two planets. In the second and third sentences Venus is the goddess of love and Mercury the god of eloquence (E. M. S.).

l. 7. *shadowes and colours.* 'Shadow' = an unreal appearance', *OED* II. 6, *fig.* a. 'Colour' = pretext.

l. 13. *Invention.* Something formally or authoritatively introduced or established; an institution, *OED* II. 10, *obs.* The reading of *Ash 826* is also possibly correct—*subventions.* 'Subvention' = a subsidy levied by the state, *OED* I, *obs.* exc. *hist.* R reads '*et postea tributa ad ipsum continuandum pendat*' (and afterwards pay tributes to continue [the yoke of sovereignty]).

l. 16. Venus *markets are so naturall.* 'Venus markets' =*OED* III, b, *attrib.* and *comb.* 'Venus' in sense 2, the desire for sexual intercourse; indulgence of sexual desire; lust, venery, *OED* 2, *obs.* Donne appears to mean general promiscuity, implying in the term 'Venus markets' the commercial nature of sex and variety of sexual partners.

l. 20. Venus *workes.* 'Venus' is used here as in '*Venus* markets', l. 16, above; Donne is saying that sexual desires are part of our nature.

ll. 20–1. (*for Marriage is chastity*). Cf. 'And mariage was not instituted to prostitute the chastity of the woman to one man, but to preserve her chastity from the tentations of more men', (*Sermons,* ii. 346–7). Cf. also 'for marriage must not be called a defilement', Milton, *Apology for Smectymnuus.*

l. 22. Sentence found only in *Ash 826, R.* The punctuation of this passage, given in the apparatus, is a correction of the faulty punctuation in *Ash 826* from the correctly punctuated *R. Ash 826* reads '. . . are workes of darkenesse Childish and vnrefined, times might thinke so . . .'. Perhaps Donne cut out this passage as being inconsistent with his preceding sentence on the naturalness of '*Venus* works'.

ll. 22–4. *In Senecas time . . . besides her husband.* This appears to be a reference to the general licentiousness of the emperor Nero and the imperial family. Seneca had tutored Nero and had been an influence upon him early in his reign. But in AD 65 Seneca committed suicide in obedience to Nero's orders. A play called *Octavia* which is based upon the activities of the imperial family used to be attributed to Seneca. See also Seneca, *Ad Helviam matrem de consolatione,* '*maximum saeculi malum, impudicitia*' (unchastity, the greatest evil of our time), xvi. 3.

l. 27. *Supererogation.* Performance of more than duty or circumstances require; doing more than is needed, *OED* I, b, *trans.* and *gen.*

COMMENTARY

l. 28. Et te spectator plus quam delectat Adulter. A rewording of 'et plus spectator quam te delectat adulter' (and the spectator pleases you more than the adulterer), Martial, *Epigrams*, i. 34. 3.

ll. 29–31. *And* Horace . . . *with looking glasses*. Cf. Suetonius, '*Vita Horati*', 'it is said that he was immoderately lustful; for it is reported that in a room lined with mirrors he had harlots so arranged that which every way he looked, he saw a reflection of venery'. Donne may have included this reference to Horace and his use of mirrors because of Seneca's reference to Hostius Quadra and his infamous use of mirrors in *Naturales quaestiones*, I. xvi. 1–9.

l. 34. Sentence found only in *Ash 826, R. her place is nearer the sunne then his, and one of her names* Lucifera. Cf. Bartholome, *De proprietatibus rerum*, 1535, Bk. VIII, ch. 26, f. cxxvii, 'Allway he is nygh the son and goth tofore him, and then he is called Lucifer a day ster, a nother time he foloweth the son, and then he is called Vesper, an eve ster.'

l. 39. *professeth*. 'profess' = the active voice *to profess*, to receive the profession of (a person), to receive or admit into a religious order, *OED* I. 1, *trans.* b.

XI. Why is Venus Starre multinominous called both Hesperus and Vesper (p. 35)

This Problem exists in two versions. The text in *Ash 826* and *R*, which I take to be the early version, is approximately half as long again as the text which I take to be the final version and which is found in all the other witnesses. Furthermore, in the material common to both long and short forms, the order in the sentences is slightly different. For these reasons, the long and the short texts are given.

The short version is printed from *O'F*, whose reading has been rejected on six occasions; on five, twice in the *title*, ll. 4, 8–9, 25, its reading is not supported by *Dob*, and on one, l. 13, it is so supported. The reading adopted in l. 13 is discussed in the notes.

The long version is printed from *Ash 826*, corrected where necessary from the text in *R*. It is headed '*Ash 826 text corrected from R*'.

Two sets of notes, one for each version, are given. The notes for the text in *Ash 826, R* follow the notes for the short version of the text.

Title. Why is Venus Starre multinominous called both Hesperus and Vesper. Although Venus is both the morning and the evening star, the planet was not known as Vesper in the evening and Hesperus in the morning as Donne appears to assume. Cf. *The Second Anniversary*, ll. 197–8:

> *Venus* retards her not, to'enquire, how shee
> Can, (being one Star) Hesper, and Vesper bee.

As Pierre Legouis, '*Sur un vers de Donne*', *Revue Anglo Américaine*, x (1932–3), 49–50 and 228–30, and *TLS*, 31 July 1937, pointed out, *Hesperus* is the

Latinized form of the Greek equivalent of *Vesper*, both of which were names given to the evening star, while *Phosphor* (also spelled *Phospher* and *Phosfer*) and *Lucifer* were names for the morning star. Legouis argued that *Hesperus* could have arisen from a copyist's writing *Hesperus* for some form of *Phosphor* which Donne had written. According to *OED*, *Phosphor* is first recorded in Cowley, and its use earlier in Donne could have caused a scribe to substitute a familiar for an unusual word.

ll. 1–2. *THE Moone ... divers governments.* Cf. Natalis Comes, *Mythologiae* (Lyons, 1605), 259:

> Cum eadem Luna sit, et Hecate, et Diana, tamen non omnes hae vires, quae per has intelliguntur, uno nomine dicuntur, et si ab uno fonte manant. Cum enim Hecate nunc Iouis, nunc Aristaei, nunc Tartari, nunc Persae filia dicatur, Luna modo Hyperionis, modo Pallantis ...
>
> (Although Luna, and Hecate, and Diana are all the same, since not all those powers, which are understood as these, are called by one name, even if they flow from one source. Since truly Hecate is called now Jove's, now Aristaeus' now Tartarus', now Perses' daughter, Luna sometimes Hyperion's, sometimes Pallas' ...).

ll. 9–10. *joyned ... for marriage.* Cf. Comes, p. 393 '*Haec eadem causa fuit cur fuerit praefecta nuptiis*' (Similarly this was the reason why she [Venus] was put in charge of marriages).

ll. 11–12. *of her Affections ... divers names.* This passage is omitted in Group II manuscripts and the editions because of eye-slip on the repetition of *names of her* and *names to her.*

l. 13. scilicet. I have adopted the full form of the word as given in the editions in preference to the various abbreviations of the manuscripts in keeping with the practice of this edition.

l. 14. *Lay incest.* incest; *Church Incest* = 'spiritual incest' (in R.C.Ch.): (a) marriage or sexual connection between persons related by spiritual affinity, or with a person under a vow of chastity, etc., *OED* 1b.

l. 15. *Mastupration.* Masturbation *OED*, *obs. Mascupration*, the reading of Group II, *S*, and *1633a* is not found in *OED*. The word appears to be a mistake arising from the similarity of 'c' and 't' in secretarial hands.

ll. 17–19. *For* Neptune *distilld and wept her ...* Vulcan *hammerd her.* Venus was born from the ocean. Donnes adaption of Venus' adultery with Mars and their capture in Vulcans' net where they are viewed by Apollo, Neptune, and Mercury, is told in Homer, *Odyssey* viii 266–367.

ll. 27–8. *Venit Hesperus ... persons of Goates.* Cf. the final line of Virgil's tenth Eclogue, 'ite domum saturae, venit Hesperus, ite capellae' (go home, fed goats, the evening star comes, go). Lando in his Problems pictured the lecherous god Pan limping on goats' feet, 'Perchè finsero i Poeti, che il lussurioso Dio Pan vada con i piedi di capra zoppicando', *Quattro libri* (1556), 18.

XI. Why is venus starre multinominous and called both Hesperus and vesper (p. 36)

Text in Ash 826, R.

Title. See note on *title*, short version above.

ll. 1–2. THE moone . . . *diverse governments.* See note on ll. 1–2, short version above.

ll. 2–3. *in Kings titles . . . Lordes names.* The full title of a monarch normally consists of various earldoms and dukedoms for which he has charge. Cf. John Selden, *Titles of Honour* (1614), 57, 'This K. *Henry* [II], it seems, following the syllables of the Bull, and his successors hence titled themselves *Lords of Ireland*, in their stile putting it before *Duke of Guienne.*'

ll. 3–6. Lactantius . . . Artem meritriciam. Cf. Comes, 391, 'Venerem amorum Deam credidit Lactantius putatam, quia laena fuerit, quae prima meretriciam artem instituerit' (Lactantius believed Venus was thought to be the goddess of lust, because she was a bawd, who first instituted the art of prostitution). Cf. Also Lactantius himself (Lucius Caelius Firmianus), *De divinis institutionibus*, I. xvii:

> What shall I say of the obscenity of Venus, a prostitute to the lusts of all, not of gods only, but of men as well? . . . She was the first, as is held in the *Sacred History* [Ennius, *Euhemerus*, fr. 13], who instituted the prostitute's art, and she was the authority for the women in Cyprus to make profit by prostituting their bodies . . . Does even she whose adulteries are reckoned more than her offspring have some divine power?

ll. 6–7. *shee is antienter . . . vitious gods.* 'Vicious' = depraved, immoral, bad, *OED* I. 1. 'If what Lactantius said is true, then Venus was the earliest of the pagan gods since they were all "vicious".'

ll. 8–10. Jubal *invented . . . another husband. R* reads, 'Nam antequam Psalterium et citharam invenisset Iubal, ipsius mater duorum virorum assumptionem invenerat'. I do not understand this reference: Jubal's mother, Adah, did not have two husbands but rather was one of two wives. Cf. Gen. 4: 19–21:

> And Lamech took unto him two wives: the name of the one *was* Adah, and the name of the other Zillah.
> And Adah bare Jabal: he was the father of such as dwell in tents, and *of such as have* cattle.

And his brother's name *was* Jubal: he was the father of all such as handle the harp and organ.

I can find no basis for Donne's assumption of Adah's polygamy. Contemporary commentaries by Andrew Willet, *Hexapla in Genesim* (Cambridge, 1605), 62, and Benedictus Pererius, *Commentariorum et Disputationum in Genesim* (Cologne, 1601), 345–9, do not mention the marital relationships of Lamech and his wives but rather deal with verses 23–4 on the killing of Cain and the meaning of the seventy-and-sevenfold revenge. Willet and Pererius summarize the writings of Catharinus, Origen, Jerome, Suidas, Theodoret, Caietanus, Ramban, Calvin, Iunius, Chrysostome, Josephus, Rupertus, Caientane, Paulus Burgensis, Oleastus. Cornelius à Lapide, *Commentaria in Pentateuchum Mosis* (Antwerp, 1616), 62, says only that Lamech was the first polygamist.

Rashi, *Commentary on the Pentateuch*, trans. J. H. Lowe (1928), 87–8, wrote that prior to the Flood men had two wives, one to bear children and the other for companionship. She who was to bear children, Adah, was neglected by her husband and mourned like a widow, while she that was meant for companionship, Zillah, was given a drink to make her barren, attired like a bride, and given sweet things to eat. Zillah appears to have usurped Adah's role as childbearer, for she bore a son Tubal-cain and a daughter Naamah (Gen. 4: 22). See also Louis Ginzberg, *The Legends of the Jews* (Philadephia, Pa., 1909), i, 116–18.

ll. 8–9. psalterium et citharam. A stringed lute-like instrument and a cithara or modern-day guitar.

l. 12. *them*[*selves*]. I have emended *them* to *themselves* because the reflexive form is required by the sense of the passage.

l. 18. *Lay incest, Church incest*. See note l. 14, short version above.

ll. 19. *mastupration*. See note l. 15, short version above.

ll. 20–1. *joyned . . . for maryage*. See note ll. 9–10, short version above.

ll. 22–5. *for* Neptune *distild . . .* Jupiters *authority secured her*. See note ll. 17–19, short version above.

ll. 27–9. *Beleive not this . . . of all fortunes*. 'The reason that Venus has two names is neither because the names symbolize all times, nor because they are, by their rising and falling, symbols of all fortunes.'

ll. 29–30. *world hath accepted . . .* summum bonum. Possibly a jibe on the Neoplatonic view that love of woman can elevate a man to love of 'the good' as expounded by Bembo in Book IV of Castiglione's *The Book of the Courtier*.

The fondness of the courtier for ladies is also seen in Spenser, 'Colin Clouts Come Home Againe', ll. 771–82.

ll. 36–42. *And because industrious . . . person of goates.* This entire passage has been omitted in *R* and replaced with the following:

si saltem Archigeni, olim praestantissimo medico, credere vultis, ut ego nondum expertus facio. Ejus sententia his versibus habetur

> *Quaerenti Hersiliae quaenam hora salubrior esset*
> *Ad venerem, medicus sic ait Archigenes:*
> *'Manè salubre magis veneris decerpere fructus,*
> *Iudice me fuerit, vespere dulce magis.'*
> *Hîc illa arridens formoso ait ore, 'voluptas*
> *Mî curae fuerit vespere, manè salus.'*

(if at least you want to believe Archigenes, once a most outstanding doctor, as I do, not yet having tried it. His sentiment is contained in these verses: When Hersilia asked what time was most salubrious for love, Archigenes the doctor speaks to her as follows, 'In the morning it would be healthier to reap the fruits of Venus, but at night, in my opinion, it would be sweeter.' To him she says, laughing with her beautiful mouth, 'In the evening I'll consider my pleasure, in the morning my health.')

The verse is by Annibal Cruceius, 'De Ersilia', *Delitiae cc. Italorum poetarum*, collected by Janus Gruterus (Frankfort, 1608), i. 860. Archigenes was a well-known and fashionable physician in Rome in the first twenty years of the second century AD. He is referred to in Juvenal's *Satires*, vi. 236, xiii. 98, and xiv. 252.

ll. 41–2. Venit Hesperus . . . *person of goates.* See note ll. 27–8, short version above.

XII. Why is there more variety of Greene, then of
other Collours (p. 38)
Omitted in HMC 26.

This Problem exists in three versions. The text in *Ash 826* and *R* has a long opening section which makes it three times as long as the text in the other witnesses. Of the two short texts, the version found in the Group III manuscripts has the same final sentence as the text found in *Ash 826* and *R*, while the other short version, found in the remaining witnesses, has an entirely different concluding sentence. I have taken the long version in *Ash 826* and *R* to be the earliest, the short version found in the Group III manuscripts to be intermediate, and the other short version containing a different final sentence, which occurs in the remaining witnesses, to be the final version of the text.

I have printed in full two complete versions of this Problem—the final version of the text followed by the earliest. The final version is printed from *TCD* whose reading is rejected twice, in ll. 7, 9. The reading adopted in l. 9

is discussed in the notes. In the apparatus of this text, the variant ending of the intermediate version which is found in the Group III manuscripts is given.

The long version is printed from *Ash 826*, corrected where necessary from the text in *R*. It is headed '*Ash 826 text corrected from R*'.

Two sets of notes one for each version are given. The notes for the text in *Ash 826*, *R* follow the notes for the short version of the text.

The Problem deals with the symbolic meanings of various shades of green. According to R. B. Kennedy, 'The Sources and Nature of Colour Symbolism in English Poetry of the mid-seventeenth Century,' Oxford B.Litt., 1974, the symbolism of colours was of considerable interest to men of the Renaissance. Several treatises written in English on this subject were engendered by half a dozen Italian works composed in the sixteenth century. While the writers do not always agree on the exact significance of every shade there is general agreement that green signifies youth, love, hope, and joy, willow-green implies extreme misery, willingness to die, and yellow-green indicates despair. The equivocal nature of this colour evidently attracted Donne.

l. 1. *Is it . . . figure of youth.* 'green' = greenness, as indicative of vigorous growth or youth, *OED* III. B. 8. Cf. also Paradox III, ll. 14–15, for the meaning of the various colours of clothes.

l. 3. *Affections.* 'Affection' =state of mind generally, mental tendency; disposition, *OED* II. 4, *obs.* in general sense.

l. 4. *wasters in Voyages.* Both speculators in shipping ventures and extravagant travellers.

l. 5. *Ennobled from Grasiers.* The generosity with which James bestowed knighthoods tripled the number of knights in the first months of his reign. Within a few years he was selling both knighthoods and baronetcies (which latter he had created in 1611) in order to raise money for the Crown. See Lawrence Stone, *The Crisis of the Aristocracy 1558–1641* (1965), ch. 3.

ll. 5–6. *Goose-greene . . . Capitoll.* The saving of Rome from destruction by the Gauls effected by geese and M. Manlius whom they awakened with their cackling was told in Livy's *History of Rome*, Bk. V, ch. xlvii.

l. 6. *pretend.* To aspire to, *OED* I. 9.

ll. 7–8. *an Age wherein they shall All hunte.* Cf. 'The Sunne Rising', l.7:
　　　Goe tell Court-huntsmen, that the King will ride.

Green was the colour associated with hunting in the sixteenth and seventeenth centuries. Cf. Spenser, *The Faerie Queene*, vi. ii, ll. 42–5:

　　　　All in a woodmans jacket he was clad
　　　　Of Lincolne greene, belayd with silver lace;
　　　　And on his head an hood with aglets sprad,
　　　　And by his side his hunters horne he hanging had

and 'The Hunt is Up', Wm. Chappell, *Old English Popular Music*, ed.
H. E. Wooldridge (1893), i. 86:

> The sunne is glad to see us clad
> All in our lustie greene.

ll. 8–9. *misdemeane . . . Willowe-Greene.* Cf. Benedick on Claudio:

> I found him here as melancholy as a lodge in a warren . . . and I offered him
> my company to a willow-tree, either to make him a garland, as being
> forsaken, or to bind him up a rod, as worthy to be whipped, *Much Ado
> About Nothing*, ii. i. 198–204.

Donne is using willow-green in connection with the rod used for whipping
rather than with the lover's melancholy.

ll. 9–11. *Magistrats . . . the Great.*

Fasces. A bundle of rods bound up with an axe in the middle and its blade
projecting. These rods were carried by lictors before the superior magistrates
of Rome as an emblem of their power, *OED* 1.

Secures. 'Securis', the executioner's axe for beheading criminals bound up
with the fasces.

Maces. The reading of the Group II manuscripts is a scribal attempt to make
sense of a word which the scribe was unable to understand. The sentence not
only differentiates between small and great offences but also between un-
important and important offenders; rods or faggots to beat the ordinary
criminal, and the axe to decapitate the offenders of high rank.

l. 9. *Or because . . . properly.* Reading of *O'F, Dob. Greene.* Of persons, their
powers or capacities: Immature, raw untrained, inexperienced, *OED* II. 8c
trans. and *fig.* Also hunting green, see note ll. 7–8 above. Simpson, *Prose
Works*, 146, considered this ending to be an attack which was 'too sweeping
a generalization, and Donne wisely decided to alter it'. Donne may well have
changed his ending because of fear of being misunderstood, but I believe his
intention was a humorous attack.

XII. Why is there more variety of greene then any other colour (p. 39)

Text in *Ash 826, R.*

This version of the Problem on the 'variety of greene' is a more exhaustive
treatise than the short version. Beginning with the classical idea of the origins
of the actual colour, it progresses through various metaphoric uses of green in
Renaissance France and Italy, and second-century AD Rome, before coming to
the passage which is found in the other witnesses; it ends with a good-humoured
attack on contemporary England.

ll. 1–2. *THAT there is more . . . is reasonable.* Cf. 'Communitie', l. 14: 'Good is as visible as greene', and Helen Gardner's note, *Elegies etc.* 157, green is the most visible colour in nature because it is the most common.

ll. 2–3. *two parts white and one halfe parte blacke.* In this colour science in which the various colours are made of black and white, black and white themselves are made, in the case of black, of heat and moisture, and in the case of white, of cold and moisture. See Bartholome, *De proprietatibus rerum*, Bk. xix. ch. 3. For the composition of green from black and white and moisture, see Bk. xix, ch. 19, f. ccclviii:

> Grene colour is gendred and bredde by werkynge of heate in a meane matter, in which moisture hath somwhat the mastrye, as hit farethe in leaves and in herbes, and in fruytes, and also in grasse and therfore the coloure is gendered, and hath moche of blacke, and is not fullye blacke of medlyng of lyght white, as yelowe is . . .

The range of colours in order between the extremes of white and black, i.e. yellow, citrine, red, purple, green, as 'Aristotle rehearseth these' are found in Bk. xix, ch. 7.

ll. 3–4. *the two lower grosser Elements.* These are earth which, when covered with vegetation, is green, and water, which also is green when it is seen in depth (E. M. S.).

ll. 4–6. [*than which the other two,*] . . . *are not so great.* The text in *Ash 826* here is corrupt, as it omits the introduction of the two higher elements (contained in *R* as *quibus reliqua duo*) which is necessary in order for the comparison to be made. 'Donne's argument appears to be that there is more green than any other colour in Nature because green is the colour of the two gross elements, earth and water. The elements of air and fire may be greater in extent (there was supposed to be a region of fire, from which meteors came, above the air), but they have no colour of their own. Compare Paradox II, ll. 21–3, where Donne says "the Starrs, the Sun, the Skye, whom thou admirest; have no color, but are faire because they seeme color'd". Air and fire when condensed may acquire colour, but in that case they lose volume, "when they are condensed and colourable are not so great" ' (E. M. S.).

l. 7. *translatitiously.* 'Translatitious' = metaphorical. *OED* 2, *obs.* (*OED* records the first use of 'translatitious' in Cotgrave's *Dictionary of French and English*, 1611, and of 'translatitiously' in Fraser's *Polichron* (1666), 2. *Translatiously*, the reading of *Ash 826* is a scribal error. *R*: supports the sense of *translatitiously*:

> Sed praeter reale viride, quam multae, queso, metaphoricae differentiae, in omnibus, in omnibus ferè rebus, ejus sunt?
>
> (But besides green proper, how many, I ask [you], metaphorical variants of it are there in all, in almost all things?)

ll. 8–9. Ronsard ... *greene eyes*. Ronsard specifically says in his first published poem 'Ode de Pierre de Ronsart à Jacques Peletier des Beautez qu'il voudroit en s'Amie', 1547,

> Noir je veux l'œil, & brun le teint
> Bien que l'œil verd le François tant adore,

that his ideal is a brunette with black eyes, not a blonde although the French-man adores a green eye so much. He expresses the same sentiment in 'Sonnet 26' of the *Amours de Cassandre*. D. Lein in a discussion of this Problem in 'Donne and Ronsard', *N&Q* ns xxi (1974), 90–2, adds to these two poems, the 'Elegie' for Madeline, Queen of Scotland, in which Ronsard prefers the darker to the fair, and also adds *Première Folastrie* in which Ronsard is unable to choose between a dark beauty and a green-eyed lady.

Lein also points out (p. 91) the ambiguity of Donne's word *inraged*. 'Enrage' comes from the French *enrager* which is only used intransitively; the transitive use in English appears to have arisen [*c.* 1600] from the past participle *enraged* [= Fr. *enragé* taken as a passive] *OED*. 'Enraged' can mean either (1) made furious, or (2) enamoured.

He regards Donne's reference to Ronsard and green eyes as a direct allusion, not as an observation founded upon a wide reading of French lyric poetry. He writes (p. 91) that the 'garbled context in which Donne put Ronsard's lines ... could easily have resulted either from a shaky recollection of the total passage or from an inaccurate or incomplete transcription of the poem in his commonplace book.'

Konsard. The reading of *Ash 826* is another example of scribal confusion of Donne's *R* and *K*. See Problem II, title, 'W. K.' for 'W. R.' and Problem X, l. 3, 'Repler' for 'Kepler'.

ll. 10–11. *prayse verdure in Lips, so in sauces and meats ... wee tast greene.* There is a pun on *verdure*, which is used to denote 'fresh or flourishing con-ditions', *OED* II. 6, *fig.* (with regard to lips); and 'taste, savour', *OED* II. 4 (in reference to sauces and meats). For 'green = taste, savour', cf. Gabriel Harvey, *Foure Letters ... touching Robert Greene*, 1592, ed. G. B. Harrison, 1922, 41, '... is not greene inough for queasie stomackes'. Harvey plays on various interpretations of the word 'green' throughout the letters.

ll. 11–12. A. Gellius ... viridem sonum. Cf. Gellius' Problem, *Noctes Atticae*, Bk. ii. 3.1:

> H litteram, sive illam spiritum magis, quam litteram dici oportet, inserebant eam veteres nostri plerisque vocibus verborum firmandis roborandisque, ut sonus earum esset viridior vegetiorque,
> (The letter *h* (or perhaps it should be called a breathing rather than a letter) was added by our forefathers to give strength and vigour to the

pronunciation of many words, in order that they might have a fresher and livelier sound.)

l. 12. *G.* The reading of *Ash 826* is obviously a scribal error.

ll. 13–15. Petrarch *sayth* . . . *Commentators agree.* The passage may refer to (*Rime* xxxiii) Petrarch's 'Sonnet XXVI', l. 9, '*quando mia speme già condotta al verde*' (When my hope [Laura] was already brought to the green), Donne having substituted *giunto* for *condotta.* The commentary on the line in *Il Petrarca con nuove spositioni* (Lyons, 1564), 63, reads:

> Già condotta al verde, al verde, cioè, al fine traslato dalle candele, quando sono arse in fino à quel poco verde c'hanno nel fine, onde Dante, Mentre che la speranza ha fior del verde, cioè punto del verde, che così si debbe legger quel luogo, e non fuor del verde, si come è stato à lungo dichiarato da colui, che compose il ragionamento havuto in Lione dal gentil' huomo Franzese, e dal Fiorentino, sopra la dichiarazione d'alcuni luoghi di Dante, del Petrarca e del Boccacio,
>
> (Already she was brought to the green, to the green, that is to the end, a metaphor from candles, when they are burnt down as far as to that little green which they have in the end, whence Dante, 'While hope has the bloom of green' [*La divina commedia*, II. iii. 135], namely the spot of green, as the passage ought to be explained, and not outside the green, as was explained at length by him who wrote down the discussion held in Lyons between the French gentleman and the Florentine, over the interpretation of some passages of Dante, Petrarch, and Boccaccio), 'Sonnet XXVI' in 1564 edition.

M. C. Linthicum, *Costume in the Drama of Shakespeare and his Contemporaries* (1936), 34–5, stated that a certain shade of green was associated with the custom of placing torches in green wood. 'When the torch had burnt to the green wood it was extinguished, hence the Italian *esser guinto al verde*, meaning to be in extreme misery or death.' Donne's *giunto al verde* appears to be a mistake for *condotta* . . . and *gionto ad verde*, the reading of *Ash 826*, provides an additional error. This reference to Petrarch is omitted in *R*.

l. 21. *refocillation.* The action of refreshment, reanimation, reinvigoration, *OED*, now *rare*. Cf. Ps.-Aristotle, *Problemata*, Bk. xxxi, ch. 19 Why does our vision improve:

> if we gaze intently on yellow and green objects, such as herbs and the like? Is it because we are least able to gaze intently on white and black (for they both mar the vision), and the above-mentioned colours come midway between these, so that, the conditions of vision being of the nature of a mean, our sight is not weakened thereby but improved?

and also the fictitious *The Problemes of Aristotle*, published in English, Edinburgh, 1595, sigs. B5–B5ᵛ:

> Why is the sight recreated and refreshed by a greene colour ... Because the greene colour doth meanly move the instrument of sight, and therefore doth comfort the sight: but this doth not blacke or white colour, because these colours do vehemently stirre and alter the instrument of the sight.

ll. 21–2. *since greene ...figure youth*. See note l. 1, short version above.

l. 23. *affections*. See note l. 3, short version above.

l. 24. *wasters in voyages*. See note l. 4, short version above.

l. 25. *innobled from grasiers*. See note l. 5, short version above.

ll. 25–6. *goose greene ... Capitoll*. See note ll. 5–6, short version above.

l. 26. *pretend*. See note l. 6, short version above.

ll. 27–8. *an age when all men should hunt*. See note ll. 7–8, short version above.

ll. 28–30. *Shee would ... properly*. It must be noted first, that this version of the text does not contain the sentence found in both of the short versions, 'And for such as misdemeane themselves a Willowe-Greene', a sentence that leads very smoothly into the ending of the final version of the text which concerns the *Fasces* and *Secures* of the Magistrates. In the second version, the concept of willow green and whipping or beating leads unpleasantly into Nature's provision of green merchants, lawyers, etc. See note for reading of *O'F*, *Dob*, l. 9, short version above.

XIII. Why doth the Poxe so much affect to undermine the nose (p. 40)

This Problem is omitted in *1633a* and *b*.

The reading of *O'F* has been rejected on thirteen occasions; on ten, ll. 6, twice in l. 7, 8, 14, 15, 24, 26, 35, 36 its reading is supported by *Dob*, and on two, ll. 13, 32, it is not so supported. One rejected reading of *O'F* which is supported by *Dob* is discussed in the notes, l. 36. Finally, three omissions in *O'F* are restored to the text, ll. 3, 6, 17–18.

Notable amongst several contemporary treatises on the nose are Erasmus's Colloquy, *De sacerdotio*, 1522, later called *De captandis sacerdotiis* and Bruscambille's 'En faveur des gros Nez', *Œuvres* (1634), 431–5. In 'Four Paradoxes by Sir William Cornwallis, the Younger', *Harvard Studies and Notes*, xiii (1931), 223, R. E. Bennett had pointed out that the nose was a popular subject with Italian Paradox writers, e.g. Annibale Caro, *Nasea*, which was published among Aretino's *Ragionamenti*, 1584. In his article Bennett printed for the first time a Paradox by Donne's friend, the younger Cornwallis, 'That a great redd nose is an ornament to the face' (E. M. S.).

ll. 1–3. *Paracelsus ... in the nose*. Cf. Paracelsus (Theophrastus Bombastus von Hohenheim, 1493–1541), *The Hermetic and Alchemical Writings*, trans. A. E. Waite (1894), ii. 232–5. He attacked the medical practices of the Galenists, 'sophistic humourists, who mingled poison with medicine, and rendered it meretricious'. Their medicine, he claimed, did not treat a specific part for its disease because they did not see that every disease had its manifestation and origins in some particular part. For the manifestation of pox in the nose, cf. no. 53 in Paracelsus's *A Hundred and fourtene experiments and cures*, 1596, 'A certaine man being long sicke of the Pox had two rumores and an ulcer in his nose, at the which everie day there came foorth great quantitie of stinking and filthie matter . . .'.

l. 2. *exaltation*. In the older chemistry and physiology: The action or process of refining or subliming; the bringing of a substance to a higher degree of potency or purity, *OED* 4, *obs*.

ll. 10–11. *mise defeate Elephants . . . theyr nose*. The animosity of the mouse toward the elephant is mentioned in *Sermons*, x. 134, while in 'Metempsychosis', ll. 381–94, and in Meditation 12, Sparrow, *Devotions*, 67, the mouse's ability to destroy the elephant is discussed. As Milgate pointed out in his note on 'Metempsychosis', *Satires etc.* 185–6, and also in 'A Difficult Allusion in Donne and Spenser'. *N&Q* ns xiii (1966), 12–14, the idea of the mouse's ability to destroy the elephant by climbing up its trunk and gnawing its brain was first told in Europe by a Portuguese physician Garçia de Orta, in a study of the spices and simples of India which was published in Goa in 1563, and subsequently published in a Latin translation by Charles de l'Escluze (Clusius) in 1567.

ll. 11–12. *this wretched Indian Vermine*. Donne rightly attributes the introduction into Europe of syphilis to Columbus's voyages to the West Indies.

ll. 13–15. *Ancient furious custome . . . Adultery*. Although Donne suggests that the injured party could cut off the noses of those offending against him, by law, he could be referring to Martial, *Epigrams*, Bk. ii. 83. 1–3:

> Foedasti miserum, marite, moechum,
> et se, qui fuerant prius, requirunt
> trunci naribus auribusque voltus.

(You have disfigured, O husband, the wretched adulterer, and his face shorn of nose and ears, misses its former self.) Cf. also iii, 85, 1. On the other hand, the reference could be to the law of the Egyptians: 'We read also that the lest punishment used by the Egyptians against adulterers, was to cut off the womans nose, and the privie parts of the man', Pierre de la Primaudaye, *The French Academie*, trans. T. B., 1586, Bk. 1, ch. 22, 227–8. Cornwallis in his Paradox on 'a great redd nose' had referred to this law of the Egyptians (Ravisius Textor, *Officina* (Basle, 1552), col. 625) (E. M. S.). The practice was also adopted in early Britain; cf. 'King *Knute* ordered that a

Wife who committed adultery should have her nose & ears cut off. Cnut. leg: can. 50', John Selden, *The Reverse or Back-face of the English Janus*, trans. Adam Littleton (pseud. Redman Westcot), 1682, Bk. i, ch. 12, 20. *deprehended.* 'Deprehend' = apprehend, *OED* 1, *trans.*

ll. 19–21. *it warnes . . . hang out one.* The reference is to the nautical use of flags for communication. The absence of a flag from its customary site could indicate a menace to a ship as much as a flag hung out to mark danger.

ll. 21–2. *Possibly heate . . . active then cold.* The rivalry between heat and cold is a theme in folklore of many countries. See Stith Thompson, *Motif Index of Folk Literature*, 6 vols. (Copenhagen, 1956), vol. 2, D 2144.2. It forms the basis for Aesop's fable on the wind, the sun, and the traveller, number 143 in the Penguin Classics edition of Aesop, ed. S. A. Handford, 1954, and is part of the argument in an undecided debate on the claims of summer and winter to superiority in the Italian work, *Il Rinaldi o vero Dialogo del Paragone tra il Verno e la State composto nuovamente dall'Accademico Bramoso . . .*, Venice, 1589. Cited by Crane, *Italian Social Customs*, 155.

ll. 24–5. *cold was able . . . noses in* Muscovy. Cf. 'Divers not onely that travell abroad, but in the very markets, and streats of their townes, are mortally pinched and killed withall [with cold]: so that you shall see many drop downe in the streates, many travellers brought into the townes sitting dead and stiffe in their sleddes. Divers lose their noses, the tippes of their eares, and the bals of their cheekes, their toes, feete, &c.', Giles Fletcher, ch. 2. 'Of the Soil and Climate', *Of the Russe Common Wealth . . .* (1591), f. 4ᵛ.

l. 24. *shewe the high wayes.* 'Mark the roads with fallen noses, like milestones,' although *straw* (strew), the reading of *Ash 826* is attractive.

ll. 29–30. Heliogabalus . . . *by the nose.* Elagabalus, b. 204, Roman Emperor AD 218–22. His perversions were described in la Primaudaye's *The French Academie* (1586), Bk. i, ch. 18, 182–3, and in Thomas Milles's *The Treasurie of Auncient and Moderne Times* (1613), Bk. vii, ch. 3, 628–9.

ll. 30–1. Albertus . . . *preferrd greate noses.* St. Albertus Magnus (Albert von Böllstadt), ?1193–1280, scholastic philosopher and teacher of St. Thomas Aquinas.

I have not been able to find a source for Donne's statement.

l. 32. *Licentious Poet was* Naso Poeta. Ovid.

l. 36. *conspicuous.* The reading of the Group III manuscripts, *O 2, S,* and *1652* is *perspicuous*, a now ? *obs.* word for 'conspicuous', *OED* 3.

XIV. Why are new Officers least oppressing (p. 42)

This Problem is omitted in *R*.

The reading of *O'F* has been rejected on three occasions; on one, l. 24, its reading is supported by that of *Dob*, and on two, ll. 24–5, 27, it is not so supported. An omission in both *O'F* and *Dob*, l. 3, is restored to the text.

The unscrupulous nature of court officers and the miserable condition of their suitors is also found in 'Satire V', ll. 7–9:

> What is hee
> Who Officers rage, and Suiters misery
> Can write, and jest?

and 'Metempsychosis', ll. 321–3:

> He hunts not fish, but as an officer
> Stayes in his court, as his owne net, and there
> All suitors of all sorts themselves enthrall.

l. 1. *old Proverbe . . . bite sorest.* 'An old dog (hound) bites sore', Tilley, D 499.

l. 20. *having drawne . . . theyr myll.* 'Every miller draws water to his own mill', Tilley, M 952.

ll. 21–31. *from the rules . . . lower rent and undervalew.* 'If they were following the rules of good horsemanship, they would think it right to begin at a moderate pace in their demands for bribes, they would gradually decrease the rate of their demands as they approached death, and they would not exact payment at an increasingly heavy rate until the end. But perhaps at the end of their tenure of office they feel that if they fail to demand at a heavy rate, they would decrease the sale value of that office both to their superior who will sell and to their prospective successor who will buy.'

ll. 22–3. *wholsomest . . . moderate pace.* Cf. 'Travaile moderately in the morning, till his winde be rack'd, and his limbes warmed, then after doe as your affaires require', Anonymous, 'The Horse', *Cheape and good Husbandry . . .,* (1614), 8.

l. 22. *jett.* To stroll, *OED* I. 2, *intr.*

l. 23. *take up.* 'Take up' means to slacken one's pace (*OED* 90, n.), cf. Fletcher, *The Captain*, iv, iii, 'take up quickly; Thy wit will founder of all four else wench, If thou hold'st this pace; take up when I bid thee', Beaumont and Fletcher, *Works* (Cambridge, 1907), v. 288.

l. 24. *mend theyr pace.* To mend (one's) pace: to travel faster, *OED* III, 12e.

XV. Why Puritans make long Sermons (p. 43)

This Problem occurs in *A 25*; it is omitted in *R*.

The reading of *O'F* has been rejected on eight occasions; on five, ll. 3, 4, 5, twice in l. 8 its reading is supported by *Dob*; on one, in the title, it is not so supported; and two rejected readings of *O'F*, ll. 2–3, 15–16, which are not

supported by *Dob* are discussed in the notes. Four omissions in *O'F* are also
restored to the text; of these one, l. 5, is supported by *Dob*, one, l. 6, is not so
supported, and two, ll. 7–8, 12–13, which are supported by *Dob*, are discussed
in the notes.

l. 2. *playne enough*. Cf. 'the Puritan insistence on a plain style in preaching,
[was] against the florid extravagances of the university and Court divines',
Christopher Hill, *Society and Puritanism in Pre-Revolutionary England* (1964),
56.

ll. 2–3. *long Sembriefe Accent . . . Crotchets*. I have accepted the reading
Sembriefe over semibreefe because it is the form which Donne used in 'Satire
IV', ll. 94–5, 'which staies A Sembriefe', although in the poem, that form may
have been chosen for metrical considerations. *Crotchets* (crotchet = a peculiar
notion on some point (usually considered unimportant) held by an individual
in opposition to common opinion, *OED* III. 9). There are also the musical
meanings of 'semibreve' (a long note equalling two minims) and 'crotchet' (a
short note of the value of half a minim, *OED* III. 7) implying respectively,
slow and rapid speech.

ll. 4–5. *pretend not . . . Torches*. A reference to the Puritan distrust of rhetoric,
see note l. 2 above.

l. 4. *pretend*. To aspire to, *OED* I. 9.

ll. 7–8. *yet spend more tyme in theyr glimmeringe*. This phrase is found only in
Ash 826 and *A 25* but it is required to make the Group II reading (except for
its error *thinke* for *stinke*) intelligible, 'then the others in their more profitable
glory'. The remaining witnesses have smoothed out the difficulty by changing
'then' to 'when' and by introducing 'are' after 'others'.

l. 8. *snuff and stinke*. When a candle is primarily burning its wick, it flickers
and smells, giving a dim irregular light.

ll. 10–11. *large measure to course ware*. 'As the qualitie of their sermons is poor,
they give longer ones.'

ll. 12–13. *Kings . . . Kings*. The complete sentence is found only in *Ash 826*,
A 25, and Group II. The other witnesses have lost the words between the first
and second 'Kings' through haplography.

ll. 15–16. *that it is . . . Auditory wake agayne*. The scribe of *O'F* appears to
have sophisticated his text here by inserting the phrase 'having brought their
Auditory a sleep'.

XVI. Why are Statesmen most Incredible (p. 44)

This Problem is omitted in *R*, *O 2*, *1633a* and *b*.

The readings of *O'F* have been rejected on seven occasions in none of which is it supported by *Dob*. These readings occur twice in l. 4, and in ll. 8, 10, 12, 15, 21. Three omissions in the text of *O'F* are restored to the text; one, l. 1, is also omitted in *Dob*, and two, ll. 24, 27 are not omitted in *Dob*.

Title. Incredible. Not credible, *OED* 1. 'Incredulous' (not ready to believe; sceptical, *OED* 1), the reading of Group II, *S 1652* and *O'F* (before the scribe crossed out '-ulous' and inserted '-ible'), is clearly incorrect.

ll. 1–5. *ARE they all wise . . . to bee beleeved.* 'Are statesmen wise enough to imitate Tiberius, who brought the Senate to be diligent and industrious to believe him, were what they say so opposite their meaning, that to be believed destroyed their true aims.' Tiberius was a master of dissimilation and also spoke obscurely as if he did not want to make his meaning clear. See Tacitus, *Annales*, i. 11. Suetonius, 'Tiberius', ch. 24. Cassius Dio lvii, 1. 'were . . . it destroyd' is idiomatic for 'were . . . it [would have] destroyed'.

l. 3. *it.* The Senate, 'even when the Senate was "opposite and diametricall" toward him, he could make it believe him'.

l. 4. *destroyd theyr very ends.* The scribe of *O'F* saw that there was a difficulty in this passage as it stood in his copy, and 'corrected' his text by crossing out 'theyr' which he had first written, and inserting 'his', thus indicating that Tiberius's aims were destroyed (which of course they were, but that is not Donne's point here).

ll. 5–6. Asinius Gallus . . . *beleeving him.* Cf. Tacitus, *Annales*, i. 12:

> Inter quae senatu ad infimas obtestationes procumbente dixit forte Tiberius se ut non toti rei publicae parem, ita quaecumque pars sibi mandaretur, eius tutelam suscepturum. Tum Asinius Gallus 'Interrogo,' inquit, 'Caesar, quam partem rei publicae mandari tibi velis.' Perculsus inprovisa interrogatione paulum reticuit; dein, collecto animo, respondit nequaquam decorum pudori suo legere aliquid aut evitare ex eo, cui in universum excusari mallet.

> (The senate, meanwhile, was descending to the most abject supplications, when Tiberius happened to say that, unequal as he felt himself to the whole weight of government, he would still undertake the charge of any one department that might be assigned to him. Asinius Gallus then said:— "I ask you Caesar, what department you wish to be assigned you." This unforeseen inquiry threw him off his balance. He was silent for a few moments; then recovered himself, and answered that it would not at all become his diffidence to select or shun any part of a burden from which he would prefer to be wholly excused.)

This passage continues on to say that Tiberius was offended as he thought that Asinius's question suggested a division of the power of the State.

ll. 6–7. *Mayour and Aldermen of London Richard the Third.* The interview between Richard III and the Mayor and Aldermen in which Richard was 'persuaded' by the Duke of Buckingham to accept the crown, took place on 25 June 1483. The dramatization of the scene is in Shakespeare's *Richard III*, III. vii. In the play, after Buckingham's speech ll. 207–18, the citizens having accepted Richard's reluctance to assume the crown, turn to leave, so in this sense they could be said to have almost deceived him. Both *S* and *1652* read 'in Richard the 3 ᵈ' implying that the reference is to the play.

l. 10. *oraculously.* 'Oraculous' = resembling the ancient oracles in the mystery, ambiguity, or sententiousness of their answers, *OED* 2b, *obs.* The earliest usage of this word recorded by *OED* is in Bacon, *Essays* (1625), 509. There is no such word as 'graculously', the Group II reading.

l. 10. *multiformly.* 'Multiform' = of many and various forms or kinds. *OED* records the first usage in 1603 in Florio's translation of Montaigne's *Essays* (1632), 458.

l. 13. Arcana Imperii. Cf. Sparrow, *Devotions,* 'Meditation 10', 56 '... certaine *Arcana Imperii, secrets of State,* by which it will proceed, and not be bound to *declare* them' (E. M. S.). The phrase also occurs in *Sermons,* v. 298, 365, vii. 124, ix, 246. In the Problem, Donne's cynical wit reduces state secrets to court gossip.

ll. 18–21. *they tell true ... in a curse.* 'Statesmen will not tell the truth about the time or the weather if these things will not aid their ambitions, in the same manner in which witches will not name Jesus in a curse, as He will not aid them in the evil they intend.'

l. 19. *disconduce.* To be non conductive *to, OED, obs.*

l. 24. *these theyr Prince.* 'The statesmen imitate Satan.'

XVII. Why doth Johannes Salisburiensis writing de Nugis Curialium handle the Providence and Omnipotency of God (p. 46)

This Problem is omitted in *R, HMC 26, TC, O 2, P, S, 1633 +* .

The reading of *O'F* is rejected on five occasions where it is without any support, ll. 3, 8, 18, 19, 20, and the rejected reading of *O'F* in the title is discussed in the notes.

Title. Johannes Salisburiensis. John of Salisbury was born at Old Sarum, the predecessor of Salisbury. Hence the variant reading *Sarisburiensis* which occurs in *O'F* and also on the title-page of *Biathanatos* along with a quotation from *Policraticus.*

John's great work was *Policraticus sive De Nugis Curialium et Vestigiis Philosophorum* (The Statesman's Book or Concerning the Toys of Courtiers and the Traditions of Philosophers) which deals, in the first half, with the ways of courtiers and, in the second, with philosophical subjects among which were included the providence and omnipotence of God.

ll. 1–6. *the Stoicks charge . . . paynes and endevours.* Cf. Bk. ii, ch. 21 of *Policraticus*, 'Unde Stoicus, omnia necessaria credit, timens evacuari posse sciententiam immutabilem. E contra Epicurus eorum quae eveniunt nichil providentiae ratione dispositum, ne forte necessitatem mutabilibus rebus inducat, opinatur. Pari ergo errore desipiunt, cum alter casui alter necessitati universa subiciat' (E. M. S.), (Hence the Stoic believes that all things are unavoidable for fear of bringing to naught immutable knowledge. On the contrary, Epicurus thinks that there are no events which are the result of the regulation of providence for fear of imposing necessity upon things subject to change. They are both equally mistaken since the one subjects the universe to chance and the other to necessity), *trans.* J. B. Pike, *Frivolities of Courtiers and Footprints of Philosophers* (Minneapolis, Minn., 1938), 105.

ll. 1, 4. *putt, putting.* 'Put' = to state assert affirm, declare as a fact, *OED* III. 30*b*, *obs.* The scribe of *O'F*, misunderstanding the meaning of *putt*, first wrote *putt downe* and *putting downe.* He later corrected his error by crossing out the *downe's.* Similarly, the scribe of *S 962* first wrote *put off.*

l. 9. *of the family of* Thomas of Becket. John was a friend of Becket's and suffered a seven-year exile from England on his account. He dedicated *Policraticus* to Becket who was then Chancellor.

ll. 10–11. *hee put hunting . . . Lay-Courtier.* Love of hunting amongst the courtiers is noted in other of Donne's works, notably 'The Sunne Rising', l. 7, 'Goe tell Court-huntsmen, that the King will ride' and 'Loves Exchange', ll. 3–4:

> At Court your fellowes every day,
> Give th'art of Riming, Huntsmanship, and Play.

John of Salisbury attacked courtiers for their love of hunting, gambling, and music in Book I of *Policraticus*.

ll. 13–14. *heavyest mettall . . . blowe it away.* The idea turns up frequently in Donne's work. Cf. 'A Valediction: forbidding Mourning', l. 24, 'Like gold to ayery thinnesse beate', also *Sermons*, vii. 403, viii. 119–20 and *Biathanatos*, Pt. 3, Dist. I, Sect. I, 155.

ll. 25–8. *That by drawing them . . . there was one.* A possible reference to *Polycraticus*, Bk. ii, ch. 29. Cf. Lawn, 68:

> By the time of John of Salisbury, if not before, the passion for disputing had begun to get out of hand, and a wrong use of dialectic was beginning to invade all fields of study, both the theological and secular. In *physica* this led to the opposing camps of the theorizing *physici* and the practitioners, so

scathingly denounced by John in the *Polycraticus*. The other tendency, then, in this field, was for the younger and more irresponsible men to indulge in vain and empty speculations which led nowhere and were often, indeed, in opposition to the Faith.

XVIII. Why doe women delight soe much in feathers (p. 47)

This Problem which is omitted in *O 2* and which was not published until 1652, occurs in two versions in the manuscripts. The short version found in Group II, *S*, and *1652*, which I have taken to be the latest form of the text, consists of three sentences extracted from three separate places in the long form of the text. The long form of the text is found in Group III, *Ash 826*, and *R*, and in this version, the three sentences which comprise the short text occupy ll. 14–15, 26–30, and 33–6.

Both long and short versions of the text have been printed in full, the long version following the short. The short version of the text is printed from *TCD*. A reading in l. 5, which is in error in all the witnesses to the short version of the text, has been corrected from the text in Group III, *Ash 826*, and *R*.

The long version of the text has been printed from *O'F* whose reading has been rejected on eight occasions where it is without any support, *title*, ll. 3–4, 15, 16, 19, 31, 34, 39. Three further readings of *O'F* are rejected; two which are supported by *Dob*, ll. 24, 41, and one, l. 32, which is not so supported. These readings are discussed in the notes. This long version is headed '*Text in O'F, Dob, Ash 826, and R*'.

Notes for both versions are given; the notes for the long version following those for the short. 'The longer form of this problem is so characteristic of Donne's satirical attacks upon women, and the shorter form is by comparison so dull that we are driven to the conclusion that the longer one represents Donne's original version. It may have been cut down because he feared that it would offend some patroness ... It is possible that this is the problem referred to in a letter:

else let this probleme supply, which was occasioned by you, of women wearing stones; which, it seems, you were afraid women should read,' (E. M. S.).

See General Introduction, p. xlv.

l. 5. Varro ... Plumarios. *Varro*, which was omitted in all witnesses to this version of the text, refers, as Evelyn Simpson noted (*Prose Works*, 144) to Varro's *Cato vel de liberis educandis*, quoted by Nonius Mariellus, *De proprietate Sermonum* 162.27 M = 239 L. The *vulgar Edition* is the *Vulgate*, Exod. 35. 35. Cf:

We have sometimes mention in *Moses* his book of *Exodus*, according to the *Romane* Translation, *Operis Plumarii*, of a kind of subtle and various workmanship, imployed upon the Tabernacle, for which it is hard to finde a proper word now; we translate it sometimes Embroidery, sometimes Needle-work, sometimes otherwise, (*Sermons*, 1. 252).

The reading of *1652*, *Pluminaries*, gave difficulties to the editors of *OED*, who, finding no other instance of the word in English, explain '? a worker or dealer in feathers'. The line is defective in all witnesses to this version of the text and has been supplied from the text in Group III, *Ash 826*, *R*.

XVIII. Why doe Woemen delight so much in Feathers (p. 48)

Text as it occurs in *O'F*, *Dob*, *Ash 826*, and *R*:

l. 1. Similis Simili. 'Like to like.'

l. 1. *round*. Fluent, easy, *OED* III. 11*b*, *obs*.

ll. 2–4. *it is besides ... this reason is*. 'It is beyond the extent of my reason in my Problems which reaches only to seeming truth (*ad verisimile*) not to an exact and indisputable truth, of which sort *Similis Simili* is.'

l. 11. *Scraping*. Scrapping or fighting.

ll. 12–14. *woemen ... communicate theyr ill*. Cf.:
    let us ... not affect the neighbourhood, nor the commerce of them who are of evill communication. Be good then, that thou mayest communicate thy goodnesse to others ..., (*Sermons*, iii. 150).

l. 19. La Gola il sonno e l'otiose piume (Gluttony, sleep, and idle feathers). Petrarch, *Sonetti e Canzoni*, Sonnet VII. 1. Petrarch's text reads 'e'l' for 'il'.

l. 24. *they*. ie. feather beds. *R* reads *illis contrarii* (their [idle beds'] contrary).

l. 24. Gregory the 13. *grewe learned in his bedd*. The witnesses disagree on whether the reference is to Gregory XIII (*Ash 826*, *R*) or Gregory III (*O'F*, *Dob*). I have adopted the reading of *Ash 826* and *R* on the grounds that these two texts are independent of each other and their agreement makes it more probable that the reading is correct. Also the temperate and moderate behaviour and hard-working nature of Gregory XIII were widely known. Cf. L. F. von Pastor, *Geschichte der Päpste seit dem Ausgang des Mittelalters* (Freiburg im Breisgau, 1923), ix. 28, '... der Papst nach solch kargem Mahle alsbald wieder an die Beschäfte gehen und daß er auch bei der größten Hitze auf eine Siesta verzichten konnte. Nach Tisch ließ sich Gregor XIII zunächst die eingelaufenen Bittschriften vorlesen' ('The Pope after such a poor meal could go straightaway again to work and that he also in the greatest heat could forgo a nap. After eating Gregory XIII caused the incoming petitions to be read aloud) and '... der Papst benutzte die späteren Abendstunden zur Durchsicht der Akten' (the Pope used the later evening hours to look through papers).

ll. 29–30. Varro ... Plumarios. See note l. 5 in notes for short version of text.

ll. 32–3. Emplumadas . . . *looser woemen*. *Emplumadas* from the Spanish verb *emplumar* meaning to tar and feather. I have adopted the spelling of *R* as its ending '-as' is feminine plural. The word means tarred and feathered women.

Emplumados. The reading of *O'F* appears to be an attempt on the part of the scribe to match the ending of the word to *Plumarios*.

l. 39. Aristotles *definition* Animal rationale. Cf. '. . . thou are but a man; and what's that: ask *Aristotle*, says S. *Chrysostome*, and he will tell thee, *Animal rationale*, man is a reasonable Creature', *Sermons*, i. 273 (E. M. S.).

ll. 40–1. Plato *or* Speusippus, Animal bipes implume. The Greek form of 'man is a two-footed animal without feathers' is found in Plato's *Definitions*, 415a (E. M. S.).

Speusippus was Plato's nephew. *O'F* and *Dob* reverse the order of *Sp-* while *Ash 826* is in error reading *Leucippus* who was the originator of the atomic theory in the second half of the fifth century BC. '*Plato or Speusippus*' implies a theory that the Platonic Definitions were in fact compiled by Speusippus.

XIX. Why did the Devill reserve Jesuits for these latter times (p. 49)

The Problem is omitted in *TC*, *O 2*, and *S*.

The reading of *O'F* has been rejected on three occasions, *title*, ll. 2, 6, where it is without any support.

The background of this Problem is probably that which Timothy Healy identified as the context for *Ignatius His Conclave*—James I's *Apology for the Oath of Allegiance . . . together with a Premonition* which works were written in answer to the two *Breves* of Paul V forbidding English Catholics to take the Oath of Allegiance and Cardinal Bellarmine's letter on the same subject to the Archpriest Blackwell. James's works generated two further answers from Bellarmine. The Oath of Allegiance was regarded as a civil document by Blackwell who was inclined to take it in the interest of peace; the Jesuits, however, were flatly opposed to the Oath. See *Ignatius His Conclave*, ed. Healy, xix–xx.

ll. 1–2. *denye the Devills possessions*. Cf. 'For he did not onely deny all visions, and apparitions . . . And was hardly drawne to beleeve any possessings; but when three *Divels* did meet him on the way', *Ignatius His Conclave*, 73. The possibility of diabolic possession was also questioned in the late sixteenth century in tracts such as S. H[arsnet]; *A Discovery of the Fraudulent Practises of John Darrel*, 1599, and *A Declaration of Egregious Popish Impostures*, 1603. See Keith Thomas, *Religion and the Decline of Magic* (1971), 489–90, and Reginald Scot, *The Discoverie of Witchcraft*, ed. Brinsley Nicholson, 1886, 430.

l. 3. *disputation of Schoolemen*. This concept appears to have been popular with Donne. Cf. 'A Feaver', ll. 13–14:

> O wrangling schooles, that search what fire
> Shall burne this world

and 'To the Countesse of Bedford' ('You have refin'd mee ...'), ll. 41–2:

> And shunne th'entangling laborinths of Schooles,
> And make it wit, to thinke the wiser fooles.

l. 4. *why the Devill could not make Lyce in Egipt.* The turning of the dust into lice was the third Plague, following the changing of the waters of Egypt into blood, and the bringing forth of frogs from the rivers. Whereas the Egyptian magicians had been able to duplicate the first two Plagues, they were unable to produce lice. The various reasons for their failure put forth by writers such as Lyranus, Thostatus, Rupertus, Caietanus, Augustine, Pererius, Pellican, and Ferus were summarized in Andrew Willet, *Hexapla in Exodum* (1608), 100–1. Cf. 'God changed the form of Dust into another form, which the Divell could never do', *Essays in Divinity*, 83.

ll. 4–5. *whether those things ... might bee true.* The possible genuineness of the works of Satan as performed by the magicians was the subject of a long debate which was summarized in Willet, 74–6.

ll. 6–7. *true and reall plague ... those Ten.* The Ten Plagues were sent by God to force Pharaoh to allow the children of Israel to leave Egypt. The devil's plague is 'true and reall'. Perhaps Donne means by this that the presence of the Jesuits will be permanent.

ll. 7–8. *greatnesse of his Kingdome ... disunion cannot shake.* This is difficult. Cf. 'If Satan also be divided against himself, how shall his kingdom stand?' Luke 11 : 18. However, according to Keith Thomas, *Religion and the Decline of Magic* (1971), 470, the seventeenth-century belief accorded enormous powers to the devil.

ll. 9–11. *our times ... another for it.* Cf. *Ignatius His Conclave*, 69:

> if this kingdome have got any thing by the discovery of the *West Indies*, al that must be attributed to our *Order* [Jesuits] ... we when wee tooke away their old Idolatrie, had recompenced them with a new one of ours.

ll. 11–13. *peradventure ... other names.* A possible reference to the equivocation of the Jesuits. Cf. *Ignatius His Conclave*, 27:

> As for those sonnes of *Ignatius* ... how justly & properly may they be called *Equivocal* men? ... they have brought into the world a new art of *Equivocation*.

III. DUBIA

These works appear in few and different witnesses. Each is treated separately.

Paradox XI. A Defence of Womens Inconstancy (p. 51)

S is the only manuscript to contain a full text of this Paradox. Extracts, consisting of ll. 5–7, 3–4, 8–12, 14–17, 72–6, 77–83, 89–91, and 87–8, appear in *Pud*. The full text appears in *1633* +. *S* is used as copy-text. The reading of *S* has been rejected on twelve occasions, and on one, l. 45 its mis-spelling has been corrected. In ll. 1, 40, 44, 93, 94 the reading of *1633* + has been preferred, and in ll. 4 (twice), 8, 11, 80, 81 the agreement of *1633* + and *Pud* has been adopted. The reading of *S* in l. 83 which has been rejected, is discussed in the notes.

The Paradox expresses a commonplace, 'Fortune (woman) is constant only in inconstancy', Tilley, F 605, which is found as early as Virgil, *varium et mutabile semper femina, Aeneid*, IV. 569–70. It echoes several of Donne's poems, including 'Change', and several of the Songs and Sonnets, such as, for example 'Communitie', 'Confined Love', 'Womans Constancy', and 'The Flea', as well as the dubious 'Variety'. Echoes of 'Goodfriday, 1613. Riding Westward' and 'Metempsychosis', ll. 191–220, also appear in 'A Defence of Womens Inconstancy'.

ll. 1–3. *THAT* Women are inconstant ... *will maintayne.* 'Maintain' = to defend (an opinion, statement, tenet, etc.), *OED* 14. The sentence means, 'I agree with any man that women are inconstant, but maintain against any man that inconstancy is bad'. However, the writer wishes to mean that he will maintain, against any man, *against* inconstancy's being a bad thing.

ll. 9–12. *Soe in Men ... more reason.* Cf. 'A wise man changes his mind, a fool never will', Tilley, M 420. A. E. Malloch, 'The Techniques and Function of the Renaissance Paradox', *SP* liii (1956), 194, noted the undistributed middle term in the argument which set out is:

> Reasonable men are changeable.
> Women are changeable.
> Therefore women are reasonable.

l. 13. *the earths dull Center.* According to the Ptolemaic system, the earth was the centre of the universe around which the sun and moon revolved. The centre was held in medieval times to be dull and dead.

l. 14. *Gould that lyeth still rusteth.* See question 273 in Luys de Escobar, *La segunda parte de las quatrocientas respuestas a otras preguntas, con las glosas y declaraciones*, Valladolid, 1552, where the possibility that gold could be corrupted and transformed over a period of years is compared with the transformation and corruption of iron which occur more rapidly. (Cited by Lawn, 137.)

l. 18. *cozen.* To cheat, defraud by deceit, *OED* 1.

ll. 19–20. *beguyled in Tryfles.* 'Trifle' = a false or idle tale, told (a) to deceive, cheat or befool, (b) to divert or amuse, *OED* 1, *obs.*

ll. 21–3. *I would you had . . . their* Smocks. Malloch, p. 194, noted that the argument depends upon a sudden switch from the intransitive to the transitive form of the verb '*change*'.

Smocks. 'Smock' = a woman's undergarment, a shift or chemise, *OED* 1, now *arch.* or *dial.*

l. 28. *The learned.* Astrologers.

ll. 36–40. Philosophie *teacheth . . . art and Nature.* Cf. Aristotle, *De caelo*, Bk. IV. 1, 'By absolutely light, then, we mean that which moves upward or to the extremity, and by absolutely heavy that which moves downward or to the centre.' Malloch, 194, noted that the argument rests upon the deliberate crossing or mixing of two metaphors. Michael McCanles, 'Paradox in Donne', *SR* xiii (1966), 278–9, noted the use of the pun on 'light' in order to prove that women do not conform to natural law.

ll. 44–6. Women *are like the Sunn . . . Course Contrary.* According to the Ptolemaic system the natural or proper motion of the sun, as of all the heavenly bodies, is from west to east, but it is carried by the diurnal motion of the *Primum Mobile* in the contrary direction from east to west. Cf. *Sermons*, vii. 222–3 and also 'Goodfriday, 1613. Riding Westward', ll. 1–10.

ll. 57–8. *makinge fooles wise . . . wise men fooles.* Cf. the question which asks, 'Does love make the wise foolish, or the foolish wise?', Giuseppe Betussi, *Il Raverta* (Venice, 1562), 133. Cited by Crane, 132.

l. 83. *is Confusyon, not diversitie.* The correct form of this reading is preserved only in *Pud.* The scribe of *S*, beginning a new page, wrote 'is as Regular' at the top of the page. Noting that this was an error, he began the page again, immediately below the error, writing 'is Confusyon, not diversitie', but forgetting to cancel the error that he had first made.

l. 90. *hornbooke.* A treatise on the rudiments of a subject; a primer, *OED*, b, *transf.* The word is also used as a pun, horn being a reference to cuckoldry.

ll. 91–5. To Conclude *. . . in the World.* 'The name, inconstancy, which has been slandered, should be changed into variety; because of variety the world is delightful, and a woman, because of her variety, is the most delightful thing in the world.' Sister Mary Geraldine in 'Erasmus and the Tradition of Paradox', *SP* lxi (1964), 62, wrote that this Paradox works on the deliberate confusing

of inconstancy with variety. She also noted that the last few lines of the
Paradox 'veer to something like Erasmian false praise'.

Paradox XII. That Virginity is a Vertue (p. 55)

This text is found only in *1652*.
Readings have been rejected on two occasions, ll. 12 and 87, where they are
clearly incorrect.

l. 16. *Engines.* 'Engine' = a snare, wile, *OED* 3; a machine or instrument used
in warfare, *OED* 5.

ll. 18–20. *Ethicke Philosophy . . . which is good.* Cf. 'Is it, then, thus in the
case of virtue also, so that, if one comes to have justice or courage to excess, he
will be worse? Surely not! . . . For virtue, though it have many other functions,
as it has, has this among the most special, to be able to make a right use of
these and the like goods when they are there', Aristotle, *Magna moralia*, Bk. II,
ch. 3.

ll. 31–2. *old Proverb . . .* lead Apes in Hell. Cf. 'Old maids lead apes in hell,
Tilley', M 37. H. W. Janson in *Apes and Ape Lore in the Middle Ages and the
Renaissance* (1952), 207–8 suggests that the possible origin of the proverb is a
Basle woodcut of 1505 by Paulus Olearius called *De fide concubinarum* which
depicts a young woman leading an ape on a rope and accepting money from a
man who is being kicked by an ass. The woodcut was readily available in
England having been printed in both Alexander Barclay's (1509) and Henry
Watson's (1517) editions of Sebastian Brant's *Ship of Fools*. The proverb
appears both in *The Taming of the Shrew*, II. i. 34, *Much Ado about Nothing*,
II. i. 43, and in many poems of the sixteenth and seventeenth centuries.

ll. 32–4. *An Ape . . . to keep an house.* Cf. Apes 'are held for a subtill, ironical,
ridiculous and unprofitable Beast, whose flesh is not good for meate as a sheepe,
neither his backe for burthen as an Asses, nor yet commodious to keepe a
house like a Dog', Edward Topsell, *The Historie of Foure-Footed Beastes*
(1607), 2.

ll. 36–9. *For surely nothing . . . were only made.* Cf. *All's Well*:

> *Parolles*: It is not politic in the commonwealth of nature to preserve
> virginity. Loss of virginity is rational increase, and there was
> never virgin got till virginity was first lost I. i. 127–3.

The parallels between the Paradox and the play were pointed out to me by
Barbara Everett.

ll. 39–41. *The Ape . . . pressing it too hard.* Cf. 'The ape kills her young with
kindness', Tilley, A 264, and 'the *Romane Church* pretends to embrace . . .
like an *Ape*, it kills with embracing', *Sermons*, vi. 252. Janson (31–2) writes
that the origin of this story lies in the Aesopic fables of classical Greece where

its purpose was to demonstrate the effects of excessive affection (*Fabulae Aesopicae collectae*, ed. Haln, nos. 366, 3 and 6b). The story ceased to be a fable and assumed the character of an actual zoological observation in Pliny, *Historia naturalis*, Bk. viii. 80; in Horapollo, *Hieroglyphica*, Bk. ii. 66; and in Oppian, *Cynegetica*, Bk. ii, ll. 605–11.

ll. 44–5. *but they also accuse their parents in condemning marriage.* Cf. *All's Well*:

> *Parolles*: To speak on the part of virginity is to accuse your mothers, which is most infallible disobedience (I. i. 134–5).

ll. 45–6. *If this application hold not touch.* 'To hold touch' or 'to keep touch' = to keep covenant, keep faith, keep one's promise or engagement, act faithfully, *OED* V. 24.

ll. 47–8. *Apes tender love ... Weasel and Ferret.* Cf. 'They love Conies very tenderly, for in England an old Ape (scarce able to goe) did defend tame Conies from the Weasell, as Sir *Thomas Moore* reported', Topsell, 5. Topsell condensed this reference from Conrad Gesner, *Historiae animalium, lib. I, de quadrupedibus viviparis* (Paris, 1551), 962. Gesner in turn copied *verbatim* from Erasmus, '*Amicitia Ephorinus, Joannes*' in *Colloquia familiaria* (*Opera Omnia*, i. 877), the story of how More's wounded monkey, while recuperating in the garden, protected the rabbits from a weasel that had loosened a board in their hutch.

ll. 61–8. *in the naturall generation ... motion and sense.* The basic theory of the gestation of the human embryo originated by Aristotle in *De generatione animalium* and *De partibus amimalium* was accepted throughout the Middle Ages and down to the sixteenth and seventeenth centuries by Church fathers, such as St. Augustine and Aquinas; physicians, such as Hippocrates, Galen, Diocles, Empedocles, Fabricius, and Polybos; and scholastic philosophers such as Duns Scotus. The theory is, in brief, that the human soul only comes into existence in the embryo when this has reached a stage of development which constitutes a truly human body. Prior to this stage of development, the foetus was generally held to be governed by the vegetable and animal souls. A recent proponent of this theory is E. C. Messenger, *Theology and Evolution*, 1949.

The teaching of the Roman Catholic Church during the Middle Ages and through the sixteenth and seventeenth centuries was that the soul entered the foetus on the fortieth day if the child were male and on the eightieth if it were female. According to *A Catholic Dictionary of Theology*, 1962, three papal bulls, (Innocent III, 1211; Sixtus V, *Effraenatam*, 1588; and Gregory XIV, *Sedes Apostolica*, 1591) dealt with the presence of the human soul in the foetus within the framework of the question of abortion.

The most commonly available early medical view of the gestation of the human embryo is that which descends through Hippocrates and Galen and which is printed in Bartholome, *De proprietatibus rerum* (trans. John de

Trevisa, 1535), Bk. vi, ch. 4, f. lxxi ᵛ. This account is copied in *Batman upon Bartholome*, 1582, Bk. vi, ch. 4, ff. 71ᵛ –72 and also appears substantially unchanged in *The French Academie*, by Pierre de la Primaudaye (trans. T. B[owes], 1586), Bk. I, ch. 2, 20. In this view there are four stages of gestation: in stage one which lasts seven days the seed is like milk, in stage two which lasts nine days the seed becomes blood and was called a foetus by 'Ipocras', in stage three which lasts twelve days the internal organs are formed but the other members are not shaped nor divided, but in stage four which lasts eighteen days the body and limbs are formed and ready to receive the soul. Then the foetus receives a soul and has life, and begins to move, and forms fingers and toes. 'Than from the day of conception, to the daye of full complicion and the fyrst of lyfe of the chylde, ben .xlvi. dayes, so that the fyrste daye and the laste be acounted in the tale' (Bartholome, f. lxxi).

This view does not appear to be that to which the writer is referring in this Paradox. His most likely source is some popularization of Diocles who agreed with Empedocles in stating that the full development of the foetus required forty days, and after twenty-seven days had passed, faint traces of the head and backbone could be seen in a moist covering. See E. D. Phillips, *Greek Medicine* (1973), 130.

ll. 82–3. (*for* Virginity *ever kept is ever lost.*) Cf. *All's Well*:

Parolles: [virginity] by being ever kept it is ever lost (I. i. 129).

ll. 95–8. *The* Paracelsians . . . *would make us immortall.* Paracelsus's theory of medicine included dependence upon arcana or secrets. 'Before, then, we treat of arcana, we must see and know why they are so called, and what an arcanum is, since it has so excellent a name, and well deserves to have it, too. That is called an arcanum, then, which is incorporeal, immortal, of perpetual life, intelligible above all Nature and of knowledge more than human . . . They have the power of transmuting, altering, and restoring us, as the arcana of God, according to their own induction . . . One arcanum, then, is of a single essence; another is the arcanum of Nature herself: for the arcanum is the whole virtue of a thing, excelling a thousandfold the thing itself. We are able, therefore, fearlessly to assert that the arcanum of a man is every gift and virtue of his which he retains to eternity.' 'The Archidoxies', Bk. V, *The Hermetic and Alchemical Writings*, Aureolus Philippus Theophrastus Bombast of Hohenheim called Paracelsus, trans. A. E. Waite, 2 vols. (1894), ii. 37–8.

ll. 95–6. *The* Paracelsians (*curing like by like*). 'Now the difference between arcana and medicines is this, that arcana operate in their own nature, or essence, but medicine in contrary elements . . . Medicines are those things wherein it is understood that cold is to be removed by heat and superfluity by purgation. Thus, there are reckoned substances of the arcana which by their natures are directed against the property of their enemy, even as one pugilist is opposed by another', ibid. 38 n.

l. 97. *taken down*. This appears to be a use of 'take' = to grasp mentally, apprehend, comprehend, understand, *OED* VII. 46.

Characters:

MSS.: Group II (*S 962*); Group III (*B, Dob, O'F*); *S*.
Editions: 'A Dunce' *1622* et seq., *1652*; 'A Scot' *1652*.

These manuscripts and editions contain the only known witnesses to the text of the Characters. There is no 'best text' of the Characters but in these works, as in the Problems, *O'F* has the most rational system of punctuation and I have used it as copy-text. In establishing the text, the agreement of Groups II and III has been accepted as having the highest authority. *S 962* represents Group II, and *Dob* both represents Group III and serves as a check on the readings of the copy-text. Readings of *S* and of the editions (*1622* and *1652* for 'A Dunce' and *1652* for 'A Scot') have also been recorded. The Character of 'A Scot' is followed by that of 'A Dunce' for that is the order in which these works occur in the Groups II and III manuscripts.

The Description of a Scot at first sight (p. 58)

The reading of *O'F* has been rejected on five occasions where it is not supported by *Dob*, title. ll. 3, 8, 10, 12. 'In 1604 and the following years there was much resentment against the needy Scots who had flocked in the train of James to the Court in England. Ben Jonson and his associates Chapman and Marston were imprisoned in 1605 for their play *Eastward Ho*, which contained an attack on the "industrious Scots" and a wish that "a hundred thousand of 'hem were in Virginia", Jonson, *Works*, eds. Herford and Simpson, iv. 570' (E. M. S.).

l. 1. Charterhouse. Name of a charitable institution or 'hospital' founded in London, in 1611, upon the site of the Carthusian monastery. The name was used for a Carthusian monastery, *OED* 1, 2.

l. 3. *stockings Gules*. red stockings. 'Gules' = red in colour, usually placed after the word which it qualifies. A term normally used in heraldry, *OED* A, B.

ll. 3–4. *One indifferent Shooe*. Possibly a single soled shoe as noted by John Taylor in *The Pennyles Pilgrimage* . . ., 1618 and quoted by J. Telfer Dunbar, *History of Highland Dress* (1962), 34.

l. 4. *Band of* Edenborough *and his cuffs of* London. 'Band' = the neck-band or collar of a shirt, . . . in sixteenth and seventeenth century, a collar or ruff worn around the neck by a man or woman, *OED* I. 4 *spec*. a. The exact meaning of this phrase is obscure. 'Edenborough' and 'London' may refer to colours (? blue and tan), fabrics, styles, or to the general bad taste shown in acquiring one's clothes in different places.

l. 6. *sodd* = sodden with rain.

l. 9. *new mount at* Wansted. Wanstead in Essex was connected with Tudor and Stuart kings from Henry VII to Charles I. The Manor at Wanstead was purchased by Robert Dudley, Earl of Leicester, in 1578 and passed through his widow Lettice, who married Sir Christopher Blount in 1590, to her son by her first marriage, Robert Devereux, Earl of Essex. Essex sold the Manor in 1598 to Charles Blount, Lord Montjoy, made Earl of Devonshire in 1603, elder brother of his stepfather, and when Devonshire died in 1606 he left the Manor to his bastard son by Penelope, Lady Rich, whom he had married in 1605, Montjoy Blount. The Manor appears at that time to have reverted to the Crown. There is no mention in the various County Histories of Essex of any erections at Wanstead during this period, and indeed the *Victoria County History* states that little change was made in the park. Although the reference appears to be geographical, it could be a pun on Montjoy Blount.

l. 13. *Sumpter.* A pack, saddle bag, *OED* 3 *obs.*

l. 15. *knight wright.* 'knight maker'. A reference to James's selling of knighthoods in return for money.

ll. 18–19. Tom Thorney. The scribe of *O'F* glosses this reference with the words 'a surgeon famed for yt'. 'Surgeon' is most probably a barber. Bear baiting was a popular sport during the reigns of Queen Elizabeth and King James, but standard works on the sport (e.g. Henslowe's *Papers*, ed. W. W. Greg, 1907, and Sir S. Lee, 'Bear bayting, Bull bayting and Cock fighting in Shakespeare's England', 1916) make no mention of 'Tom Thorney'.

Character of A Dunce (p. 59)

The reading of *O'F* has been rejected on eleven occasions; on two, ll. 10, 37, it is supported by *Dob*, and on nine it is not so supported (ll. 5, 6, 7, twice in l. 9, 13, 30, 41, 50). On one further occasion, ll. 12–13, a passage omitted in *O'F* is restored to the text.

l. 16. animatum Instrumentum. 'An animated instrument'.

l. 19. *Monsters.* 'Monster' = something extraordinary or unnatural; a prodigy, a marvel, *OED* A. 1, *obs.*

l. 27. Hecatombs. 'Hecatomb' = a great public sacrifice (properly of a hundred oxen) among the ancient Greeks and Romans, *OED* 1.

l. 45. Apothegms. Apophthegm = a pithy or sententious maxim, *OED.*

l. 51. Terminorum positione. 'In setting of boundaries'.

ll. 61–2. *His hearers ... turne.* The manuscripts here have the true reading while the readings of the editions ('Heel i.e. he will ... turn', *1652*, and 'He ... turns', *1622*) do not make sense.

l. 63. *from side ... to leaning.* This passage is omitted in both *S* and the editions.

An Essaie of Valour (p. 62)

MS.: *S*.

Editions: *1622 et seq., 1651, 1652.*

These texts are the only known witnesses of the Essay. I have used *S* as the copy-text because it contains the entire text, which *1651* does not (*1651* omits ll. 1–25 and ll. 117–19), and because it is better punctuated than *1622*, *1652*. In establishing the text, the agreement of *S* and *1651* has been accepted as having the highest authority, because these texts appear to be independent of each other and yet agree in readings from which the texts in *1622*, *1652* appear to have deteriorated. Readings of *1622*, *1652* have been recorded.

Minor readings of *S* have been rejected on twelve occasions, ll. 23, 32, 33, 42, 46, 54, 63, 69, 81, 94, 95, 113, and its peculiar spelling has been altered twice, ll. 36, 98. Five further readings of *S* have been rejected, ll. 28–9, 38, 64–5, 66, 80–1, and the readings adopted are discussed in the notes.

l. 16. *It yeilds the wall.* 'Valour gives a protected place'.

l. 23. *futures.* 'Future' = loosely used for: Subsequent (to a specified past epoch), *OED* A. 3.

l. 27. *better. Nothing.* At first sight the reading of *1651* '... better. Nothing draws a Woman like to it. Nothing ...' appears to be the correct reading which the other witnesses have omitted through an eye slip on 'Nothing'. However, the phrase copied at this point in *1651* appears in ll. 24–5 in the texts of the other witnesses, in that section of the text which is omitted in *1651*.

ll. 28–9. *are free from the daunger of yt.* John Sparrow has suggested that *are free ...* is the correct reading from which the *we free ...* in *S*, *1622*, *1652* is caused by a simple scribal error changing 'we' to 'are'. The sense of the sentence is that women are protected by men's valour and are free from the danger of being ravished because of this valour. This sense is expressed in the emendation, *and in a free way too, without any danger*, in *1651*.

l. 38. *we.* There is general disagreement in this reading; *1622* reads 'we', *S*, *1652* reads 'he', *1651* reads 'the world'. The reading 'we' has been adopted because the reference throughout the sentence is to non-valorous men called 'we': 'our shamefacedness gives women the idea of being modest, inasmuch as it is cunning rhetoric to persuade women that they are that which we want them to be'.

l. 45. *Age of witt, and wearinge Blacke.* i.e. the present age when wit and feigning melancholy could win a lady.

l. 47. *rydinge through* Forrests. A cryptic reading which is expanded in *1651* to 'Riding to seeke Adventures through dangerous Forrests'.

l. 50. *Inundatyon*. An overspreading or overwhelming in superfluous abundance, *OED* 2 *trans*. and *fig*.

ll. 63–5. *bee hee of grym Aspect, and such an one as a glasse scarse dares take, and shee will desyre him.* John Sparrow has suggested that this might be the original reading from which the reading in *S*, *1622*, *1652* has deviated and whose corrupt state was emended by the printer of *1651*. *bee hee* is probably correct for *S*, *1622*, *1652* reads *bee* and *1651* reads *he*. The other and major emendation is *an one as a glasse scarse dares take*. The omission of 'as' an 'in one as a' is easy to understand, and 'scarse' coming between 'glasse' and 'dares' might easily be omitted by a copyist. I have accepted Sparrow's emendations, and have supplied commas in the passage.

l. 66. *mole is*. 'is' which is found only in *1651* is necessary to make the comparison with the 'skar' complete gramatically.

l. 73. *be not there Rivall*. The reading of *1651* has the same meaning, 'corrive not therewith'. 'Corrival' = to rival, *OED* 1 *trans*., *obs*.

ll. 80–1. *a good diversitie, then*. This reading of *1651* appears to be correct. The construction means 'if Ovid . . . would allow it . . . then . . .', which is not as clear in the reading of *S*, *1622*, *1652* 'good a diversitie, That'.

ll. 94–5. *alwais stand . . . of Clothes*. This reading is omitted in *1622*, *1652* because of an eye slip on 'Clothes'.

ll. 112–13. *a privie Coat of Defence*. i.e. concealed armour.

ll. 113–14. *such as made Bucklers*. 'Buckler' = a means of defence; protection, protector, *OED* 2, *fig*. The meaning of the entire sentence is obscure. It appears to mean, with the preceding sentence, that 'I do not consider a man valorous who fights only when drunk or angry, or provoked, etc., for if this were a valorous man, then those who offer defence against him would be considered "Catalines".'

l. 114. Catalines. From Catiline (Lucius Sergius Catilina), a patrician and soldier whose ambitions in government were thwarted in part by rumours of his involvement in conspiracy against the state. He became the champion of the poor and discontented, particularly of the dissolute aristocrats, and was involved in a conspiracy against Cicero and Rome. He was killed in 62 BC. The reading of *1651*, 'very scum' is a gloss on 'Catalines'.

Newes from the very Country (p. 67)

MS.: *Bur*, extracts, now preserved in L. P. Smith, *The Life and Letters of Sir Henry Wotton*, Oxford, 1907.
Editions: *1614* et seq., *1650*.

These are the only known witnesses of the text of the News. There is little

difficulty with the substantive or accidental readings of either *1614* or *1650*.
I have used *1614* as the copy-text and have recorded the variant readings of
1650. Readings of *Bur* have not been included as its text is incomplete and
some of the anecdotes are slightly abbreviated.

l. 1. *fripery*. A place where cast-off clothes are sold, *OED* 3, *obs.*

l. 4. *falls*. 'Fall' = the timber cut down at one season, *OED* III. 14.

l. 8. *Pike*. A voracious fish.

l. 9. *lesse vices*. 'Lesser or smaller vices'.

l. 10. *stomacke*. i.e. appetite.

ll. 11–13. *debtors . . . house*. It is difficult to know whether this is a specific
reference.

l. 17. *Christmas Lords*. Lords of Misrule in Christmas festivities.

ll. 21–4. *That sentences . . . snares*. 'Sentences, like hair in a horse's tail, agree
in their source, but being removed singly can act as traps.'

l. 23. *springes*. 'Spring' = a snare or noose, *OED*, sb³, *obs. exc. dial.*

ll. 25–6. *cotton and stones . . . hawke*. Cf. Anon., *Cheape and Good Husbandry*,
1614, 'But for long winged Hawkes, the best casting is fine Flannel, cut into
square pieces of an inch and a halfe square, and all to jagged, and so given with
a little bit of meat. By these castings you shall know the soundnesse and un-
soundnesse of your Hawke', p. 136. 'If your Hawke by overflying, or too
soone flying, be heated and inflamed in her body as they are much subject
thereunto, you shall then to coole their bodies give them Stones', p. 137.

l. 28. *three pilde mischiefe*. 'Best quality mischief'. Cf. *Measure for Measure*, I.
ii, 30–1:

    And thou the velvet; thou art good velvet; thou'rt a three-piled piece.

l. 33. *default. Spec.* in *Hunting*, failure to follow the scent; loss of the scent or
track by the hounds, *OED* II. 6, *obs.*

l. 34. *Favourites course . . . in view*. 'Coursing is the pursuit of the hare with
greyhounds, by sight, as distinct from the hunting of the hare by scent (see
Shakespeare's England, ii. 362)' (E. M. S.).

l. 36. *Sparrow*. Cf. 'As lustful as Sparrows', Tilley, S 715.

l. 38. *up and down*. Sparrow, *London Mercury*, xviii (1928), 41 noted ' "up
once and down forever", parallel to "peremptory", which seems to mean
"with a fixed and inevitable end" . . . to be opposed to "vicissitudes" '.

APPENDIX

LODEWIJK ROUZEE

In the preface, '*Ad Lectorem*', to his book of Problems, *Problematum miscellaneorum, Antaristotelicorum, centuria dimidiata* . . ., Rouzee wrote that he was of Arras by origin, Antwerp–Brabant by birth, French by education, almost English by manners (through a ten-year assimilation and intercourse), and in 1616, of Leiden by residence (sigs. *2–*2 ᵛ). He is not recorded in the standard dictionaries of national biography of any of these countries.

He was born *c*.1586, matriculated as a student of medicine in Leiden on 27 October 1615, and took his MD degree on 24 September 1616. He is listed in *English Speaking Students of Medicine at the University of Leyden*, R. W. Innes Smith, 1932. His name appears on his incorporation as MD Oxon. on 12 July 1625 in Wood's *Fasti Oxonienses*, edited by Philip Bliss, 1815, and also in *Alumni Oxonienses 1500–1714*, Joseph Foster, 1891. His family name appears variously was Rouzee, Rouseus, Rozaeus, Rosaeus, Rowse, Rouse, Rowze, Rowzee, and Rouverius. His Christian name appears as Ludovic, Ludovicus, Lodovick, Lodowick, and Lewis.

R. C. Bald discovered that Rouzee became a British subject early in 1630.[1] He also pointed out that in his Problem, *Cur Gallum in suo famulitio habere tantoperè affectant Nobiles Angli*, the author suggested that he may have spent his early years in England attached to some noble household.[2]

In 1632, while practising as a physician in Ashford, Kent, Rouzee published a book called *The Queenes Welles. That is, A Treatise of the Nature and Vertues of Tunbridge Water*, 1632, which he dedicated to the second Viscount Conway. In his dedication to this work Rouzee wrote that the first Viscount, Edward Conway, had been his friend both in England and in the Brill, and that he had stayed with Conway twenty-six years previously (*c*.1606). Edward Conway was a lifelong friend of Donne's and was one of the persons to whom Donne sent his works; he had had *Biathanatos* around 1608.[3] It is likely that Donne lent Conway other works, including the Problems, and since Rouzee was with Conway around the year 1606, a year which is included in the period during which the Problems appear to have been composed, it is

---

[1] 'A Latin Version of Donne's Problems', *MP* lxi (1964), 198-203. The record appears in SP, Dom., Chas. I, 1629-31, 178, and in Patent Rolls, 6. Car. I, pt. II.

[2] Ibid. 199.

[3] A letter to Sir Henry Goodyer which is dated ?1608 reads: 'The day before I lay down, I was at *London*, where I delivered your Letter for *Sir Edward Conway*, and received another for you, with the copy of my Book . . .', John Donne, *Complete Poetry and Selected Prose*, ed. John Hayward (1929, [rpt. 1962]), 452–3.

not unlikely that Rouzee was able to copy the Problems, either from Donne's holograph or from a copy of it which Conway had caused to be made.

Rouzee knew the identity of the author whose works he translated, and he may have punned on his name, using the verb *dono* for render or translate, in his preface.[1] He claimed to have come across the Problems some six or seven years before (1609–10) and said that they were composed in English but never printed. Rouzee also wrote that their author was a most learned gentleman and endowed with the keenest intellect, but he would not wish to acknowledge the Problems as his because he had embraced a most dignified career. Donne was ordained deacon and priest in January 1615.

Two of Rouzee's translations have been chosen for reproduction in full. The first shows Rouzee taking liberties with his text, while the second is more faithfully rendered. In both, it may be noted that the Latin text is approximately as long as Donne's original versions—a tribute to the economy of Donne's prose.

Cur Veneris aster est πολυώνυμος et vocatur tum Hesperus, tum Vesper?

XXII. (XI in Donne)

Aeque varia quidem nomina habet luna, non tamen ut est stella, sed quatenus diversa munera exercet, sicut videmus in Regum titulis, Ducum, Comitum, et dominorum nomina. Lactantius Firmianus cum hanc dominam Stellam vituperare cuperet, eam magis quam ullus ex ejus Idololatrarum numero honoravit; Dicit enim Venerem primò artem meretriciam invenisse. Quod si verum sit, ea certè cunctis, qui è vitiosorum deorum prosapia unquam extiterunt, immo,credo, etiam musicae inventore antiquior erit; Nam antequam Psalterium et citharam invenisset Iubal, ipsius mater duorum virorum assumptionem invenerat. Si igitur Venus id fecit, multiplicia nomina idcirco fortè habet, ut prostitutis suis discipulis exemplum det, quae tam frequenter sua nomina mutare debent, aut ut imponant magistratibus, ne illis innotescant, aut ut scortatoribus novae, et antea inauditae appareant; Nam haec ars alijs omnibus planè contraria est, quia in his quo experientia et artis usu magis pollent artifices, eo magis apud omnes aestimantur, in illa verò novitiae et artis omninò rudes semper plurimi fiunt, exercitatisque praeponuntur. Fortasse diversa nomina assumit diversarum functionum, quas habet, ratione, sicut enim suprema est imperatrix omnigeni amoris, seu libidinis, cujus plures sunt species, quam ullius alius vitij, utpote pollutio, fornicatio, adulterium, Laicus incestus, incestus spiritualis, raptus, Sodomia, mastupratio &c; Sic quoque eam cum Junone, Diana et alijs matrimonio praesidere faciunt omnes mythologi. Potest etiam fieri, ut hoc significare velit suam facilitatem ad se diversis

---

[1] The passage concerning Donne's Problems reads: 'nisi forte 12 vel 13, quae non omninò mea sunt, sed ante annos 6 vel 7 in manus meas Anglicè conscripta, nunquam tamen excusa, venerunt. Illa autem ob insignem, quam habebant, venustatem, paucis in quibusdam eorum immutatis, latinitate donavi, nec nomen Authoris, Viri Doctissimi, acutissimoque ingenio praediti, hîc reticerem, nisi vererer eum nunc illa tanquam sua agnoscere nolle, quia gravissimum vitae genus iam amplexus est', sigs. *9–*9ᵛ.

hominibus applicandam, quam ab origine habuit: Neptunus enim ipsam
lachrymavit et destillavit, Apollo calefecit et emollivit, Vulcanus conflavit et
malleavit, Mercurius persuasit et Sacramento alligavit, Jupiter denique
authoritatem dedit. Sed quòd specialiter haec duo nomina, Hesperus et
Vesper, illi indita sint, hanc non puto esse rationem, nempe quod omnia
tempora includant, emblamataque, per ortum et occasum, omnium fortunarum
sint; Verùm quia mundus hoc, pro *summo bono*, accepit, rationi consentaneum
videtur, ut omnes gradus, omnia membra illius boni recipiat, iis solummodò
exceptis, quae illi ex diametro opposita sunt, ipsiusque destructionem
moliuntur, sicut *Bonum honestum* facere videtur. Idcirco illa, quatenus
Hesperus, *bonum utile* vobis profert, quia matutino tempore venus saluberrima
est, quatenus Vesper autem, *bonum delectabile* vobis commendat, quia
vespertino tempore maxime delectat, si saltem Archigeni, olim praestantissimo
medico, credere vultis, ut ego nondum expertus facio. Ejus sententia his
versibus habetur

> *Quaerenti Hersiliae quaenam hora salubrior esset*
> *Ad venerem, medicus sic ait Archigenes:*
> *'Manè salubre magis veneris decerpere fructus,*
> *Iudice me fuerit, vespere dulce magis.'*
> *Hîc illa arridens formoso ait ore, 'voluptas*
> *Mî curae fuerit vespere, manè salus.'*

Cur plumis tantoperè delectantur mulieres?
Probl. XXXVIII. (XVIII in Donne)

Simile simili dicere, nimis quidem tritum, et id etiam foret praeter rationum
nostrarum in hisce problematibus scopum, ille enim ad verisimile tantùm sese
extendunt, non verò ad expressam et individuam veritatem, qualis haec ratio
est. Non inficias iri possumus, quin quibusdam viris etiam plumae placeant, sed
isti sunt, vel milites, vel aulici, qui quamvis vitae genere, institutis suis ex
diametro sibi invicem planè oppositi sint, in hoc tamen concurrunt, quod et hi
et illi mulierosi sint, gaudeantque sese mulieribus assimilare. Mirum sanè est
mulieres nihil prorsus sibi proprium habere posse, quod quandoque sibi viri
non arrogent: Principes namque falsitatem usurpant, eorum ministri corradunt,
ecclesiastici rixantur, quamvis haec omnia propriè, et de jure ad mulieres
pertineant, quae cum communicabiles sint creaturae, et boni nihil habeant, sua
mala nobis communicant. Aut putant plumas allas imitari, et sic inquietudinem
et instabilitatem suam indicare volunt; Aut plumas gestando plumaeve existendo
titulum habere volunt ad locum cujusdam versus, quo Petrarchus res, quae
virtutem relegarunt Bocacio enumerat, *La gola, il somno, & l'ociose piume.*
Petrarchus enim non adeò tautologus est, ut quod iam dixerat per hanc vocem,
somno, statim repetat; nec etiam plumeos lectulos, qui virtutem in exilium
dederunt, otiosos appellasset, otiosi quippe lecti non tantum adversus virtutem
fecère, atque illis contrarij, imò Gregorius 13 Pontifex maximus doctus in

lecto evasit. Per plumas igitur, aut aliquid mulieribus inseparabiliter junctum, aut mulieres ipsas exprimit. Fortasse sicut re ipsa sunt, sic etiam nomine similes esse volunt illis curiosarum vanitatum artificibus, quos sub uno nomine comprehendit Varro, vocatque Plumarios; Nam credere non possum, eas tam humiles, tamque bonae esse conscientiae, ut hoc fateantur se meruisse esse *Emplumadas*, quod genus poenae est apud Hispanos, quo dissolutiores mulieres castigantur. Aut forsan plumas amant eadem ratione, qua semper indignissimos viros diligunt, nempe ut inconstantia sua et frequens mutatio excusabilis videatur. Aut denique hoc pacto ex omni hominis definitione sese penitus excluserunt. Cum viderent enim Aristotelis definitionem, *Homo est animal rationale*, sibi non competere, placuit quoque illam, quae est Platonis vel Speusippi, *Homo est animal bipes implume*, à se amovere.